Focus Groups, Volume I

A Selective Annotated Bibliography: Art and Humanities, Social Sciences, and the Nonmedical Sciences

Graham R. Walden

With an Introduction by David L. Morgan

The Scarecrow Press, Inc.
Lanham, Maryland • Toronto • Plymouth, UK
2008

SCARECROW PRESS, INC.

Published in the United States of America
by Scarecrow Press, Inc.
A wholly owned subsidary of
The Rowman & Littlefield Publishing Group, Inc.
4501 Forbes Boulevard, Suite 200, Lanham, Maryland 20706
www.scarecrowpress.com

Estover Road
Plymouth PL6 7PY
United Kingdom

British Library Cataloguing in Publication Information Available

Library of Congress Cataloging-in-Publication Data

Walden, Graham R., 1954–
  Focus groups : a selective annotated bibliography / Graham R. Walden.
     p. cm.
  Includes bibliographical references and index.
  ISBN-13: 978-0-8108-6117-6 (v. 1 : pbk. : alk. paper)
  ISBN-10: 0-8108-6117-8 (v. 1 : pbk. : alk. paper)
  eISBN-13: 978-0-8108-6230-2
  eISBN-10: 0-8108-6230-1
  1. Focus groups—Bibliography. 2. Social sciences—Research--Methodology—
Bibliography. 3. Humanities—Research—Methodology—Bibliography. 4. Research—
Methodology—Bibliography. I. Title.
  Z7164.F64W35 2008
  [H61.28]
  016.0014'33—dc22
                                                                    2008005788

∞™ The paper used in this publication meets the minimum requirements of
American National Standard for Information Sciences—Permanence of Paper
for Printed Library Materials, ANSI/NISO Z39.48-1992.
Manufactured in the United States of America.

Contents

Contents

Acknowledgments

First, and foremost, I would like to thank David L. Morgan, university professor, Portland State University, for contributing the Introduction. Professor Morgan is one of the most prolific and frequently cited authors in the field of focus group research.

Martin Dillon and Andrew Yoder, Scarecrow Press editors, have been helpful and responsive throughout the project, and they have been open to various modifications suggested along the way.

Resources to assist with the project were provided by The Ohio State University Libraries in the form of a three-month special research assignment, as well as a grant to cover the costs of the manuscript preparation. Both were administered through the Advisory Committee on Research. Thanks to Jim Bracken, assistant director for Collections, Instruction, and Public Services, and Joe Branin, director of University Libraries, for their continued support of my research endeavors.

Appreciation is extended to Jennifer Kuehn, interlibrary loan coordinator, and staff members Tonya Maniaci and Jody Faught for quickly providing many resources from far afield. Additional thanks to the members of the Circulation Department, coordinated by Tony Maniaci, for the smooth functioning of our OhioLINK borrowing environment. Many volumes came to Ohio State from the participating member libraries throughout the state of Ohio. Anne Fields, coordinator for research and reference, graciously assisted by working my desk hours while I was away on the special research assignment.

The mother/daughter team of Tammy and Taryn Jones word-processed the manuscript. Their flexibility and responsive efforts were very helpful.

Preface

This annotated bibliography provides the reader with access to the realm of applications of focus group methodology in a variety of nonmedical subjects from the past decade. The intended users include professional focus group practitioners, scholars in the areas covered, graduate and undergraduate students, and others wishing to conduct this type of qualitative inquiry. This is volume one of a two-volume set; the second book will deal exclusively with the medical and health sciences literature. The reason for the division is because the medical community has demonstrated extensive usage of the approach, with their applications exceeding all other subject disciplines combined in terms of published academic book and journal article production. (Market researchers undoubtedly represent the largest segment of users, but their research is primarily proprietary and not published for public access.) The annotations in this volume, averaging 160 words, are intended to both describe the content and enable the reader to gain a clear understanding as to whether pursuing the full text for the particular item is appropriate.

SCOPE

In broad terms the types of materials include the following categories: instructional guides, handbooks, reference works, textbooks, and the academic journal literature. The subject disciplines covered in the arts and humanities are linguistics, music, religion, and sports and leisure studies. In the social sciences the following disciplines have entries: anthropology, business, cartography, communication, demography, education, law, library science, political science, psychology, and sociology. The nonmedical sciences addressed are agriculture, biology, engineering, environmental studies, and physics. The subject areas represented were not selected as such, but rather were included because they are the appropriate studies available in each category. Stated another way, disciplines not found in this bibliography are absent due to a lack of publicly available documentation.

The entries selected have a minimum of four pages. Generally speaking, shorter articles are either opinion pieces or of such brevity as to not merit inclusion alongside the more substantial academic literature.

Throughout the development of the focus group methodology in this country, the vocabulary used to describe the technique has included the following: group interview, group depth interview, group discussion, focus group, focus group discussion, focused interview, focus group interview, nominal group interview, and qualitative group discussion. European variants include psychodynamic market research group and cooperative research. Since the 1980s, the most frequently used terms in print and online databases are focus group(s), focus group interview(s), and focused group interview(ing).

Modified, and in some cases rewritten, entries from the author's two published articles in the field have been incorporated into this bibliography. These are "Focus Group Interviewing in the Library Literature: A Selective Annotated Bibliography 1996–2005" (*Reference Services Review*, vol. 34, no. 2, 2006, pp. 222–241), and "Recent Books on Focus Group Interviewing and Mass Communication" (*Communication Booknotes Quarterly*, vol. 37, no. 2, Spring 2006, pp. 76–93).

The bibliography has the following counts by category of inclusion: 29 books, 50 book chapters, 349 articles, and 10 pamphlets, totaling 438 entries.

COVERAGE

The bibliography focuses on the core academic literature published from 1997 through 2006 as found in books, book chapters, journal articles, and significant pamphlets from the United States, Canada, the United Kingdom, Australia, New Zealand, India, and other countries where the document has been made available in English (this means that some articles appear in their translated form). The cited authors include individuals from many countries beyond the scope of the English-speaking regions of the world. All items can be publicly accessed, and each is available from at least one location via interlibrary loan. A partial list of materials specifically excluded incorporates the following: book reviews, conference proceedings, critical works, editorials, Internet resources (including journals available only online), letters, mass-market periodicals, master's theses and doctoral dissertations, newspaper articles, and opinion pieces.

METHODOLOGY

The annotations are descriptive and nonevaluative. Both the citations and the annotations follow the guidelines found in *The Chicago Manual of Style* (15th edition) (an exception is the way numbers are presented).

APPENDIX

The appendix lists all source journals found in the citations, with the appropriate item numbers provided. There are 245 individual journal titles listed.

INDEXES

The author index lists the name of all authors, coauthors, and editors found in the citations, with the appropriate item numbers provided. The aim of the subject index is to reference unique terms. The detailed contents pages, with multiple subheadings, are intended as the primary approach to access the entries in this bibliography.

Introduction

Since the 1980s, there has been an extremely rapid growth in the use of focus groups. Many researchers have discovered that focus groups create the potential for a "good return on investment" by generating high-quality data with modest resources. For those working in the social sciences and related areas, this provides the opportunity to do solid work that does not require large grants. For those working in applied areas, focus groups can produce valuable insights into program improvement without straining budgets that are already stretched thin.

The rapid growth in the literature on focus groups also has a downside, however, because it has become very difficult to track the state of this research area as a whole—let alone to locate the items in that larger literature that provide interesting alternatives to current practices. Most of the current sources on focus groups are textbooks that remain at a relatively introductory level, but the nature of the field is dynamic while the content of textbooks is static. This would be less of a problem if there were sources that regularly published methodological articles or reviews on focus groups, but unlike some other methods, there are no journals that typically carry this kind of work. As a result, there is a systematic lack of access to the focus group literature, and the great value of this book is to fill this gap.

From the point of view of the field as a whole, one major value of this book is to help us grasp where we stand in terms of routine practices. Beyond that, it will also help us locate both new developments and useful adaptations of existing approaches, while saving us from inadvertently duplicating existing work. The interdisciplinary nature of the material covered here will be especially valuable for these goals, by increasing the chance for cross-fertilization of practices from different fields. Thus, for methodologists who are actively working on focus groups or for experienced practitioners who want to extend their skills, this book offers a treasure trove of opportunities for new knowledge.

In addition, it may well be even more valuable for those who are relatively new to focus groups. For those who are in the process of mastering a method, it is often particularly useful to study the experiences of others who have worked on similar issues—especially as a way to move beyond the broad-stroke advice from textbooks. Similarly, students will also benefit from the ability to locate studies that match their own interests, so they can learn from the best examples of existing work in their field. Thus, for those who are learning how to apply focus groups to specific projects, this book gives access to a wide variety of "lessons learned" from previous research.

The ability to benefit from these strengths is greatly enhanced by the skills that the author, Graham Walden, brings to this book. Based on his experiences in creating a related series of books in the area of survey research, Walden has the expertise both to search the existing literature effectively and to summarize the results in a meaningful way. In terms of searching, the contents cover a very wide range of journals, books, and book chapters, at the same time that his selection criteria weed out the less useful material that contains only incidental mentions of focus groups. I would also like to applaud Walden's decision to divide his work into two separate volumes, where the second one will be limited to work in the health-care fields. This matches my own experience in searching this literature, where half or more of the articles that use focus groups are devoted to health care. Hence, the division into two volumes will make things easier for those who either are or are not looking for health-related topics.

Some people approaching a reference tool such as this are likely to ask: Couldn't I just find all this material by doing my own database searches? As someone who has used computerized searches to locate literally thousands of articles on focus groups, I am quite happy to point out the unique contributions of an annotated bibliography such as this. One major advantage I have already noted is that this book eliminates the "false hits" where some field in some database contains the phrase "focus groups," despite the fact that this method is only an incidental topic in the reference being cited. Even more valuable is the actual content of entries, which are not just reprints of the original abstracts; instead, the entries concentrate on the parts of the article or chapter that are actually relevant to focus groups. In addition, the careful use of keywords and detailed indexing makes it easy to find the entries that match your needs. So, the simple answer is that this volume goes well beyond mere database searching by not only giving direct access to the most relevant articles but also giving you the content you need to evaluate those articles.

Overall, I am sure that other readers—whether you are searching for a broad overview of focus groups as a field or assistance in developing your own specific project—will join me in the thanking Graham Walden for the wonderful resource that he has created for us.

David L. Morgan, Ph.D.
Portland State University
September 2007

I.

Methodology

1.1 COMPREHENSIVE

Books

1. Barbour, Rosaline S., and Jenny Kitzinger, eds. *Developing Focus Group Research: Politics, Theory and Practice*. London: Sage, 1999. 225p.

   This collection contains 13 chapters written by 21 contributors (nine of the chapters have two or more authors). The editors, both senior lecturers at Glasgow University, contributed chapter 1 ("Introduction: The Challenge and Promise of Focus Groups"), in which they review the basics of the focus group technique: appropriate uses, sample size, participant selection and recruitment, moderator/facilitator skills, data analysis and presentation, ethics, and the politics of focus group research. For entries selected from the Barbour and Kitzinger volume, see the Author Index under these names: Baker, Bloor, Cunningham-Burley, Das, Farquhar, Frankland, Green, Hart, Hinton, Kerr, Kitzinger, Macnaghten, Michell, Myers, Pavis, Waterton, Wilkinson, and Wynne.

2. Billson, Janet Mancini. *The Power of Focus Groups: A Training Manual for Social and Policy Research*. 4th ed. Barrington, RI: Skywood Press, 2004. 153p.

   Billson, a sociologist and head of her own consulting firm, provides a highly detailed, pragmatic, and applied approach for conducting research in the field. Directed toward both the neophyte and the experienced researcher, the organization of the material follows the stages of a focus group project—the initial designing and planning phase, the recruitment of participants, moderating the discussion, data analysis, and report preparation. The last chapter (12) deals with professional ethics, with the author acknowledging that even though focus groups generally pose minimal risks, the rights of participants must be protected throughout the research process. Information is given on verbal and/or written explanations of the project, informed consent forms, and assurances of anonymity and confidentiality. Visual aids, in the form of examples, "tips," and frequently asked questions, are found throughout. Six appendices include sample screeners, protocols, reports, and executive summaries and recommendations.

3. Bloor, Michael, Jane Frankland, Michelle Thomas, and Kate Robson. *Focus Groups in Social Research*. Introducing Qualitative Methods. London: Sage, 2001. 110p.

Although the volume is intended as a textbook for undergraduate and postgraduate research methods courses, it is also relevant for social researchers in areas such as medicine, social work, education, and nursing. The goal is to provide a practical step-by-step guide to the intricacies of focus group methodology, including initial design; optimal group size and composition; preparation, facilitation, and conduct of the session(s); and transcription and analysis. Examples and exercises appear as the final entry of each chapter. In chapter 5, the authors address virtual focus groups—how to administer them, the strengths and weaknesses of computer-mediated discussions, and the ethical issues accompanying online research. (The reader is cautioned to take account of any prevailing relevant population biases of Internet users in relationship to the target population of the research.) Virtual focus groups are viewed as a "new dimension" of an established method—one that offers quick, convenient, and low-cost options for gathering qualitative data from geographically difficult-to-convene populations. Bloor et al. conclude that focus groups are best used as ancillary to other research design techniques.

4. Fern, Edward F. *Advanced Focus Group Research*. Thousand Oaks, CA: Sage, 2001. 254p.

Directed toward both the academician and the practitioner, this book has four goals: (1) to stimulate more research on the focus group method by encouraging researchers to test the hypothesized relationships presented; (2) to motivate and facilitate experience sharing among researchers across a variety of disciplines; (3) to seek appropriate methods for specific research purposes; and (4) to examine various technological issues and offer new perspectives. Fern's presentation parallels the logical progression of a focus group research project, beginning with group composition and then moving to the research setting, the moderator, the factors that have an impact on the discussion, methodological issues, and the exploratory, experiential, and clinical tasks associated with the method. In the last chapter, the author establishes a conceptual framework, based on four groups of variables, for planning research on focus groups: inputs, organizing concepts, process variables, and focus group outcomes. Comments are made concerning the reporting of focus group results, noting that it is "impossible" to synthesize knowledge from existing poorly reported published research reports that have failed to provide the minimum information necessary to replicate results or determine the validity of the data produced.

5. *Focus Group Kit*. Thousand Oaks, CA: Sage, 1998. 6 vols.

The *Focus Group Kit* contains selections written primarily by David L. Morgan, a sociologist and professor in the Institute on Aging at Portland State University's College of Urban and Public Affairs, and Richard A. Krueger, a professor in the College of Education and Human Development at the University of Minnesota and an evaluation specialist in the university's extension service. The six-volume set is intended for both novice and expert working within a wide variety of disciplines. The goal is to guide the reader through the steps of a focus group project—from the initial planning phase to strategies for analyzing and reporting the results. Each volume contains references, icons, checklists, examples, and indexes. The members of the kit have been separately annotated in this bibliography, and are listed below:

1. *The Focus Group Guidebook*/David L. Morgan;
2. *Planning Focus Groups*/David L. Morgan with Alice U. Scannell;
3. *Developing Questions for Focus Groups*/Richard A. Krueger;
4. *Moderating Focus Groups*/Richard A. Krueger;
5. *Involving Community Members in Focus Groups*/Richard A. Krueger and Jean A. King;
6. *Analyzing & Reporting Focus Group Results*/ Richard A. Krueger.

6. Greenbaum, Thomas L. *The Handbook for Focus Group Research*. 2nd ed. Thousand Oaks, CA: Sage, 1998. 262p.

Directed toward the marketing professional, this book provides comprehensive coverage of the focus group interviewing technique—the research decisions that need to be made, the challenges frequently encountered, and how to maximize the overall effectiveness of the approach. The four chapters new to the second edition contain information on topics and trends that were emerging at the end of the past millennium. Chapter 6 covers two technological developments, namely, satellite videoconferencing and the use of the Internet to conduct this type of qualitative inquiry. In chapter 9, Greenbaum offers guidelines for conducting focus groups beyond U.S. borders, as many corporations now take a global view of their products and services. Chapter 11 identifies some of the differences associated with conducting focus groups with an important market segment—the physician. Another new chapter considers how moderators or client organizations can better manage the field service aspect of a project. The author includes an 84-item glossary of key terms in the field.

7. Krueger, Richard A., and Mary Anne Casey. *Focus Groups: A Practical Guide for Applied Research*. 3rd ed. Thousand Oaks, CA: Sage, 2000. 215p.

The 11 chapters cover the range of elements in the focus group experience—the questioning schedule, the selection of participants, the skills needed for successful moderating, and how to analyze and report the results of a focus group project. Also discussed are focus group styles, adapting the technique for specific audiences, modifications to the traditional moderating style, and a consideration of the quality of the research format (Is it scientific? Are the results generalizable? How is validity determined?). This edition provides additional information on the analysis component, as well as a new chapter that compares and contrasts four different approaches to focus group research: market research, academic, nonprofit, and participatory. Throughout most of the volume emphasis is placed on "how-to" strategies, although the authors note that their advice is intended to be flexible. The book is designed to be a reference for those conducting focus groups, for teaching purposes, and for researchers. Examples, icons, illustrations, and checklists are provided throughout the text.

8. Litoselliti, Lia. *Using Focus Groups in Research*. Continuum Research Methods series. London: Continuum, 2003. 104p.

Litoselliti presents the key elements in the use of focus groups as a qualitative research method for the social sciences. The goal is to communicate the value of this technique for a variety of audiences: undergraduate and graduate students planning a focus group project, as additional reading for general social science research methods courses, and for researchers designing funded studies. The author examines the advantages and disadvantages of the method, discusses the planning and organization of a focus group project, offers suggestions for developing and asking the questions, and considers the intricacies involved in conducting the sessions. The analysis of focus group data, described as "the most difficult stage," is the topic of the last chapter, with the author emphasizing that this step must be a collaborative and continuous process among researcher, moderator, and analyst.

9. Morgan, David L. *The Focus Group Guidebook*. Focus Group Kit 1. Thousand Oaks, CA: Sage, 1998. 103p.

The initial volume in the kit provides a pragmatic overview for those wishing to carry out a focus group project. Morgan introduces the reader to the basics of the technique. These include the most appropriate applications for different settings, the contributions of other social science disciplines, and how to develop reasonable expectations concerning the results produced. Also discussed are the resources required (time, personnel, and funding) for the successful completion of a project. Costs can vary widely depending upon the type of facility chosen, the selection and recruitment of the participants, the number of sessions needed to accomplish the goals of the research, and the level of expertise of the moderator. Morgan addresses the ethical issues that may arise during a focus group project. These primarily concern the relationships among sponsors, researchers, and participants; how to protect the privacy of the participants; and ways to minimize the impact of stressful discussions. Accompanying the text are icons, examples, and checklists.

10. Morgan, David L. *Focus Groups as Qualitative Research*. 2nd ed. Qualitative Research Methods Series, vol. 16. Thousand Oaks, CA: Sage, 1997. 80p.

The volume provides an overview of the focus group process for scholars, practitioners, and students who conduct focus groups as part of a research assignment. Morgan places focus group methodology within the larger realm of social science research, comparing this data-gathering technique to participant observation, individual interviews, surveys, and experiments. The practical aspects involved in conducting focus groups are examined—preplanning, project design, criteria for participant recruitment, conducting the sessions, analyzing the data, and reporting the results. The author emphasizes that a balance must be maintained between participants' direct quotations and the summary of their discussions. Also considered are some additional applications of focus groups, the challenges faced by researchers, the importance of sharing existing knowledge, and how new approaches may advance the state of the art.

11. Morrison, David E. *The Search for a Method: Focus Groups and the Development of Mass Communication Research*. Luton, Bedfordshire, UK: University of Luton, 1998. 294p.

Morrison, a British scholar at the University of Leeds, has also been involved in the commercial sector of a large media research organization. Over half the book traces the background of focus group research—from the founding fathers to the book publication date—emphasizing the contributions of Paul Felix Lazarsfeld. Discussed in detail are Lazarsfeld's move in 1933 from Vienna, Austria, to the United States; his innovations in the field of mathematics and their applications to social and mass communication research; and his research methods, which created a framework for the development of focus groups by Robert Merton. (Lazarsfeld and Merton were close colleagues at the Bureau of Applied Social Research at Columbia University in New York City in the 1940s, and collaborated on many projects ranging from radio research to troop morale for the War Department.) The author discusses some problematic aspects, reviews positive and negative practices, and comments on various ethical issues relating to focus group interviewing. Information is provided from personal interviews with Lazarsfeld, as well as from private papers, correspondence, and archival materials.

12. Simon, Judith Sharken. *The Wilder Nonprofit Field Guide to Conducting Successful Focus Groups: How to Get the Information You Need to Make Smart Decisions*. The Wilder Nonprofit Field Guide Series. Saint Paul, MN: Amherst H. Wilder Foundation, 1999. 70p.

Although written specifically for leaders of nonprofit organizations who wish to better connect with their constituents and communities, this book can be utilized by a wider audience. Simon describes the focus group methodology and offers suggestions as to when it can be used most effectively: for developing a long-term strategic or marketing plan, as an aid in departmental reorganization, and for service evaluation and improvement. In addition, the technique is viewed as beneficial for the nonprofit management environment because of the goodwill that is created when people perceive their opinions to be valued by the organization. Ten easy-to-follow steps are provided for conducting a focus group project. An appendix includes examples, worksheets, and answers to frequently asked questions.

Chapters in Books

13. Barbour, Rosaline S., and John Schostak. "Interviewing and Focus Groups." In *Research Methods in the Social Sciences*, edited by Bridget Somekh and Cathy Lewin, 41–48. London: Sage, 2005.

The authors place focus groups within the larger realm of interviewing and then identify the role that focus group research has in the social sciences. A theoretical discussion of the key concepts involved in face-to-face interviewing is presented, and the implications of focus groups for overall research design are highlighted. Focus groups are described as "a social process through which participants co-produce an account of themselves and their ideas which is specific to that time and place" (p. 43). The challenges presented to the researcher are outlined. A final section in the chapter was written solely by Barbour. Titled "Stories from the Field," it recounts several of Barbour's experiences while conducting focus groups in the United Kingdom. The value of pilot work and pretesting, the logistical problems presented when selecting participants and conducting the sessions, and the credibility of participants' accounts are among the topics discussed relative to the health-care environment.

14. Berg, Bruce L. "Focus Group Interviewing." In *Qualitative Research Methods for the Social Sciences*, 123–45. 5th ed. Boston: Allyn & Bacon, 2001.

This textbook was designed to be used in quantitative as well as qualitative research methods courses. Berg defines focus group interviewing, traces its development from World War II, lists some benefits and limitations, and compares and contrasts the methodology to face-to-face interviewing, participant observation, and unobtrusive measures. Eight steps for conducting a focus group research project are outlined and discussed. The author recommends the use of the *extended focus group* (a procedure that includes a pregroup questionnaire administered to participants) because of its advantages to the key players. Berg completes the chapter with a consideration of participant confidentiality and videoconferencing.

15. Bristol, Terry. "Enhancing Focus Group Productivity: New Research and Insights." In *Advances in Consumer Research*, edited by E. J. Arnold and L. M. Scott, vol. 27, 479–82. Provo, UT: Association for Consumer Research, 1999.

Bristol reports on three papers presented at an annual conference of the Association for Consumer Research. The session had two purposes: to summarize some of the most recent empirical, theory-based research on focus group methodology, and to address a variety of challenges encountered with this qualitative format. Kim Corfman's paper examined how factors such as participant traits (self-esteem and gender), group size, topic relevance, and compatibility with the moderator have an impact on data quality. The second presentation by Terry Bristol focused on gender, acquaintanceship, and self-disclosure issues. Ann Schlosser's research investigated the role of gender on the data-collection method (face-to-face versus computer-mediated interviews). Following the presentations, a roundtable discussion considered three topics: practices and trends in usage, effective interviewing strategies, and directions for future research.

16. Bryman, Alan. "Focus Groups." In *Social Research Methods*, 345–62. 2nd ed. New York: Oxford University Press, 2004.

The discussion is organized into five major sections. Initially, the focus group method is compared and contrasted to individual interviews, *focused interviews* (in which participants are selected based on their involvement in a particular situation), and other forms of group interviewing. Bryman reviews some possible uses of focus groups, discusses their applicability and adaptability to qualitative research projects, outlines the pragmatic aspects of conducting a focus group, and suggests appropriate strategies for asking questions in a semi- or unstructured environment. The importance of interaction among the participants is highlighted in the third section. Three aspects of focus groups that lend themselves to the politics and ethics of feminist research are discussed: data are gathered in a more naturalistic environment that encourages interaction, the concept of *decontextualization* (a scenario in which the individual is examined in isolation rather than in a social context) is avoided, and the risk of a power relationship between the female researcher and the female respondent is reduced. Limitations of the method include less moderator control, the data are challenging to manipulate, sessions are difficult to organize, transcription is time consuming, group effects must be controlled for, and participants may be uneasy in certain environments.

17. Buddenbaum, Judith M., and Katherine B. Novak. "Focus Groups." In *Applied Communication Research*, 217–40. Ames: Iowa State University Press, 2001.

This textbook is intended for upper-level undergraduate and graduate students taking research methods courses. Although the emphasis is on communication applications (organizational communication, journalism, public relations, advertising, and marketing), the approach is interdisciplinary. Buddenbaum and Novak discuss the planning process, the recruitment of participants, the characteristics of an effective moderator, and the logistics involved in scheduling and recording the sessions. One section covers three alternatives to the "true" focus group: the nominal group technique (in which a consensus must be reached); the Delphi technique (participants never meet each other but much reach a final consensus); and Q-methodology (people work alone to rank statements). The differences between quantitative and qualitative analysis are explained, with the goal of the latter being "to extract all potentially useful information from the available record" (p. 233). In a discussion of quality control, the authors advise that reliability may be enhanced by using a well-trained moderator. Internal validity can be improved by working with matched pairs of groups. External validity can be established by combining focus group findings with those gathered via other methodologies [that is, the process of triangulation].

18. Cunningham-Burley, Sarah, Anne Kerr, and Stephen Pavis. "Theorizing Subjects and Subject Matter in Focus Group Research." In *Developing Focus Group Research: Politics, Theory and Practice*, edited by Rosaline S. Barbour and Jenny Kitzinger, 186–99. London: Sage, 1999.

Two epistemological paradigms, positivist and interpretivist, and their relationship to focus group research are compared and contrasted. The positivist tradition, which emphasizes documenting consumers' views, underlies much of the use of focus groups in market research as well as in the social sciences in general. The interpretivist framework emphasizes involvement and dialogue among participants as active players in the research process. It views reality as socially constructed. The authors explore the issue of empowerment, critique the positivist model, and consider the role of the social researcher in a "nexus of power relations between funders, consumers and citizens" (p. 186). Several examples illustrate the authors' commitment to the interpretivist position through the various focus groups they have conducted. They believe that much research is manipulated by planners, policymakers, and managers who do not necessarily act on the results, but merely provide "the appearance of public participation in decision-making, without generating any real change" (p. 192).

19. Dickson, David. "The Focus Group Approach." In *Handbook of Communi-cation Audits for Organisations*, edited by Owen Hargie and Dennis Tourish, 85–103. New York: Routledge, 2000.

The function of focus group research is described as uncovering "the meanings and interpretations that individuals, in their own terms, place upon their experi-ences" (p. 103). Focus groups collect qualitative data, serve as a medium for closely examining a topic or issue, and create information through group discus-sion. The popularity of focus groups as a qualitative data-collection approach is discussed. In a section considering the use of the method in auditing communi-cation, Dickson offers three possible scenarios: focus groups as part of a multi-method strategy; focus groups in a subsidiary role to an alternate data-gathering technique; and focus groups as the sole technique. Half the chapter is devoted to a step-by-step analysis of how focus groups should be conducted, along with a presentation on data analysis and report writing.

20. Green, Judith, and Laura Hart. "The Impact of Context on Data." In *Develop-ing Focus Group Research: Politics, Theory and Practice*, edited by Rosa-line S. Barbour and Jenny Kitzinger, 21–35. London: Sage, 1999.

Green and Hart suggest that, instead of attempting to reproduce more "natu-ralistic" talk in discussion groups, researchers should address such issues as sampling strategies, the research environment, relationships, and language. In contrast to traditional focus groups, discussion groups seek to bring together peers—ideally people who knew one another prior to the research setting. The authors report on the methodology used for their Children and Risk study (1996), which examined children's knowledge and views about accident risks. A total of 99 boys and girls between the ages of 7 and 11 participated in 16 discussion groups. Parental consent forms were obtained (one section of the chapter deals with ethics). The research demonstrates how different contexts (for example, for-mal versus informal) and different group compositions (for example, the number and gender of participants, gender mix, friendship and nonfriendship groups) affected the resulting data.

21. Hennick, Monique, and Ian Diamond. "Using Focus Groups in Social Re-search." In *Handbook of the Psychology of Interviewing*, edited by Amina Memon and Ray Bull, 113–41. Chichester, England: Wiley, 1999.

The authors describe this qualitative research paradigm as a "non-directive interview technique which encourages discussion between participants" (p. 114). The emphasis on interaction among group members distinguishes the technique from the group interview, in which the moderator poses the questions and re-spondents individually provide answers. Following a discussion of the benefits, limitations, and appropriate applications of focus groups, the key features of the methodology are covered: (1) defining the research problem; (2) participant selection through purposive and convenience sampling and other techniques; (3) issues related to group size, the number of sessions needed to achieve the goals of the research, and the meeting venue; (4) question design; (5) the crucial role of the moderator in managing the group; and (6) data analysis and reporting the findings to the client. The last step is viewed as "complex" and "time consuming" due to the large volume of textual data produced. Various approaches to analysis are discussed, including computer software such as Ethnograph, NUD*IST, QualPro, and Atlas-ti.

22. Hughes, Diane L., and Kimberly DuMont. "Using Focus Groups to Facilitate Culturally Anchored Research." In *Ecological Research to Promote Social Change: Methodological Advances from Community Psychology*, edited by Tracey A. Revenson et al., 257–89. New York: Kluwer Academic/Plenum, 2002.

The intended audiences for the volume are master's and doctoral students in research methods courses, researchers and scholars in community psychology and other subdisciplines of psychology, and social scientists in general. Hughes and DuMont discuss the merits of focus groups, noting that they "provide researchers with direct access to the language and concepts participants use to structure their experiences and to think and talk about a designated topic" (p. 258). The central components of a focus group project are described as sample selection, instrumentation, and data analysis. The authors provide an example of how focus groups were used to facilitate a culturally sensitive research project — specifically, work and parenting issues in African-American dual-earner families. A total of 43 such parents residing in the New York metropolitan area participated in six focus groups. Participants' narratives were categorized into descriptive statements, stories, and abstract generalizations, and then analyzed. The focus groups they conducted proved valuable for their contributions to culturally anchored research.

23. Kamberelis, George, and Greg Dimitriadis. "Focus Groups: Strategic Articulations of Pedagogy, Politics, and Inquiry." In *The Sage Handbook of Qualitative Research*, edited by Norman K. Denzin and Yvonna S. Lincoln, 887–907. 3rd ed. Thousand Oaks, CA: Sage, 2005.

The authors approach focus groups both conceptually and from a transdisciplinary point of view. The implementation of focus groups by Paulo Freire in Brazil and Jonathan Kozol in New York is considered in relation to collective struggle and social transformation. Feminist consciousness-raising groups are discussed as examples of focus groups. Collective testimonials and group resistance narratives have been generated through focus groups as significant elements of feminist work. The transformation of first-wave feminism prior to World War II through post 2000 third-wave feminism is addressed. The authors trace the beginnings of focus group interviewing to 1941 with the work of Paul Lazarsfeld and Robert Merton, and summarize the uses of the methodology as a research technique. In a critical review it is observed that "large quantities of material [can be generated] from relatively large numbers of people in a relatively short time" (p. 903). The chapter closes with both a look back and a view to the future, in terms of focus groups as sites where pedagogical, political, and interpretative methodology converge.

24. Kleiber, Pamela B. "Focus Groups: More than a Method of Qualitative Inquiry." In *Foundations for Research: Methods of Inquiry in Education and the Social Sciences*, edited by Kathleen deMarrais and Stephen D. Lapan, 87–102. Mahwah, NJ: Lawrence Erlbaum, 2004.

Although this textbook is designed for students in introductory research methods courses, the editors write that more experienced researchers will also find the book useful. The development of focus group interviewing is traced to the 1940s with the contributions of Paul Lazarsfeld and Robert Merton, to its widespread use by market researchers, to acceptance as a primary research methodology in the social sciences. Kleiber comments on the basics of focus group design, discusses some practical considerations for conducting a focus group project, and presents two scenarios that characterize two different contexts for their use. The author observes that very little attention has been paid to the impact of a focus group experience from the participants' perspective. The advantages and limitations of the method are evaluated.

25. Millward, Lynne J. "Focus Groups." In *Research Methods in Psychology*, edited by Glynis M. Breakwell, Sean Hammond, and Chris Fife-Schaw, 303–24. 2nd ed. London: Sage, 2000.

Millward discusses the appropriateness of the focus group method for social science research, the type of evidence that it yields, the meaning of "focal stimuli," and how focus groups can be utilized in conjunction with surveys. A framework is presented for conducting a focus group project. The framework, which follows the logical progression of carrying out this form of qualitative research, consists of design and planning (issues of sampling, recruitment, group size, and venue); implementation (the role of the moderator and the topic guide); data collection and transcription; and content analysis (divided into qualitative, quantitative, and structural). Final comments allude to future technological developments, namely, online discussion groups that cross "cultural, spatial and temporal boundaries."

26. Morgan, David L. "Focus Group Interviewing." In *Handbook of Interview Research: Context & Method*, edited by Jaber F. Gubrium and James A. Holstein,141–59. A Sage Reference Title. Thousand Oaks, CA: Sage, 2002.

This chapter appears in part 1, "Forms of Interviewing," which covers survey, qualitative, in-depth, and life-story interviews. Morgan traces the development of focus group methodology, emphasizing its "migration" from the field of market research to widespread use within many disciplines in the social sciences. (These disciplines had traditionally been dominated by quantitative techniques.) The various approaches to moderating (less versus more structure) are considered. The author notes that the choice between the options requires careful decision making. Focus group interviewing and individual interviews are compared and contrasted in terms of whether one is more "naturalistic" than the other; whether the data produced are similarly detailed, valid, and reliable; and whether the two can be used interchangeably as qualitative research procedures. Comments are made concerning future directions for focus group research—how to both build on existing knowledge and create new ways for using the technique, such as discourse analysis, participatory action, and the impact of cross-cultural variations.

27. Rea, Louis M., and Richard A. Parker. "Utilizing Focus Groups in the Survey Research Process." In *Designing and Conducting Survey Research: A Comprehensive Guide*, 73–85. 3rd ed. San Francisco: Jossey-Bass, 2005.

Focus group interviewing is considered in terms of its use both as an alternative data-collection technique and as an adjunct to survey research. The discussion is organized around the first three components of the focus group research process: planning, recruiting, and implementation. In planning the project, decisions must be made concerning the number and type of participants needed, the number of sessions required to accomplish the goals of the research, the type of facility most conducive to interaction, whether incentives should be used, and how best to schedule the meetings. Rea and Parker offer suggestions for recruiting appropriate participants. The third component, implementation, is divided into two sections: preparation and the actual conduct of the session. Focus groups are also discussed in chapter 2 (questionnaire development), chapters 8 and 9 (sampling), and chapter 13 (the interrelationship of qualitative and quantitative findings).

28. Stewart, David W., and Prem N. Shamdasani. "Focus Group Research: Exploration and Discovery." In *Handbook of Applied Social Research Methods*, edited by Leonard Bickman and Debra J. Rog, 505–26. Thousand Oaks, CA: Sage, 1998.

This chapter is an "updated adaptation" of Stewart and Shamdasani's *Focus Groups: Theory and Practice* (1990) and Shamdasani and Stewart's "Analytical Issues in Focus Group Research," *Asian Journal of Marketing* 1, no. 1 (1992):

27–42. The authors explore several philosophical perspectives, review the relative advantages and disadvantages, and provide detailed information on how to design, conduct, analyze, and interpret the data generated from a focus group project. Emphasis is on the analysis component, with discussion of two formats: the cut-and-sort technique; and formal content analysis, including computer-assisted content analysis approaches such as KWIC, TEXTPACK V, the Oxford Concordance Program, and the Keyword-in-Context Bibliographic Indexing Program. A recent development is the electronic focus group, a format that uses a real-time, interactive computer system to enhance group discussion. Examples such as OptionFinder and GDSS allow the inclusion of demographically diverse participants in the same focus group.

29. Sudman, Seymour, and Edward Blair. "Conducting Focus Groups and Depth Interviews." In *Marketing Research: A Problem-Solving Approach*, 183–204. Boston: McGraw Hill, 1998.

Chapter 8 in this textbook provides an overview of focus groups, a qualitative data-collection methodology commonly used in the market research field. The authors define the concept and review the general procedures. The discussion centers on a wide range of issues: the role of the moderator; appropriate applications; how to select a proper venue for the discussions; recruiting the desired population (based on the goals of the research); and analyzing and reporting the results to the client, with emphasis on ideas, themes, and relationships (that is, a "nonquantitative" approach). Strengths and weaknesses are evaluated, and comparisons are made to surveys and individual interviews. Boxed material, exhibits, tips, and case studies serve to highlight important points. Individual interviews are considered on pages 196–202. The chapter ends with a list of suggested readings, discussion questions, a market research "challenge," an Internet exercise, and references.

30. Wilkinson, Sue. "Focus Groups." In *Qualitative Psychology: A Practical Guide to Research Methods*, edited by Jonathan A. Smith, 184–204. London: Sage, 2003.

This textbook is intended for undergraduate and graduate students, as well as for advanced researchers. Wilkinson observes that it is the method of data collection, rather than data analysis, that distinguishes focus groups from other qualitative approaches. The versatility of focus groups is emphasized. Using examples from her current research on women's experiences with breast cancer, Wilkinson guides the reader through the essential stages of conducting a focus group project: preplanning and design, selecting the participants and the venue, managing the discussion (Wilkinson served as the moderator), transcription, and data analysis. The last step of the process is discussed in terms of two contrasting ways of analyzing focus group data—content and discursive analysis. The

relevance and strengths of each are described, with the author concluding that
the choice depends upon the theoretical framework of the research and the type
of question being addressed.

Journal Articles

31. Hamel, Jacques. "The Focus Group Method and Contemporary French Sociology." *Journal of Sociology* 37, no. 4 (December 2001): 341–53.

Hamel (University of Montreal) briefly traces the development of the focus group method, noting that it is "back in fashion" in the social sciences—especially in sociology. The method, tied to social innovation, involves these components: a purpose, diversified actors, an innovative practice, and an assessment. Methodological issues include the representativeness of the group, the objectivity of the data produced, and the possible biasing effects of the researcher on group interaction. The author reviews the key characteristics of the technique, writing that the focus group "aims at a collective definition of problems and at remedying them through concrete action formulated as the analysis unfolds" (p. 343). The relationship between focus groups and the nominal group technique (a ranking exercise) is considered. For the rest of the article, the author discusses an extension or variant of the focus group technique—the sociological intervention approach devised by Alain Touraine, a French sociologist.

32. Hartman, Jackie. "Using Focus Groups to Conduct Business Communication Research." *Journal of Business Communication* 41, no. 4 (October 2004): 402–10.

In the initial portion of the article, Hartman defines and explains the areas in which focus groups have been used to gather qualitative data. Approximately half the article considers the value of, and the necessary steps in, focus group research. This section covers each element: the purpose, the client for whom the information is being sought, the nature of the interviewing structure, moderator selection, location choice, and the "opening" of the session. The balance of the article provides an example of focus group research applied to a business communication issue—specifically one dealing with "organizational alignment messages." Hartman maintains that focus groups are "relatively inexpensive, data-rich, flexible, and stimulating" (p. 408).

33. Ledingham, John A., and Stephen D. Bruning. "Ten Tips for Better Focus Groups." *Public Relations Quarterly* 43, no. 4 (Winter 1998/99): 25–28.

Ledingham and Bruning suggest 10 ways to avoid having focus groups fail. These are as follows: (1) use focus groups for problem solving (specific problems, issues, or conceptual approaches); (2) employ the technique to determine how people think and feel, and to explore perceptions; (3) recruit 6 to 10 participants per group, and conduct sufficient sessions (too many is better than not enough); (4) utilize focus groups only when alternatives are still being considered (if a decision has already been made, omit the focus group approach); (5) videotape the sessions; (6) inform participants about taping and observation—observers may need to be "managed" by a member of the focus group team; (7) decide if a focus group facility is really necessary—it is possible that other locations will suffice; (8) retain the services of an experienced moderator; (9) use focus groups for legitimate research, not for "show"; and (10) avoid participants' "follow the leader" behavior by having them write down some thoughts before verbal responses begin to a particular question.

34. Matoesian, Gregory M., and James R. Coldren Jr. "Language and Bodily Conduct in Focus Group Evaluations of Legal Policy." *Discourse & Society* 13, no. 4 (July 2002): 469–93.

The authors explore the role of verbal and nonverbal speech in focus group interviewing—"the linguistic presuppositions and discursive technologies" found at the core of participants' interaction in the group discussion environment. The context for the study is an assessment of a community-policing program that emphasizes partnerships between the police and the community, such as neighborhood watch groups, training for community members, and evaluation of that training. The focus group conducted was designed to assess the effectiveness of legal change and social policy initiatives. Matoesian and Coldren discuss how language and other communication strategies (for example, bodily motion, gaze, gesture, and voice pitch) shape the interaction among those involved—the moderator, members of the evaluation team, and the community participants. To demonstrate the use of these verbal and nonverbal cues, the authors provide a highly detailed analysis of an excerpt from a focus group discussion. The implications of these features of dialogue for miscommunication and misunderstandings are examined.

35. Parker, Andrew, and Jonathan Tritter. "Focus Group Method and Methodology: Current Practice and Recent Debate." *International Journal of Research & Method in Education* 29, no. 1 (April 2006): 23–37.

The authors have written a review article outlining the methodological background of focus groups and addressing key areas such as recruitment, interaction, and sampling. Focus groups are perceived to be more cost effective than "traditional" methods, adaptable, and particularly useful when studying policy-related topics. Parker and Tritter are at the University of Warwick in the United Kingdom and cite the fact that successive U.K. governments have promoted the value of focus groups as effective mechanisms for determining public opinion. The authors stress the differences between "group interviews" and focus groups (group interviews are seen as investigative, with the researcher asking the questions and controlling the dynamics of the group, whereas in focus groups the researcher facilitates or moderates the discussion among participants). The discussion concerning recruitment covers (1) the issue of providing incentives; (2) methods of sampling such as the "snowball" technique, which involves using participants who know each other; (3) the commercial market research approach, which has tended to use strangers; and (4) the selection of participants from members of preexisting social groups. Data-analysis techniques are reviewed, as well as the ethical considerations of data sensitivity and confidentiality.

36. Quible, Zane K. "A Focus on Focus Groups." *Business Communication Quarterly* 61, no. 2 (June 1998): 28–38.

Quible encourages the use of the focus group process in business communication courses. A description of the technique includes sections on the participants and the role of the moderator. Specific discussion incorporates the planning, conduct, and analysis and reporting stages. Several advantages and disadvantages of the technique are noted. Four suggested topics for classroom use are listed. The author cites the origin of the process as being in the 1950s, the product of focused interviewing and group therapy techniques practiced by psychiatrists. The smallest and largest focus groups are suggested to be, respectively, 6 and 12 participants. In the analysis phase Quible suggests using a three-element coding scheme broken down by individual, consensus, and areas of agreement and disagreement. A two-page appendix provides an example of a focus group report.

37. Wilkinson, Sue. "Focus Group Methodology: A Review." *International Journal of Social Research Methodology* 1, no. 3 (1998): 181–203.

Wilkinson (University of Loughborough) traces the development of focus group methodology, observing that prior to the late 1970s the technique was used primarily for the evaluation and marketing of products, programs, and services. In the 1980s, health researchers found the method applicable to a wide range of topics in health education and health promotion, such as HIV/AIDS, smoking cessation, family planning, and sexual behavior and attitudes. In the following decade, the technique was adopted by researchers in a variety of disciplines including education, feminist research, anthropology, linguistics, and sociology. Focus groups have been utilized as a stand-alone method, as an adjunct to other qualitative or quantitative designs, and as a form of participatory action research. The author evaluates the benefits and limitations of focus groups and reviews three defining characteristics—all emphasizing the interactive nature of the data gathered. Wilkinson discusses some of the issues involved in the analysis of focus group data, which she considers a neglected area in the published research. Two approaches are explained: content and ethnographic.

38. Wooten, David B., and Americus Reed II. "A Conceptual Overview of the Self-Presentational Concerns and Response Tendencies of Focus Group Participants." *Journal of Consumer Psychology* 9, no. 3 (2000): 141–53.

The authors present a conceptual model that encourages researchers to "challenge" some of the conventional wisdom regarding focus groups. According to the model, the amount and quality of information that people convey about themselves depend upon the degree to which they wish to make desired impressions on others, and, if highly motivated to do so, may present biased images of themselves or provide evasive or deceptive answers. Wooten and Reed identify and discuss five factors that may heighten self-presentational concerns among participants, thereby affecting group participation. These are (1) group characteristics (issues of size, homogeneity, and acquaintanceship of members); (2) individual characteristics (such as the degree to which participants are concerned about what others think of them); (3) the discussion topic (especially if the topic is of a sensitive nature); (4) the moderator (verbal and nonverbal cues can affect responses); and (5) the facility (issues such as the seating arrangement and physical layout). Implications of the model for future research endeavors are discussed.

Pamphlets

39. American Statistical Association. Section on Survey Research Methods. *What Are Focus Groups?* ASA series What Is a Survey? Alexandria, VA: American Statistical Association, 1998. 12p.

The association defines focus groups as "in-depth qualitative interviews with a small number of carefully selected people, brought together to discuss a host of topics ranging from pizza to safe sex" (p. 1). Although focus groups are viewed as an "important companion" to sample surveys, there are distinct differences between the two data-collection methodologies. The data generated from the former is through the give and take of group discussion, rather than the one-way flow of information that characterizes the survey. Topics discussed include potential users, participant selection, the role of the moderator, appropriate types of questions for group discussion (open-ended, as opposed to those requiring "yes" or "no" responses, are advocated), the recommended size of the group, and the actual conduct of the sessions. Methods for recording the discussion are audiotaping, videotaping, manual note taking, or some combination of the three. Advantages and disadvantages are noted, and comments are made about how the results produced compare to those from surveys.

40. Chalofsky, Neal. *How to Conduct Focus Groups.* Info-line: The How-to Reference Tool for Training & Performance Professionals. Alexandria, VA: American Society for Training & Development, 1999. 16p.

While emphasizing product, service, and program development and evaluation, the author introduces the basics of focus group methodology, identifies applicable situations, and offers suggestions for planning and conducting a focus group project. Instructions are provided for writing open-ended questions; recruiting the appropriate participants, moderator, and recorder; facilitating the sessions; and analyzing and reporting the results to the client. Chalofsky provides a sample focus group protocol and an example of a typical discussion. A consideration of seven "myths" surrounding the use of the methodology completes the pamphlet.

41. Fabiano, Patricia, and Linda Costigan Lederman. *Top Ten Misperceptions of Focus Group Research.* Working Paper 3: A publication of The Report on Social Norms. Garfield, NJ: Paper Clip Communications, 2002. 8p.

The authors identify the misperceptions, provide examples of each, examine the assumptions associated with them, and counter with methods and standards that will contribute to solid research and valid results. The common misunderstandings discussed center on these points: that focus groups are easy to conduct, take little time to complete, are low in cost, do not require specific participants or numbers of participants, and can be conducted by untrained personnel. The next four items concentrate on focus group data, namely, that it can supplant survey questionnaires, is generalizable, is of higher quality than data produced by quantitative methodologies, and can be easily compiled and reported. The last misperception concerns the view that focus groups pose no risk to participants.

1.2 ANALYSIS

42. Frankland, Jane, and Michael Bloor. "Some Issues Arising in the Systematic Analysis of Focus Group Materials." In *Developing Focus Group Research: Politics, Theory and Practice*, edited by Rosaline S. Barbour and Jenny Kitzinger, 144–55. London: Sage, 1999.

The difficulties of analyzing focus group data with techniques designed to address data produced by other qualitative approaches, such as depth interviews and ethnographic field notes, are highlighted. *Analytic induction*, also known as *deviant case analysis*, is advocated. First adopted in 1934, the purpose is "to derive propositions which apply generally across all the data to the entire universe of relevant cases or transcript items" (p. 150). Analytic induction is discussed in terms of its benefits and limitations for application to focus group data—in this case, data from a study of adolescents, peer pressure, and smoking behavior. As part of a larger smoking cessation intervention program, 12 focus groups were conducted with students ages 12 to 14 attending four secondary schools in South Wales. The discussions were audiotaped and transcribed, the latter practice highly recommended to preserve the "richness" of the dialogue. Resulting data were indexed, coded, entered into Ethnograph (a computer program designed to facilitate data analysis), and interpreted by analytic induction.

43. Hydén, L.-C., and P. H. Bülow. "Who's Talking: Drawing Conclusions from Focus Groups—Some Methodological Considerations." *International Journal of Social Research Methodology* 6, no. 4 (2003): 305–21.

The Swedish authors write from the perspective that focus group participants may speak and interact in many capacities (and shift between modes), thereby producing "a central methodological question" when analyzing group discussions. Participants may interact as individuals, as members of a small group, or as people who temporarily share a situation that focuses their attention. Hydén and Bülow summarize the problem of "who's talking" by questioning how the utterances of individual members of the group should be interpreted. The authors conducted three focus groups with a total of 18 general practitioners, schoolteachers, and social workers—all deemed to be at risk for job "burnout." Data were analyzed using techniques from ethnomethodology and conversation analysis. The discussion centers on whether people respond as individuals or as members of a small group, and the implications for analysis and interpretation.

44. Krueger, Richard A. *Analyzing & Reporting Focus Group Results*. Focus Group Kit 6. Thousand Oaks, CA: Sage, 1998. 138p.

Krueger makes the point that approaches for analyzing qualitative data are quite different from those required for quantitative studies, the latter typically being subjected to statistical analysis. The author discusses the basic principles and techniques involved in the focus group process, noting the special difficulties encountered when analyzing responses to open-ended questions and interaction among participants. Also considered are various strategies for analysis, a review of the tools and equipment that may aid the process, and suggestions for writing the results document. Included in the volume are five essays written by experts in the field, who share their thoughts and experiences with manipulating large quantities of narrative data. The book is directed toward academic audiences, practitioners, and moderators. Many examples, icons, and exercises are found throughout the text.

45. Myers, Greg, and Phil Macnaghten. "Can Focus Groups Be Analysed as Talk?" In *Developing Focus Group Research: Politics, Theory and Practice*, edited by Rosaline S. Barbour and Jenny Kitzinger, 173–85. London: Sage, 1999.

Based on principles drawn from conversation analysis, the authors recommend that researchers direct more attention to analyzing focus group transcripts as talk. They observe that although content analysis can indicate what participants talked about, conversation analysis can reveal how they discussed a topic, as well as other information. Three examples demonstrate how opinions are offered in context, how topics are redefined, and how moderator intervention keeps the discussion on target. Myers and Macnaghten state that the work of the moderator "is rendered invisible when the published reports on the research quote only the utterance of the participant, and not those leading up to it" (p. 181). Additional analysis, with longer quotations from the transcripts, is advocated. Full conversation analysis would include indications of volume, speed, quality of voice, pauses, breathing, and intonation—a much more time-consuming process than a simple transcription.

46. Schmidt, Marcus. "Using an ANN-Approach for Analyzing Focus Groups." *Qualitative Market Research* 4, no. 2 (2001): 100–112.

The analysis of focus group data can be very time consuming. Schmidt discusses various software programs designed to ease the challenge, and the theoretical underpinnings to a number of these. In particular, he concentrates on an artificial neural network (ANN)-based software called CATPAC 4 Windows from Terra Research, describing the data-preparation procedures and the empirical value of the approach. The aim of such programs is to begin to quantify data by examining elements such as frequency of keywords as part of the text analysis. Schmidt advises that it may take a week to analyze 10 to 15 pages of text—a time period that may be acceptable to a social scientist but which may be considered overly long for a research consultant working in a commercial environment. The author views these quantitative methods as supplementing well-established qualitative approaches, rather than replacing them.

47. Smithson, Janet. "Using and Analysing Focus Groups: Limitations and Possibilities." *International Journal of Social Research Methodology* 3, no. 2 (2000): 103–19.

Smithson examines some of the methodological issues involved when focus groups have been chosen to carry out qualitative social science research. The context for the study was young adults' expectations of the future with regard to work and family in five European countries: Ireland, Norway, Portugal, Sweden, and the United Kingdom. Approximately 10 focus groups were conducted in each of the countries (the present analysis is based on data from the 14 U.K. focus groups). A total of 82 men and women participated, with 20 percent representing ethnic minorities. The author recruited the participants, and moderated, audiotaped, and transcribed the discussions. The defining characteristic of the method, interaction, is discussed in terms of dominate voices, "constructing the other" (this refers to moderator bias), normative discourses, and conflicts and arguments. Smithson emphasizes that these central interactive features must be taken into account in the analysis phase. Moderator strategies and analysis approaches are discussed. Extracts from the transcripts are used to highlight the methodological concerns.

48. Warr, Deborah J. "'It Was Fun . . . but We Don't Usually Talk about These Things': Analyzing Sociable Interaction in Focus Groups." *Qualitative Inquiry* 11, no. 2 (April 2005): 200–225.

Warr writes that the nature of the dialogue generated in focus groups is "a mixture of personal beliefs and available collective narratives that are flavored by the local circumstances of participants' lives" (p. 200). Due to the interaction ("layers of talk") among participants that characterizes the technique, the researcher is faced with a variety of complicated analytical and interpretative challenges. The standard analytic methods for qualitative research (content and thematic analyses) require modification to include this interaction. These modifications are discussed in context of a focus group study undertaken in Victoria, Australia. A total of 54 individuals from socioeconomically disadvantaged areas participated in eight 60- to 90-minute focus groups. The moderator (Warr) asked a series of broad, open-ended items focusing on love and intimacy. Some theoretical issues that informed the research are discussed, and the three phases required to analyze the material are described. Ten excerpts serve to illustrate key points. In the author's view, the data produced in focus groups offer "valuable sociological insights" (p. 223).

49. Wiggins, Geoffrey S. "The Analysis of Focus Groups in Published Research Articles." *Canadian Journal of Program Evaluation* 19, no. 2 (Autumn 2004): 143–64.

Using the Ebsco and LexisNexis journal "search engines" (for the terms "focus," "group," and "groups"), a total of 72 citations were retrieved: 29 from health education, 22 from sociology, and 21 from education. With an emphasis on the analysis component, Wiggins presents a summary of the article findings in table 1. Authors and date of publication are provided in the first column. The second and third columns indicate whether focus groups were utilized alone or in combination with some other qualitative or quantitative technique, and whether this information is supplied in the text. Under "Application," the fourth column, Wiggins lists whether quotations and ideas from the focus group discussions were used, or whether a coding scheme assisted in organizing and analyzing the data (44 percent of the articles employed either manual or computer assistance). The nature of the coding scheme, emergent or preordinate, is provided in column five. The "yes" and "no" headings in the "Quality Check" column indicate the use of an interrater reliability check when analyzing the transcripts (14 percent). Column seven lists the dominant area of study of the article (health, education, or sociology). Evaluators are advised that the goals of the research dictate the choice of analytic technique.

1.3 MODERATING

50. Bystedt, Jean, Siri Lynn, and Deborah Potts. *Moderating to the Max: A Full-Tilt Guide to Creative, Insightful Focus Groups and Depth Interviews.* Ithaca, NY: Paramount Market Publishing, 2003. 143p.

Based on their experiences, the authors describe some innovative alternative approaches for use with focus groups and in-depth interviews. These include such techniques as free association, sorting, perceptual mapping, storytelling, and on-site interviews. The concept of *laddering*, a qualitative methodology introduced in the mid-1980s, is defined as "the systematic explanation of the links" between service attributes and the "meanings, feelings, and associations they impart" (p. 65). Subsequent chapters cover emotions, imagery, and associations. A "junk drawer" consists of observations not included elsewhere, such as the "power of introductions" and introductory questions. The recommendations offered are intended to be modified to meet individual requirements. The text is accompanied by the liberal use of graphics in the form of line drawings, black-and-white photographs, boxes, and charts.

51. Cowley, James C. P. "Strategic Qualitative Focus Group Research—Define and Articulate Our Skills or We Will Be Replaced by Others." *International Journal of Market Research* 42, no. 1 (Winter 1999/2000): 17–38.

The Australian author concentrates exclusively on the role of the moderator/facilitator in conducting market research focus groups. Cowley emphasizes the need for moderators to possess a high level of competency for performing their duties. In addition, a taxonomy of skills must be developed that indicates what traits are necessary to attain this level of competency. It is observed that market research companies have established "no required entry qualifications or agreed frame of knowledge and no competency criteria" (p. 23) for moderators. To fill this void, a research case study was undertaken. Focus groups were conducted with a sample of 19 leading male and female strategic qualitative market researchers (SQMRs). A taxonomy of skills was developed from the SQMRs' descriptions of derived skills, a literature review, and the researcher's own experience as a market research moderator. Competency was attributed to hard work and experience.

52. Greenbaum, Thomas L. *Moderating Focus Groups: A Practical Guide for Group Facilitation.* Thousand Oaks, CA: Sage, 2000. 249p.

Designed for facilitators of focus groups, interviewers, or those conducting general business meetings, this book deals with every aspect of the topic from simple to advanced, and all related components of moderating. Greenbaum discusses the central role of the moderator, planning and preparation, participant recruitment, and pre- and postgroup briefings. Subsequent chapters cover the discussion guide, the use of external stimuli, the written report, and the basics of a pricing strategy. Consideration is given to unique moderating situations, that is, those that involve special categories of participants such as physicians, employees, children and teens, senior citizens, and the uneducated. The personal and professional skills required for handling sensitive topics are reviewed. One chapter is devoted to global focus group research, with the author noting that anticipating problems is important for successful assignment completion. The controversy as to which method (focus groups or individual in-depth interviews) is more effective for producing qualitative research information is addressed. A glossary of 91 entries is provided.

53. Krueger, Richard A. *Moderating Focus Groups*. Focus Group Kit 4. Thousand Oaks, CA: Sage, 1998. 115p.

This volume is a highly pragmatic presentation covering all aspects of the topic. It is directed to both the newcomer for the task of moderating a focus group discussion, as well as to the experienced practitioner who needs to improve her or his moderating skills. The important role of the moderator/facilitator in the focus group process is discussed in terms of the training and skill level required, the variety of interviewing techniques an effective moderator can utilize, and the strategies this individual can employ for managing difficult situations. Details are provided on how to choose the recording equipment, select the facility and arrange the room, and deal with disruptive, quiet, shy, inattentive, and disrespectful participants. The responsibilities of the assistant moderator include recording the sessions, for example, note taking, flip charts, audiotaping, and videotaping, the last deemed "obtrusive and usually not worth the effort." Many icons, examples, and checklists are included.

54. Krueger, Richard A., and Jean A. King. *Involving Community Members in Focus Groups*. Focus Group Kit 5. Thousand Oaks, CA: Sage, 1998. 94p.

Although many texts and journal articles deal with the role of the moderator/facilitator in the successful conduct of focus group interviews, little research has been devoted to training moderators to teach others—that is, volunteers—the skills required for such an activity. Krueger and King trace the development of participatory evaluation during the past several decades and discuss the practical, historical, and psychological rationale underlying the use of volunteers as moderators in focus group studies. The advantages of involving community members in this capacity are the following: participants feel more comfortable while sharing their thoughts and opinions; studies are more cost effective; volunteers may be more interested in the outcome of the research; and there may be personal and collective benefits to those serving in this role. Subsequent chapters cover how to form the research team, set up a training schedule, and conduct the sessions. Exercises, checklists, and icons are found throughout the text.

55. Langer, Judith. *The Mirrored Window: Focus Groups from a Moderator's Point of View.* Ithaca, NY: Paramount Market Publishing, 2001. 256p.

The author covers many aspects of the moderator's role in conducting qualitative market research, specifically the focus group interview. Suggestions are offered as to when qualitative approaches would prove most successful, such as for gauging consumers' feelings and for developing new products. Also considered are the advantages and disadvantages of online focus groups; how to define the task and devise a hypothesis; the intricacies of managing the fieldwork; how to write the screener questionnaire and interview guide; moderator behavior and special techniques; and the challenges of analyzing and reporting qualitative data. In a chapter titled "15 Myths about Qualitative Research," Langer addresses such issues as group size, the optimal time of day to conduct group sessions, and the degree to which the topic guide (or "script") should be followed.

56. Prince, Mel, and Mark Davies. "Moderator Teams: An Extension to Focus Group Methodology." *Qualitative Market Research* 4, no. 4 (2001): 207–16.

Prince and Davies write from the perspective that traditionally conducted focus groups (that is, those led by a single moderator) can contribute to moderator bias. Some of the problems arising from traditional focus groups are discussed. The authors consider the interpersonal qualities, or "cues," that moderators possess, that in spite of self-awareness may be subjectively assessed by participants "beyond face value." These qualities include appearance, values, dialect, choice of words and phrases, and verbal and nonverbal behavior. To reduce the difficulties associated with using a single moderator, the authors propose a new approach: the Serial Moderating Technique (SMT). This method involves a series of complementary moderators who facilitate the discussion, sequentially, over the course of the session. Specifically, three to five moderators lead each group for 20 to 40 minutes. The common element among them is the interview schedule, with each moderator specializing in a specific section and/or the overall session. A multidisciplinary team is recommended. The authors discuss the advantages of the SMT, provide a brief case study of its successful application in the market research field, and suggest some caveats (primarily cost) to effective usage.

57. Puchta, Claudia, and Jonathan Potter. *Focus Group Practice.* London: Sage, 2004. 174p.

Puchta and Potter concentrate on the interaction that occurs between the moderator and the participants in a focus group discussion. The intended audiences are market research practitioners, secondarily for social scientists, and thirdly for individuals engaged in tasks involving group interviews. The goal is to assist moderators in developing an understanding of the concept of interaction by presenting two relatively new perspectives: conversation analysis and discursive psychology. The chapters highlight the ways in which the moderator can foster an informal atmosphere—one that will encourage participation and the accurate and forthright expression of both opinions and descriptions. In the last chapter the prospective research is channeled from strategy to practice. Deficiencies in current focus group practice are noted, and comments are made concerning focus group methodology and the future of market research. Throughout, the authors provide examples of actual conversations from focus group sessions. Each chapter ends with a summary and a set of practical suggestions.

58. Puchta, Claudia, and Jonathan Potter. "Manufacturing Individual Opinions: Market Research Focus Groups and the Discursive Psychology of Evaluation." *British Journal of Social Psychology* 41, no. 3 (September 2002): 345–63.

The authors provide background information on (1) traditional conceptualizations of attitudes and opinions; (2) the discursive social psychology (DSP) approach, that is, the application of tenets from discourse analysis to issues in social psychology; (3) the theoretical and analytic perspective of conversation analysis (CA); and (4) rhetorically organized speech versus freestanding opinions and enduring underlying attitudes in focus group interaction. The authors investigate the techniques that moderators use for "discovering the traditional notion of opinion within participants, while overly eliciting it from them" (p. 346). These techniques include how moderators deal with rhetorically developed opinions, how they can encourage respondents' freestanding opinion packages, and what procedures can be employed to "strip off" the rhetorically embedded nature of evaluations. Data for the analysis came from videotapes of eight 90-minute market research focus groups on cigarettes conducted by six experienced moderators. All discussions were in German, transcribed in German, and then translated into English. The analysis was performed on the German original, using techniques from CA and DSP. Moderators helped participants produce freestanding opinions by ignoring side comments between and/or among members.

59. Puchta, Claudia, Jonathan Potter, and Stephan Wolff. "Repeat Receipts: A Device for Generating Visible Data in Market Research Focus Groups." *Qualitative Research* 4, no. 3 (2004): 285–309.

Puchta et al. consider how focus group data are produced for market research clients through the use of *repeat receipts*, a technique in which the group moderator repeats the participants' remarks—either word for word or by shortening them. The device serves a number of functions, such as emphasizing central terms, removing rhetorical relations, and covering conflict. The authors discuss how moderators use repeat receipts to help shape focus group interaction and why the "phenomenon" is necessary to guide this interaction "in a way that makes opinions, beliefs and attitudes clearly *visible*" (p. 287). The applicability of the technique is demonstrated by 13 videotaped market research focus groups (9 German, 4 English) conducted by 11 different moderators. In addition, eight audiotaped German social science focus groups were conducted by three different moderators. All sessions lasted 90-plus minutes. There were 7 to 11 participants per group. Analysis indicates that repeat receipts were used between 15 and 20 times in each market research group, while none were found in the social sciences groups. A comparison of repeats in focus groups, surveys, and news interviews concludes the article.

1.4 MULTIPLE SESSIONS

60. Lindsay, A. C., and Anita M. Hubley. "Conceptual Reconstruction through a Modified Focus Group Methodology." *Social Indicators Research* 79, no. 3 (December 2006): 437–54.

The issue of age identity was examined with a modified version of focus group methodology. The authors conducted one focus group with six female university students who attended multiple sessions (in this case three). The sessions lasted for one hour and were spaced one week apart. Between each session the authors conducted a detailed transcription process requiring approximately 10 hours. At the second session each participant read the transcript, and was then asked if she wanted to "clarify, revise, or extend" her comments, with the moderator probing each person to seek explanations for any ambiguities. The process was repeated with the third session, at the end of which the authors believed that they had reached "informational redundancy." A poststudy questionnaire was administered. While none of the participants were willing to choose a number to represent the age they felt during the focus groups, participants in other question-naire research selected their age "relatively easily."

1.5 ONLINE

61. Anderson, Terry, and Heather Kanuka. "Focus Groups." In *e-Research: Methods, Strategies, and Issues*, 102–19. Boston: Allyn and Bacon, 2003.

Focus group interviews are "focused" in two ways: the group participants are similar in some aspect, and the goal is to collect data about a single topic or a narrow range of topics. The technique is frequently used for in-depth and collaborative examination of an issue and for redefining the research topic. Four types of Internet (Net)-based focus groups are identified and discussed: synchronous and text-based; synchronous and audio- and/or video-based; asynchronous and text-based; and asynchronous and audio- and/or video-based. (Most Net-based focus groups are conducted using text-based synchronous or asynchronous software.) The merits of traditional face-to-face interviewing versus Net-based focus groups are evaluated. Among the advantages of the latter are that individuals from different geographical areas can participate from their homes or offices; no costs are incurred for travel, food, or facility rental; the discussions from the sessions do not need to be transcribed; and participant anonymity is ensured. Disadvantages include poorer quality data, the lack of nonverbal cues, and more challenging data analysis. A variety of theoretical and practical issues of interest to the e-researcher are discussed.

62. Choe, Pilsung, Chulwoo Kim, Mark R. Lehto, Xinran Lehto, and Jan Allebach. "Evaluating and Improving a Self-Help Technical Support Web Site: Use of Focus Group Interviews." *International Journal of Human-Computer Interaction* 21, no. 3 (2006): 333–54.

Three focus group interviews were conducted with 19 students and technical marketing and support personnel to aid in the development of a user-friendly Web site. The discussions generated 90 comments, which could be divided into 28 usability categories. A postdevelopment experiment validated the usefulness of the focus group approach, with the changes resulting in substantial improvement as compared with the original site. The authors note that the moderator not only needs to be expert with focus groups but also should have technical knowledge and a background understanding of the Web site under consideration. When selecting participants for the focus groups, one should be sensitive to choosing appropriate users for the particular type of Web site being evaluated. Participants' prior familiarization of the site improved the interviews, as well as the capability for simultaneous viewing during the sessions. The authors found focus groups to be an "easy and efficient" method for Web site evaluation—when questions are prepared in detail and when the organizational approaches described above are followed.

63. Easton, George, Annette Easton, and Michael Belch. "An Experimental Investigation of Electronic Focus Groups." *Information & Management* 40 (September 2003): 717–27.

The authors review the defining characteristics of both traditional focus groups and focus groups supported by Group Support Systems (GSS) technology ("a term synonymous with the combination of computer, communications, and decision technologies" [p. 718] to affect group processes and outcomes). An empirical study was undertaken to compare the two formats in terms of unique ideas, on-task ideas, levels of participation, and the impact of group size. A total of 120 undergraduate students were assigned to either six traditional or six GSS focus groups. In the latter, the moderator verbally conducted the sessions; students responded via workstations. Although the same moderator and interview guide were used for both approaches, group size was varied. The results indicate that GSS group members had higher participation rates and generated a greater number of unique and higher-quality ideas. Mixed support was found relative to group size. The authors conclude that "GSS group methodologies may provide a superior methodology to traditional focus group methodologies" (p. 726).

64. Franklin, Kathy K., and Catherine Lowry. "Computer-Mediated Focus Group Sessions: Naturalistic Inquiry in a Networked Environment." *Qualitative Research* 1, no. 2 (2001): 169–84.

The authors define and discuss the terms generalizability, reliability, and validity, and provide a philosophical perspective for each. An overview of the traditional focus group method is given, with the term "rapporteur" used to describe the researcher/moderator role (as used by J. F. Templeton in the 1987 work titled *Focus Groups: A Guide for Marketing and Advertising Professionals*). The advantages and disadvantages of the approach are described. By contrast, the positives and negatives of computer-mediated focus groups are presented. Positive aspects include the improvement of the objectivity of the data collection, the reduction in discomfort while addressing sensitive topics, and the potential to better manage challenging participants. A study is described that used doctoral students enrolled in a qualitative research course at the University of Arkansas at Little Rock as the rapporteurs, with 28 professors as the participants. The subject of the study was the faculty attitude toward the use of instructional technology in the college classroom. Four focus groups were conducted using 14 networked computer workstations. Six benefits and four challenges with the computer-mediated format are discussed in detail.

65. Gaiser, Ted J. "Conducting On-Line Focus Groups: A Methodological Discussion." *Social Science Computer Review* 15, no. 2 (Summer 1997): 135–44.

The implementation of online focus groups using technology available in 1997 is addressed. Although chat groups, multiuser dimensions, and Web conference pages are cited as the most likely places to conduct focus groups, these areas are "superficial and playful," and it may be difficult for them to be used for serious discussion. Bulletin boards are suggested as likely successful sites, but these too have researcher limitations, in that probing issues would be a challenge. Gaiser explores the methodological efforts to date. Techniques for participant recruitment, informed consent, and response time are discussed: a one-week period gives respondents time to be reflective. The development of guides for online focus groups is briefly considered, as are the relative merits of face-to-face versus the computer environment. The selected level of moderating is considered to be of importance, and needs to be expressed (but which can be varied within a particular study). Flexible expectations, awareness that contention may arise with respect to subject matter and methodology, and that the moderator needs to be emotionally "as present to the situation . . . as possible" are noted as points to consider.

66. Harris, Cheryl. "Developing Online Market Research Methods and Tools—Considering Theorizing Interactivity: Models and Cases." *Marketing and Research Today* 25, no. 4 (November 1997): 267–73.

Theoretical and methodological problems and issues in the online research environment are explored. The first half of the article considers online surveys, with an outline summary of perceived benefits and limitations. Harris then discusses online qualitative research, again providing pros and cons related to online focus groups. It is noted that sessions of an hour or less with six to eight participants are the most effective. The challenge of recruitment in the online environment is observed, with potential participants not granting the same level of commitment to an online appointed time as participants involved in face-to-face group sessions. Harris wonders whether the significant advantage that the online mode has through the perceived sense of anonymous communication will endure once participants may be visually represented, with what are described as "respondent avatars" (such as cartoon characters, or photographic representations of the respondent). The ethics of online research are discussed, with several codes of conduct cited.

67. Hughes, Jerald, and Karl R. Lang. "Issues in Online Focus Groups: Lessons Learned from an Empirical Study of Peer-to-Peer Filesharing System Users." *Electronic Journal of Business Research Methods* 2, no. 2 (2004): 95–110.

Information on the beliefs and attitudes about peer-to-peer file-sharing systems by members of the MP3 user community, industry experts, and parents of children using MP3s were researched using two online focus groups. Hughes and Lang were primarily seeking to establish future directions for their investigation. The article reviews the state of online research, places the issue of file-sharing in context, and discusses the application of online focus groups. With visual maps, the authors demonstrate the "multi-threaded simultaneous conversations" that occur online. Through the use of arrows connecting conversation text, the reader can trace the flow of the communication—seen as packages of words linked one to another, instead of a simple logged transcript by time. The authors present a chart of 10 major criticisms of Internet-based group communication and then respond to each. Future areas for research using Internet focus groups include issues of group size, composition, session length, time per question, moderation approaches, location (as in a laboratory versus users' own computers), data collection, time zone issues, and member interaction.

68. Lim, Cher Ping, and Seng Chee Tan. "Online Discussion Boards for Focus Group Interviews: An Exploratory Study." *Journal of Educational Enquiry* 2, no. 1 (2001): 50–60.

The authors explore the use of Blackboard, an online discussion board, as a medium for focus groups. Information and communication technologies used to gather qualitative data at the Singapore National Institute of Education—specifically in an instructional technology course required for the postgraduate diploma in education. The focus group was conducted online for 12 days with 19 participants, for a total of 60 postings (an average of 2.5 postings per participant), with an average length of 128 words. The advantages of online discussion boards are the following: (1) greater convenience—scheduling problems are eliminated and participants can choose when and where to access the group; (2) reduced social interference—in face-to-face sessions some participants hold back responses; (3) reduced "groupthink," a situation that can arise from dominant, loud, aggressive, or persuasive participants; (4) the ability to reflect before responding; (5) the greater control available to the moderator; and (6) the ready-made record of all communication. Limitations include disjointed transactions (responses out of sequence or without reading previous discussions), lack of nonverbal cues, and the need for participants to have access to the proper equipment and the necessary skills.

69. Monolescu, Dominique, and Catherine Schifter. "Online Focus Group: A Tool to Evaluate Online Students' Course Experience." *Internet and Higher Education* 2, nos. 2–3 (2000): 171–76.

The researchers report on a pilot study designed to examine factors that contribute to students' level of satisfaction with Internet coursework. Monolescu and Schifter believe that a different research paradigm is necessary when evaluating online experiences. Two data-gathering approaches were utilized: virtual focus groups and the Delphi method, "a systematic communication technique, mainly used for forecasting" (p. 173). Recruitment yielded a total of eight students, whose anonymity was preserved throughout the project. All contact between researchers and participants was via e-mail. Student communication was asynchronous, that is, they did not have to be online at the same time. (The "uniqueness" of the study is said to be related to the integration of asynchronous communication and focus group methodology.) In phase two of the three-phase project, students could read the comments posted by others. Virtual focus groups are presented as a "flexible" and "powerful" research tool.

70. Montoya-Weiss, Mitzi M., Anne P. Massey, and Danial L. Clapper. "On-Line Focus Groups: Conceptual Issues and a Research Tool." *European Journal of Marketing* 32, nos. 7–8, (1998): 713–24.

The role of technology is discussed in relation to focus group composition, controversial topics, and the impact of the moderator. The authors observe that as of 1998 there is a need for research into the effects of anonymity, leanness (the absence of cues such as body language and verbal tone), and parallel communication (multiple simultaneous topics being pursued at the same time). Montoya-

Weiss and coauthors developed a tool called IntFG to enable researchers to study the nature of online focus groups. The questions raised by this resource include how the depth and quality of the discussions are influenced and the degree to which input quantity by participants is adjusted. The ability of the moderator to achieve a desirable balance is noted as a key issue.

71. O'Connor, Henrietta, and Clare Madge. "'Focus Groups in Cyberspace': Using the Internet for Qualitative Research." *Qualitative Market Research* 6, no. 2 (2003): 133–43.

Using a software conferencing technique called Hotline Connect, the authors investigated whether virtual synchronous group interviews could be successfully conducted. The advantages are low costs, the ability to obtain a record of activities, and the possibility of conducting international research. The challenges are that the traditional interviewer/interviewee relationship is quite different (including the power dynamic), visual pointers are absent, and rapport building and question probing are more difficult. The pilot project research, titled Cyberparents, was designed to measure the impact of Web sites on parenting practices. The authors maintain that online research is an "attractive option"—despite the noted limitations.

72. Oringderff, Jennifer. "'My Way': Piloting an Online Focus Group." *International Journal of Qualitative Methods* 3, no. 3 (September 2004): 1–10.

Online focus groups (OFGs) were conducted with geographically dispersed populations, thus enabling the collection of data from people in multiple time zones. Oringderff explains the experiences she had in implementing OFGs in an academic setting and highlights both the advantages and the pitfalls of the approach. The project was designed to consider "the effects accompanying expatriate spouses have on the success of an international assignment" (p. 1). The article includes the following six guidelines for "best practice": (1) recruit participants who are comfortable with the online environment; (2) establish clear procedures to be followed by the moderator and the participants; (3) select a moderator who is capable and knowledgeable; (4) determine how participants will be selected; (5) keep the discussion focused (participants tend to wander off the topic); and (6) indicate the study time frame and what will occur at the end (such as shutting down the site). The author points to the many benefits of OFGs and maintains that the limitations are surmountable.

73. Parent, Michael, R. Brent Gallupe, Wm. David Salisbury, and Jay M. Handelman. "Knowledge Creation in Focus Groups: Can Group Technologies Help?" *Information & Management* 38, no. 1 (October 2000): 47–58.

The use of face-to-face Group Support Systems (GSS) as a mechanism to increase knowledge creation in focus groups is explored. Two experiments were conducted. The first, with 40 subjects, sought to determine if the GSS technique is relevant to knowledge creation in focus group methodology. The authors found that GSS led to a greater number of relevant ideas. The second experiment, with 193 subjects, found that the approach generated a greater number of higher quality ideas, with improved consensus achievement—but at the expense of a lower satisfaction level than groups not using GSS. The GSS environment involves "same-place-same time" configurations with networked computers arranged around a U-shaped table. One of the reasons for this modified focus group approach is to counter some of the perceived negatives of focus groups, namely, their subjectivity, inconsistent results, and moderator variation. Overall, the authors found that the use of GSS was appropriate as a knowledge creation support system for focus groups.

74. Reid, Donna J., and Fraser J. M. Reid. "Online Focus Groups: An In-depth Comparison of Computer-mediated and Conventional Focus Group Discussions." *International Journal of Market Research* 47, no. 2 (2005): 131–62.

This 30-page comparison of face-to-face (FTF) focus groups versus computer-mediated communication (CMC) concludes that CMC can be seen as a "viable alternative." One drawback of CMC is that it requires twice as long to produce the same number of ideas as FTF focus groups. The study compared the two approaches on process, objective, and subjective measures. The authors considered the amount of communication, equality of participation, uninhibited communication, group interaction, self-disclosure, the number of ideas generated, and the subjective experience. The authors tested these issues through an experimental study involving 48 undergraduates, divided into 16 three-person groups. The FTF groups were videotaped, with the text transcribed for analysis. The CMC groups were conducted at computers in the four corners of a computer lab (participants could hear but not see each other). Of the participants in the study, approximately 50 percent preferred each medium, with a small percentage suggesting that either would be acceptable.

75. Schneider, Sid J., Jeffrey Kerwin, Joy Frechtling, and Benjamin A. Vivari. "Characteristics of the Discussion in Online and Face-to-Face Focus Groups." *Social Science Computer Review* 20, no. 1 (Spring 2002): 31–42.

The formats of face-to-face and online focus groups are compared and contrasted. Considered for both approaches are the merits and drawbacks, the nature of communication, the differences in participant behavior, and the concept of social presence. To evaluate some health-related Web sites produced by the federal government, four face-to-face focus groups were conducted with 29 participants, and four online focus groups were conducted with 59 participants. The study found that the online participants contributed more comments per group—but this seeming advantage was negated when the longer time utilized by the online groups was taken into account. Online participants contributed fewer words and were more likely to send brief messages of agreement with a previous statement. In the face-to-face groups the participation level varied, with some individuals contributing a great deal more than others.

76. Sweeney, Jillian C., Geoffrey N. Soutar, Douglas R. Hausknecht, Raymond F. Dallin, and Lester W. Johnson. "Collecting Information from Groups: A Comparison of Two Methods." *Journal of the Market Research Society* 39, no. 2 (April 1997): 397–411.

The Group Support Systems (GSS) technology involves participants using computers connected to a local area network (with participant inputs and responses displayed), and a moderator and a "chauffeur" who assist with technical issues. GSS technology groups versus traditional focus groups were compared in Perth, Western Australia, with two groups consisting of 16 and 18 participants, respectively. Group members were recruited as a random sample with no significant differences in the group profiles. The study sought to collect ideas on cognitive dissonance. The GSS groups cost 25 percent more, but the results were immediately available, whereas the traditional focus groups needed to have the output transcribed. The GSS groups took 1.75 hours on average, versus 1.5 hours for the regular focus groups. The benefits of the GSS approach were that all participants could respond equally (avoiding the pitfalls of a dominant respondent in the traditional focus group mode). In addition, they gained confidence, were enthusiastic, and produced a considerable breadth of information.

77. Sweet, Casey. "Designing and Conducting Virtual Focus Groups." *Qualitative Market Research* 4, no. 3 (2001): 130–35.

This article contains pointers on how to achieve success with virtual focus groups. Sweet compares virtual groups with in-person approaches from a variety of standpoints, including screeners, recruitment, virtual facilities, client observers, invitations and preparation, discussion guide development and design, show rates and selection, moderating, what the respondents see, and analysis and reporting. A section titled "unanswered questions" provides 10 tips for those conducting virtual groups for the first time, as well as 10 tips for avoiding technical problems. Four answers to frequently asked questions follow, concluding with an 11-entry glossary.

78. Tse, Alan C. B. "Conducting Electronic Focus Group Discussions among Chinese Respondents." *Journal of the Market Research Society* 41, no. 4 (October 1999): 407–15.

The advantages and limitations of online focus groups are summarized. Tse writes that the method may be particularly effective when conducting research on sensitive topics in a Chinese cultural environment, because Internet-based focus groups afford participants the opportunity to respond anonymously (an important consideration in this culture). One online focus group was conducted with 71 second-year students enrolled in a marketing management course at the Chinese University of Hong Kong. The discussion concerned a sensitive topic: counterfeit products. Students were then asked to complete a questionnaire about the focus group experience. As compared with traditional face-to-face discussion groups, the students in the online format responded more openly and interacted more vigorously. Implications for market researchers are discussed.

79. Turney, Lyn, and Catherine Pocknee. "Virtual Focus Groups: New Frontiers in Research." *International Journal of Qualitative Methods* 4, no. 2 (June 2005): 1–10.

The authors examined whether online discussion boards in Blackboard could be used as virtual focus groups. Specifically, Turney and Pocknee determined that Blackboard and WebCT are highly appropriate for such applications. Researchers would need training in online communication skills. The approach is of special value for populations that are difficult to recruit and/or access. Additionally, virtual research is useful for individuals or groups who are "hesitant or unable to participate in face-to-face focus groups" (p. 8). Anonymity and confidentiality are ensured because access to Blackboard and comparable systems is limited to personnel determined by the academic unit. The article compares the virtual approach to criteria specified by Krueger for focus groups, and systematically addresses these points.

80. Underhill, Christina, and Murrey G. Olmsted. "An Experimental Comparison of Computer-Mediated and Face-to-Face Focus Groups." *Social Science Computer Review* 21, no. 4 (Winter 2003): 506–12.

The purpose of this study was to compare computer-mediated with face-to-face focus groups. The participants were 156 sailors (81 percent were male) from the Naval Training Center in Great Lakes, Illinois. The protocol called for three formats: the traditional in-person focus group; a computer environment in which the participants could see and hear each other in a single room, but were to communicate only via the computer; and a simulated Internet situation where the members of the group were in the same room but could neither see nor hear others (headphones and partitions were used). The authors found that the computer-based focus groups produced the same quantity and quality of information as the face-to-face focus groups. The latter format generated more words, but "the amount of unique ideas produced by each was not significantly different" (p. 511). The computer groups veered from the topic more frequently than the face-to-face groups. Participants' social presence ratings were similar—they enjoyed the focus group experience. The nature of the participants may limit the generalizability of the study findings.

81. Walston, Jill T., and Robert W. Lissitz. "Computer-Mediated Focus Groups." *Evaluation Review* 24, no. 5 (October 2000): 457–83.

Walston and Lissitz refer to computer-mediated (CM) focus groups as an environment in which all communication in the group is conducted via the computer. The theoretical basis for this approach is presented, along with a summary of the steps involved in focus group research and experiences with computer-administered surveys. An examination of the nature of CM focus group is provided, including comparisons with face-to-face (FTF) focus groups. Academic dishonesty was the topic for both the CM and FTF focus groups. The purpose was to ascertain the ways in which students cheat and their attitudes about cheating. Three CM groups (8, 9, and 20 undergraduate students) and two FTF groups (7 and 8 students) were convened. The CM groups were held in one room with 20 networked computers. A table displays the reactions of the students to each format. Portions of the CM transcripts are provided. The authors include nine recommendations for CM focus groups. The questions asked by the moderator appear as an appendix. The conclusion states that CM focus groups have great potential.

1.6 PARTICIPANT RECRUITMENT

82. Valdez, Avelardo, and Charles D. Kaplan. "Reducing Selection Bias in the Use of Focus Groups to Investigate Hidden Populations: The Case of Mexican-American Gang Members from South Texas." *Drugs & Society* 14, nos. 1–2 (1999): 209–24.

Hidden populations refer to small subpopulations or subpopulations of individuals who, due to their involvement in certain socially stigmatized behaviors, are unwilling to disclose themselves, such as heroin addicts, drug users, and gang members. Sampling and recruitment of members of such groups is seen as a methodological challenge for social science researchers. Selection bias is a prime concern because it affects both internal and external validity, as well as the generalizability of study results. A number of issues relating to selection bias arose during a focus group study of Mexican-American gang members in South Texas. A total of 24 focus groups were conducted with a diverse group of male and female participants—from gang members to law enforcement personnel. The sessions were moderated by one of the principal investigators, who was assisted by community "researchers." Six strategies for reducing sources of selection bias are discussed. The authors highlight the importance of community gatekeepers and researcher immersion into the social world of the participants.

1.7 PLANNING

83. Morgan, David L. *Planning Focus Groups.* Focus Group Kit 2. Thousand Oaks, CA: Sage, 1998. 139p.

According to the author, the essence of the planning component is an awareness of the desired goal of the research, as well as wise decision making throughout the process. Morgan advises the reader, whether novice or experienced, of
the options that must be considered when undertaking a focus group project; the
attention that needs to be paid to issues such as recruiting the participants and
defining the role of the moderator; and the importance of personnel and budget-
ing, with separate scenarios presented for smaller and larger projects. Subsequent
chapters concentrate on the details of group composition and size, the desired
structure of the interview questions, and the location of the interview venue (such
as public meeting rooms, office buildings, and private homes). The text includes
checklists, icons, and examples of budgets and timelines.

1.8 QUESTION DESIGN

84. Krueger, Richard A. *Developing Questions for Focus Groups*. Focus Group
    Kit 3. Thousand Oaks, CA: Sage, 1998. 107p.

As in the conduct of survey research methodology, the writing of concise, easily understood, and clearly worded questions and their sequencing on the survey
instrument or interview schedule is critical for collecting quality data that meet
the goals of a focus group project. Krueger covers the guiding principles of asking
questions, including the different categories, how to phrase and arrange them for
effective use, and the role of probe, follow-up, and unplanned questions. (Probe
questions are designed to elicit additional information from a participant who has
provided cryptic or vague comments in need of clarification or enhancement.) In
the final part, the author considers another kind of question-asking strategy—one
that requires the participant to become actively engaged in the process. With
this technique, participants are asked to write, draw, speak, debate, and so forth,
with the hope that useful information will emerge from such experiences. Other
data-eliciting strategies include listing, rating, and the use of analogies, personification, fantasy and daydreams, and role-playing. The book contains examples,
icons, and 16 complete focus group scripts previously used by the author.

1.9 SPECIAL TECHNIQUES

85. Freeman, Melissa. "Nurturing Dialogic Hermeneutics and the Deliberative
    Capacities of Communities in Focus Groups." *Qualitative Inquiry* 12, no. 1
    (February 2006): 81–95.

As part of a larger study designed to examine the impact of state standardized
testing on teaching and learning in the state of New York, one focus group was
conducted with five parents whose children attended an urban school. Freeman

used this context to examine the nature of dialogue, a "primary component of philosophical hermeneutic theories of understanding" (p. 81). (Hermeneutics is the study of the methodological principles of interpretation.) The author believes that social scientists have paid more attention to focus groups as a data-gathering strategy than to their potential for collecting human interaction, "where meaning is understood as being coconstructed in the interaction itself" (p. 83). The central question for the research is whether focus groups can serve as a means for enhancing communication among people. The author describes an alternative elicitation technique in which she borrows the key ideas and perceptions from the transcripts of one group, converts them into "poetic displays," and reads them aloud for another group.

86. Martinec, Radan. "Concept Evaluation in Focus Groups: Semantic Fields and Evaluative Strategies." *Semiotica* 147, nos. 1–4 (2003): 357–88.

The evaluation of market researcher-generated ideas by participants in focus groups is the realm of Martinec's article. The goal of the research was to determine the criteria that focus group participants employ to evaluate proposed ideas. The ideas were presented to the groups using stimulus material or concept boards that contain verbal text and images. Part of the evaluation criteria involved these boards, which are conceptualized as semantic fields. Six three-hour focus groups were conducted with 48 16- to 24-year-old men who responded to a toiletries company wishing to expand beyond aftershave for young men. Martinec explains the nature of semantic fields and the evaluative strategies. The evaluation of the concept boards is considered in significant detail. One idea presented to the focus groups was a "smartcard" for shopping. Evaluative strategies in relation to the card are elaborated upon. The author concludes by observing that "a model has been developed of the process of evaluation of complex ideas in focus groups" (p. 335).

87. Sato, Steve, and Tony Salvador. "Playacting and Focus Troupes: Theater Techniques for Creating Quick, Intense, Immersive, and Engaging Focus Group Sessions." *Interactions* 6, no. 5 (September–October 1999): 35–41.

"Focus troupes" are described as a method that combines "theater techniques and groups of end-users in new product development" (p. 36). The format is similar to traditional focus groups except that the introduction provided by the moderator establishes the context for a dramatic vignette (a 6- to 10-minute skit) that will follow. The intent of the vignette is to capture how the new product concept can be used. The participants discuss the product, with a live actor's monologue reflecting positive or negative audience comments. Further discussion and interaction continue. The technique is meant to be used early in the product development process. The product designers are present during the focus troupe session to answer questions (thus assuming some of the moderator's usual duties). Analysis is based on judgment—weighing the comments of the audience against "what the developers know to be true" (p. 37). The authors describe 16 techniques for incorporating theater into group research.

1.10 TERMINOLOGY

88. Boddy, Clive. "A Rose by Any Other Name May Smell as Sweet but 'Group Discussion' Is Not Another Name for a 'Focus Group' nor Should It Be." *Qualitative Market Research* 8, no. 3 (2005): 248–55.

The following terms may be used interchangeably, but according to Boddy, inappropriately so: focus group, group discussion, group interview, group, focus group interview, focus group discussion, qualitative group discussion, and nominal group interview. The author explains the nature of the confusion, discusses the historical and geographic sources for the varying terms, and proceeds to individually define focus group discussions (FGDs) and focus group interviews (FGIs). FGDs involve group consideration of an area of interest using a moderator and involving participating discussion in which both the breadth and depth of interchange among the members of the group can be maximized. Boddy defines FGIs as groups in which the facilitator manages the group more closely, with members acting more as respondents rather than as participants. In the FGI model, group respondents may use handheld electronic devices to vote, or mini-questionnaires may be administered. The two approaches are compared, and a review of differing scientific traditions is presented.

II.

Arts and Humanities

2.1 LINGUISTICS

89. Brown, Courtney L. "Sociolinguistic Dynamics of Gender in Focus Groups." In *How and Why Language Matters in Evaluation*, edited by Rodney K. Hopson, 55–67. New Directions for Evaluation, no. 86. San Francisco: Jossey-Bass, 2000.

The research considers the question of whether men and women participate equally in evaluations in mixed-gender focus groups. This topic was examined by analyzing 11 archived videotapes, audiotapes, and transcripts from focus groups conducted at two different East Coast living history museums. All participants were white, upper-middle class, and well educated. Qualitative and quantitative approaches were part of the study protocol. Codes and categories were determined and a case study was written on each of the focus groups, which were identified as predominately male or predominately female. The cross-case analysis produced the following themes: body language, talking time, floor-taking strategies, topic raising, and leadership emergence. The author found that the conversational styles used by men and women were different, with men creating an imbalance of participation through dominating and assertive behaviors. Men displayed these tendencies whether they were the majority or minority gender in the group. Mixed-gender focus groups are not recommended.

90. Myers, Greg. "Displaying Opinions: Topics and Disagreement in Focus Groups." *Language in Society* 27, no. 1 (1998): 85–111.

Myers discusses the distinctions between ordinary conversation and the dialogue produced in focus groups, noting that the effectiveness of the latter depends on "tension" between the moderator's constraints and participants' interactions.

For example, although the moderator typically presents and defines the topics to be considered, participants can "shift, close, and interpret" these topics. In addition, the moderator can encourage disagreement, but participants manage their own disagreement by using the moderator as an audience, and by employing various conversational devices. Myers views focus groups as "a complex collaborative project operating under the shared assumption that the purpose of the discussion is to display opinions to the moderator" (p. 85). The mechanisms and strategies participants employ to orient themselves to topics, and acknowledge and manage disagreement, are emphasized. The comments are based on transcripts drawn from seven focus groups designed to explore how people discuss issues related to environmental sustainability. The implications of group dynamics for analysis are considered.

91. Puchta, Claudia, and Jonathan Potter. "Asking Elaborate Questions: Focus Groups and the Management of Spontaneity." *Journal of Sociolinguistics* 3, no. 3 (August 1999): 314–35.

The premise of the research is that moderators can manage the dilemma of leading both a highly focused discussion on predefined topics while, simultaneously, encouraging spontaneous participant conversation and interaction. According to the authors, effective question design—that is, the use of "elaborate" questions—can resolve this "tension" between research approaches. Elaborate questions, defined as those that "include a range of reformulations and rewordings" (p. 314), promote participation by offering respondents a portfolio of question components from which to choose. Participants can then elect to spontaneously focus on one or more of the presented elements. To demonstrate the application of the concept, Puchta and Potter report on eight market research focus groups conducted in German by six experienced moderators. The transcripts were then translated into English. Pauses, emphasized elements, and other speech characteristics were transferred from the original language to the English version. Extensive examples and excerpts illustrate how elaborate questions provided the types of responses deemed desirable for the project.

2.2 MUSIC

92. MacDonald, Raymond, and Graeme Wilson. "Musical Identities of Professional Jazz Musicians: A Focus Group Investigation." *Psychology of Music* 33, no. 4 (2005): 395–417.

The authors discuss (1) the central role of improvisation in jazz; (2) the psychological underpinnings of this form of music; and (3) the formation of musical identity—both individual and group. The article was written from the perspective that "further knowledge of how musicians conceive of themselves and their music will elucidate the psychological processes that lie at the heart of a unique creative process" (p. 395). To inform the topic of musical identities, two one-hour audiotaped focus groups were conducted with 11 Scottish professional jazz musicians: five men in the first group, and six in the second. The musicians, all instrumentalists, ranged in age from their early 20s to the mid-60s. All were recruited from established jazz venues in Glasgow and Edinburgh. The discussions were transcribed using minimal phonetic conventions, and then coded. The main themes identified center around two ideas—one relating to the music (improvising and composing, swing, collective processes, and instrument differences) and to the musicians themselves (social context, professional context, being in a group, self, and others). Focus groups were found to be a "useful" method for gathering the perspectives of these musicians. The implications of the research for jazz education are discussed.

2.3 RELIGION

93. Krause, Neal, Linda M. Chatters, Tina Meltzer, and David L. Morgan. "Negative Interaction in the Church: Insights from Focus Groups with Older Adults." *Review of Religious Research* 41, no. 4 (2000): 510–33.

Focus group interviewing was selected as the method of choice for assessing elderly people's perspectives on the types of troublesome social relations that may be encountered in the church environment. The authors write from the perspective that "a good deal may be missed by current closed-ended items" (p. 514) that fail to reveal the content domain of such interaction and its impact on health-related outcomes of this population. A total of eight focus groups were conducted with 63 men and women, residing in Washtenaw County, Michigan, who were recruited by means of a random probability sampling procedure. The female moderators, trained by Morgan, were matched to the race of the participants (white and African American). A certified court reporter assisted with transcription. Unpleasant encounters, a significant source of distress among the study population, fell into three categories: interpersonal conflicts between or among parishioners, conflicts between church members and their pastors, and conflicts relating to church doctrine, church policy, or religious teaching. Coping strategies were also identified. The methodology provided a "wealth of information" on the topic.

94. Krause, Neal, Linda M. Chatters, Tina Meltzer, and David L. Morgan. "Using Focus Groups to Explore the Nature of Prayer in Late Life." *Journal of Aging Studies* 14, no. 2 (June 2000): 191–212.

The authors review a variety of quantatitive research methods that have been employed for the measurement of prayer as a coping strategy, namely, survey questions, scales, and indices—none of which were specifically developed for examining the elderly. With the goal of creating a close-ended survey instrument appropriate for this population, a total of 63 Christian, white and African-American males and females (average age 73.08 years) were recruited from Medicare lists in Washtenaw County, Michigan. Each received $25 for her or his involvement in the research. Eight audiotaped focus groups (four rounds) were conducted over a three-month period. Morgan comoderated the first round and trained the other moderators—all female and matched to the race of the group participants. A certified court reporter transcribed the discussions. Three major themes emerged from the project: how prayer "operates," the distinctions between group prayer and individual prayer, and the impact of age-related issues in prayer. Although five shortcomings of the methodology are reviewed, the participants provided "rich insights" into this aspect of religious life.

95. O'Connell, Kathryn A., and Suzanne M. Skevington. "The Relevance of Spirituality, Religion and Personal Beliefs to Health-Related Quality of Life: Themes from Focus Groups in Britain." *British Journal of Health Psychology* 10, no. 3 (September 2005): 379–98.

The purpose of the research was to determine whether spirituality, religion, and personal beliefs are important as related to quality of life (QoL) and well-being. Nine focus groups with 55 participants explored the following 18 facets of the QoL measurement instrument: "kindness to others, acceptance of others, forgiveness, a code to live by, freedom to practice beliefs and rituals, faith, hope and optimism, experiences of awe, spiritual strength, control, inner peace, meaning of life, connection to a spiritual being or force, wholeness and integration, detachment and attachment, death and dying, divine love and specific religious beliefs" (p. 382). The results indicate support for the concept of spirituality, religion, and personal beliefs in QoL, as well as a biopyschosociospiritual model of health. Limitations of the focus group work include that the participants were mostly well educated and came from one geographic area (southwest England) and that the subgroup comparisons were based on small numbers.

96. Scannell, Alice Updike. "Focus Groups Help Congregation Improve Its New Member Ministry." *Review of Religious Research* 45, no. 1 (September 2003): 68–77.

Focus groups were used to determine how new members at St. Michael and All Angels Episcopal Church (St. Michael's), located in Portland, Oregon, perceived the welcoming process (brunches, informal gatherings, letters, and home visits) they had received upon joining the congregation. St. Michael's is an urban church with about 770 members, who are primarily European American (80 percent), middle class, and college educated. Scannell, a member of St. Michael's, and the church team sampled and recruited 22 people who had become members within the past five years. These newer members participated in one of two two-hour focus groups that utilized a predetermined script of seven topics. The major finding was that people have different needs and expectations when joining a new congregation. Scannell posits that the focus group discussions provided the team with insights and information that would have been difficult to achieve with face-to-face, telephone, or mail surveys. The recommendations produced became a "catalyst" for change in some of the church procedures.

2.4 SPORTS AND LEISURE STUDIES

97. Burton, Laura J., and Jennifer E. Bruening. "Technology and Method Intersect in the Online Focus Group." *Quest* 55, no. 4 (November 2003): 315–27.

Sport science is the setting for the work of Burton (Department of Parks, Recreation, and Tourism Management at North Carolina State University at Raleigh) and Bruening (Department of Kinesiology at the University of Connecticut at Storrs). The "traditional" focus group methodology is outlined as a preamble to a presentation of the eight positive and the seven negative features of online focus groups. A fall 2001 study is described involving 64 students (43 women, 21 men) who were divided into five focus groups based on the number of credits they had in online coursework. Another set of four focus groups was formed in spring 2002 with 43 students (26 women, 17 men). The asynchronous focus group method was used, as the subject of the research was the experiences of students in an asynchronous learning environment. The second group involved the issue of motivating factors related to attending football games at a new football stadium located a 30-minute drive from the main campus. The authors summarize the six "lessons" that they learned from conducting this research.

98. Hurtes, Karen P. "Social Dependency: The Impact of Adolescent Female Culture." *Leisure Sciences* 24 (2002): 109–21.

Two qualitative data-gathering approaches were used to identify the critical elements that make up adolescent girls' culture and to determine the impact of this culture on leisure behavior in an adventure camp environment. The author was seeking a "multifaceted" view of the girls' culture by examining the differences between "stated reality" (that is, the way the girls say they behave) and "actual reality" (that is, the manner in which they actually behave). To achieve this end, 12 hours of focus groups (1 to 2.5 hours long) were conducted with 16 15-year-old girls attending a residential camp in the Northeast. Six important elements of culture were identified. (Eight other girls were the focus of 36 hours of participant observation.) Four phases of the analysis process are explained. The findings suggest that adolescent girls view the world "in terms of absolutes" and have an "overriding" desire for status, popularity, and social acceptance. Until social acceptance is achieved, it is unlikely that two other innate psychological needs, competency and self-determination, will be addressed. Because these needs are "often the goals of adventure and other recreation programs" (p. 117), there are implications for professionals working in these areas.

99. Warner-Smith, Penny, and Peter Brown. "'The Town Dictates What I Do': The Leisure, Health and Well-Being of Women in a Small Australian Country Town." *Leisure Studies* 21 (2002): 39–56.

Many factors are seen to contribute to the lack of leisure opportunities for women: limited employment choices, poor public transportation, few facilities, isolation, family transience, and the "often exclusionary politics of small communities" (p. 41)—exclusions based on class, age, ethnic, regional, and gender differences. To investigate the contribution of leisure to individual health and well-being, the authors selected a small country town in New South Wales. This research is part of a broader quantitative (mail surveys) and qualitative study (focus groups), the latter involving 12 sessions with 62 women. Information for the present paper was obtained from a focus group with five women between the ages of 48 and 53. All were of western European origin. The discussion centered on the themes listed above, which were identified as significant for women in isolated areas. The results are discussed in terms of the commonalities among the women and the impact of explicit and implicit constraints, cultural exclusions, and changing economic forces.

100. Yuen, Felice C. "'It Was Fun . . . I Liked Drawing My Thoughts': Using Drawings as a Part of the Focus Group Process with Children." *Journal of Leisure Research* 36, no. 4 (2004): 461–82.

Noting that there has been little research in leisure studies that has utilized children's drawings as a data-gathering method, the author (University of Waterloo) identifies and discusses four contexts in which focus groups can assist in this process: (1) for facilitating a relaxed environment; (2) for eliciting information on children's thoughts and feelings; (3) for providing structure for the discussion; and (4) for reducing "groupthink" (that is, group conformity). As part of Yuen's master's thesis, six 75-minute focus groups were conducted at an international summer camp (located in Canada) with 32 11-year-old boys and girls from 12 different countries. Because most of the children did not speak English as their first language, drawing was selected to help them describe their perspectives about the camp experience. The author served as moderator for the audiotaped sessions. The drawings were presented and discussed by the group. Although there were some limitations, the drawing alternative was found to be a "natural" form of communication—one best used in conjunction with verbal interaction approaches.

III.

Social Sciences

3.1 ANTHROPOLOGY

101. Baker, Rachel, and Rachel Hinton. "Do Focus Groups Facilitate Meaningful Participation in Social Research?" In *Developing Focus Group Research: Politics, Theory and Practice*, edited by Rosaline S. Barbour and Jenny Kitzinger, 79–98. London: Sage, 1999.

The authors base their observations on two anthropological research reports carried out in Nepal. Over an 18-month period, Baker studied street children residing in Kathmandu, while Hinton lived for one year with refugee families from Bhutan in camps in Eastern Nepal, with follow-up research seven months later. The purpose of the projects was to explore areas within health and well-being that were considered problematic by members of the community and service providers. Focus groups were used to identify concerns, formulate hypotheses, and as a comparison to the findings from other methods (for example, interviews, surveys, an appraisal instrument, clinic data, and participant observation). The authors examine a variety of factors that affect the dynamics between participants and researchers during each component of the focus group process. These include the four stages of participatory research, the importance of planning, the value of alternative methodologies, and how a research partnership can serve all involved.

102. Hollander, Jocelyn A. "The Social Contexts of Focus Groups." *Journal of Contemporary Ethnography* 33, no. 5 (October 2004): 602–37.

The basis for the article is the view that focus group discussions are "deeply affected" and "shaped" by the larger social contexts in which they occur. The resulting data are similarly affected in ways not yet widely acknowledged. Hollander used data from a focus group study on the effects of violence on daily

45

living to analyze four "multiple and overlapping" contexts: (1) associational (the common characteristic that brings participants together); (2) status (issues of gender and social hierarchies); (3) conversational (refers to the topics considered); and (4) relational (the degree of participants' prior acquaintance). These contexts lead to both problematic silences (that is, respondents' failure to disclose information) and problematic speech (that is, respondents' failure to convey their "real" thoughts in the group environment). The latter problem involves issues of conformity, "groupthink," and social desirability. Hollander's comments are based on a project involving 13 two-hour focus groups conducted with 76 participants residing in the Seattle area. Focus groups are described as "an excellent site" for analyzing social interaction processes.

103. Schensul, Jean J. "Focused Group Interviews." In *Enhanced Ethnographic Methods: Audiovisual Techniques, Focused Group Interviews, and Elicitation Techniques*, by Jean J. Schensul, Margeret D. LeCompte, Bonnie K. Nastasi, and Stephen P. Borgatti, 51–114. Ethnographer's Toolkit 3. Walnut Creek, CA: Altamira Press, 1999.

Schensul observes that applied ethnographic research can be a valuable tool for practitioners as well as for researchers working in a variety of disciplines. Focus group interviews permit the ethnographer to interview more than one individual at a time and to utilize the interaction of group members to produce qualitative data on people's insights, beliefs, and opinions. The technique is to be used in conjunction with other formats designed to comprehend a particular cultural setting. A wide range of topics is covered: organizing and preparing for the interviews; selecting a target population; identifying and training the interviewers; conducting the sessions (including question asking and data recording); and analyzing and reporting the data. The text is accompanied by checklists, key points, and 18 case studies, such as one comparing the validity of data collected via focus groups and surveys.

3.2 BUSINESS

Accounting

104. Myers, Roslyn. "CPAs Get into Focus." *Journal of Accountancy* 193, no. 2 (February 2002): 28–33.

The following quotation from Frank Lutz appears on the first page of this article: "Roughly 70% of all consumer-research dollars are earmarked for qualitative research, and it is nearly impossible to find a *Fortune* 500 company that does not use focus groups" (p. 28). Myers discusses the uses of focus groups by CPAs, indicating how they are appropriate for such areas as strategic planning, attitude determination, developing new services, evaluating pricing, and for gaining a better understanding of clients. An outline of the steps involved in focus group research is provided, along with an executive summary covering six key points.

Directory

105. GreenBook. *Worldwide Directory of Focus Group Companies and Services.* 14th ed. GreenBook, vol. 2. Bradenton, FL: American Marketing Association, New York Chapter, 2005–2006. 334p.

The directory has entries for 641 companies, including 68 foreign country listings. Entries include the address (including e-mail and Web), telephone, and FAX, as well as a paragraph describing the available facilities, the nature of services offered, and other specialty elements, such as language skills and translation capabilities. Company logos are provided. The book is divided into six indexing sections: (1) geographic listing of participating companies; (2) types of research (with headings for advertising, brand, competitive intelligence, customer satisfaction, product, omnibus surveys, package, media, retail, strategic, syndicated, and trend); (3) research services (with headings for focus group facilities, moderating, questionnaire design, recruiting, videoconferencing, and usability testing laboratories); (4) audience, industries, and markets; (5) online research and computer software (with headings for online focus groups, online copy testing, Web site analysis, video streaming/Internet, broadcasting, survey recruiting, and online moderating); and (6) principal personnel and company name.

Finance

106. Johnson, Brandt. "Keeping the Client in Focus." *Financial Planning* 28, no. 4 (April 1, 1998): 123–26.

Focus groups and surveys are recommended as effective techniques for identifying and understanding the needs of those who seek the services of a financial planner. As a first step in conducting a focus group, Johnson advises that a clear picture of the knowledge desired will dictate both the choice of questions and the selection of participants. A skilled professional moderator should lead the sessions, which may include existing or prospective clients. Costs are broken down into recruiter and moderator fees, incentives for participants, facility rental, refreshments, audiotape transcription, and data analysis—a total of approximately $3,000 to $3,500 per session. Also considered are ongoing client advisory boards and, for a quantitative approach, telephone, mail, and face-to-face surveys (the last referred to as "intercept" surveys in the article).

107. Lewis Alan. "A Focus Group Study of the Motivation to Invest: 'Ethical/ Green' and 'Ordinary' Investors Compared." *Journal of Socio-Economics* 30, no. 4 (2001): 331–41.

As part of a larger project carried out in the United Kingdom, this research explores how two different groups of investors explain their motives to invest and whether they face any "moral dilemmas, confusions or inconsistencies" in making the choices they do. Focus group methodology, described as "an innovation in this area of research," was selected to provide insight. Fourteen 45-minute audio-taped focus groups were conducted: seven sessions with 45 "ordinary" investors, and seven sessions with 49 "ethical/green" investors. The majority of the male and female participants were over age 50. Each participant received a small payment to cover travel and expenses. The research officer on the project performed the moderating duties. NUD*IST software assisted in the analysis. Among the results are the following: (1) neither group cited purely economic gains as a motive for investing, but instead mentioned "foresight," "independence," and the desire to bequeath; (2) "ethical/green" investors avoided companies that manufacture munitions, are exploitative, and that pollute; (3) "ordinary" investors were sympathetic to the environmentally conscious groups; and (4) many "ethical/green" investors had mixed portfolios, thus creating a moral dilemma.

Human Resources

108. Bader, Gloria E., and Catherine A. Rossi. *Focus Groups: A Step-by-Step Guide.* 3rd ed. San Diego, CA: Bader Group, 2002. 61p.

This comprehensive review guides the reader through all components of the focus group process: the key players, the agenda, techniques for recording the discussions, the selection of the facility, and data analysis and reporting. Throughout, the authors provide examples of how the staff of the Human Resources Department of Winners' Ink, a fictional company, successfully utilized the focus group approach to solve a number of personnel problems. The advantages and disadvantages of three recent technological developments—online focus groups, teleconferencing, and videoconferencing—are discussed by Lisa Hart. The last chapter, "Materials and Samples," offers examples of appropriate questions, an outline of focus group roles and responsibilities, a sample invitation, an agenda planner, a 22-item planning checklist, an action planning matrix, and references.

109. Byrne, Alistair, and Bill Rhodes. "Employee Attitudes to Pensions: Evidence from Focus Groups." *Pensions* 11, no. 2 (February 2006): 144–52.

Focus groups were selected as the qualitative method of choice to gain insight into employees' knowledge of and perspectives about their pension plans. Four 90-minute focus groups were conducted with a total of 36 employees of a listed distribution company that has a large number of relatively small branches located across the United Kingdom. The company manages several different plans having different terms and conditions. Participants were grouped according to the similarities of their plans. The results indicate that the employees' knowledge of pensions in general and their plan in particular was "quite limited." Employees expressed the desire for more information and advice. The changes to the Pensions Act 2004 are discussed.

110. Cyphers, Gary. "Staff Focus Groups." In *Workforce Data Collection Field Guide for Human Service Agencies: Practical Recommendations for Conducting: Staff Exit Interviews, Staff Focus Groups, Employee Surveys*, 8–12. [n.p.]: American Public Human Services Association, 2003.

In fall 2000, the American Public Human Services Association, the Child Welfare League of America, and the Alliance for Children and Families conducted a workforce survey of state, county, and private child welfare agencies. The issues examined included staff recruitment, employee turnover, and staff development. The purpose of this field guide is to help public human service agencies implement the survey recommendations. The section on staff focus groups offers the user a number of practical considerations for gathering essential workforce data. These include design and planning (including participant recruitment), obtaining the services of a professional moderator, conducting the sessions, preparing a formal report for the sponsoring agency, and estimating the total costs. There are five appendices.

111. Hall, Julia. "Focus Groups." In *Gower Handbook of Customer Service*, edited by Peter Murley, 138–50. Aldershot, England: Gower, 1997.

Hall identifies three customer service areas that are highly appropriate for focus groups: determining customer expectations in terms of service, examining their feelings about the organization and its services, and ascertaining how new customer-service initiatives can be developed. The reader is advised on techniques for forming a focus group (selection and number of respondents, and number of groups); the conduct of the sessions (venues, recording options, length, and incentives); the advantages and limitations of the method; and analysis and interpretation of the data. Focus groups are also seen as an effective method for assessing the views of customer-service staff and for strategy development within an organization.

112. Herington, Carmel, Don Scott, and Lester W. Johnson. "Focus Group Exploration of Firm-Employee Relationship Strength." *Qualitative Market Research* 8, no. 3 (2005): 256–76.

To gain a greater understanding, from the employees' perspective, of the key elements contributing to good employee-employer relationships, focus group methodology was selected as the data-gathering method of choice. Four one-hour audiotaped focus groups were conducted with 20 employees recruited from a large Australian regional city. The participants were predominately female, between the ages of 23 and 55, and represented a wide range of professions and work environments. One of the researchers served as moderator. Data were collected via whiteboard summaries, which were digitally photographed to aid content analysis. The participants identified six elements as important to relationship strength: cooperation and empowerment; communication; attachment; shared goals and values; trust; and respect. These characteristics are "in line with what was found in the non-marketing literature rather than what was found in the marketing literature" (p. 271). Implications of the exploratory study for management are discussed, and a model is proposed.

113. Kretovics, Mark A., and James A. McCambridge. "Determining What Employers Really Want: Conducting Regional Stakeholder Focus Groups." *Journal of Career Planning and Employment* 58, no. 2 (Winter 1998): 25–29.

The setting for the study was Colorado State University (CSU), an institution that has traditionally relied on national survey data to identify employers' desired traits for new employees. To examine whether selection criteria were similar for local and regional employers, as well as the ranking of the criteria, a qualitative study was undertaken. Four 90-minute audiotaped focus groups were conducted with a nonrandom sample of 21 employer representatives from four areas: manufacturing, service, small business, and metropolitan. The authors served as moderators. The principles of grounded theory assisted in the analysis. Three areas—technical skills, communication skills, and personality characteristics/attributes—were identified as the most important criteria. Implications for CSU's College of Business and career center staff are discussed.

114. Lockwood, Diane, and A. Ansari. "Recruiting and Retaining Scarce Information Technology Talent: A Focus Group Study." *Industrial Management & Data Systems* 99, no. 6 (1999): 251–56.

Information technology (IT) talent is competitively sought after. This article explains the findings of a 4.5-hour focus group conducted with 14 senior IT practitioners, and facilitated by a PhD academic who participated in the session. The purposes of the focus group were to establish what factors, past and present, are important to recruits; to identify recruiting paradigms; and to determine the recruiting and retention strategies that have been particularly successful. Areas discussed include money (the single most important factor), training, benefits, and flexible work schedules. In terms of recruiting practices, employee referral programs, dedicated IT recruiters, acquisitions, speed hiring, local advertising, Web sites, and college job fairs are discussed. Retention strategies considered include raising salaries, bonuses, career advancements and promotion, training, personal recognition, and time off.

115. Weber, Paula S., Elaine Davis, and Richard J. Sebastian. "Mental Health and the ADA: A Focus Group Discussion with Human Resource Practi-

tioners." *Employee Responsibilities and Rights Journal* 14, no. 1 (March 2002): 45–55.

In 1997, the Equal Employment Opportunity Commission (EEOC) released new guidelines to clarify implementation of the mental health regulations under the Americans with Disabilities Act (ADA). The purpose of the research was threefold: to investigate human resource professionals' knowledge and understanding of the guidelines, to identify the types of mental health situations encountered by organizations, and to determine potential compliance issues. To gather this information by qualitative means, one audiotaped focus group was conducted with 13 human resource directors, who represented 16,400 employees from over a dozen corporations located in the Midwest. The results are discussed in terms of training related to ADA, experiences with claims and accommodations, and workplace violence. The underreporting of mental health claims was the "most significant" issue identified. Also discussed are the impact of demographics, misreporting, and societal and economic factors on mental health.

Market Research

General Sources

116. Calder, Bobby J. "Focus Groups and the Nature of Qualitative Marketing Research." *Journal of Marketing Research* 14, no. 3 (August 1977): 353–64.

Calder considers focus group methodology from a "philosophy of science" perspective—"to analyze the type of knowledge sought by qualitative research, be it scientific knowledge or otherwise, to determine what this implies about the use of the focus group technique" (p. 354). Three discernible, "though often blurred," approaches to focus group research in current practice are discussed: the exploratory, the clinical, and the phenomenological. The exploratory approach, frequently used prior to a quantitative research project, seeks to generate prescientific constructs and validate the knowledge gained against everyday experience. In the clinical approach, the most scientifically oriented of the three, quasi-scientific knowledge is desired. Self-reports are considered unreliable, and clinical judgment is necessary. The goal of the phenomenological approach is to yield everyday knowledge in order to understand the everyday experiences of the consumer. Calder comments on the issue of generalizability and concludes by stating that validity can best be assessed by the use of multiple methods. Implications for marketing research practitioners are discussed.

117. Carson, David, Audrey Gilmore, Chad Perry, and Kjell Gronhaug. "Focus Group Interviewing." In *Qualitative Marketing Research*, 113–31. London: Sage, 2001.

Focus groups are described as an "extremely useful," "cost-effective," and "versatile" method for obtaining people's insights about a research topic. The authors provide a step-by-step framework for applying this qualitative approach, emphasizing its use in the marketing management research environment. Group interaction (also termed *group effect*, *group dynamic*, or *synergy*) is the most important and unique feature of the method. Discussed are the components involved in carrying out a focus group project: problem definition; preplanning; participant, moderator, and site selection; the conduct of the sessions; and analyzing the data collected. Limitations include bias on the part of the key players and the nongeneralizability of the results.

118. Crocker, Paul. *Focus Group Research for Marketers: What Marketers Need to Know about This Popular Research Technique to Use It Safely, Effectively and Wisely.* Philadelphia: Xlibris, 2001. 202p.

Crocker's book provides an overview of the focus group process—an "all-steps" presentation for the beginner and a reference tool for others. Discussed are effective interviewing techniques, the possibility of bias and its impact on the resulting data, the vital role of the moderator, moderator briefing strategies, the importance of respondent screening, group composition, and the costs associated with selecting the focus group approach for promoting the marketing of products and services. In a chapter titled "Pest Control in Focus Groups," various categories of problem participants are identified. Suggestions are offered for dealing with each, including nonverbal cues, interruption, intervention, respondent censure, put-downs, and dismissal.

119. Edmunds, Holly, and American Marketing Association. *The Focus Group Research Handbook.* Lincolnwood, IL: NTC Business Books, 1999. 276p.

This book is designed for two audiences: the layperson who needs to contract with a professional marketing research vendor for a focus group study, and moderators and project managers with modest experience. The full range of issues pursuant to a focus group research project are addressed: design and planning, selecting the facility, the tasks of the moderator, and preparing an appropriate report for the client. Consideration is given to the challenges involved when interviewing special groups, such as children, teenagers, or senior citizens. The authors present a checklist for conducting focus groups abroad, including sampling and recruiting requirements, how facilities and amenities may vary from country to country, and the language barriers and cultural differences that may be encountered. A chapter on ethics covers the expectations of the client, the vendor, and the participants. A glossary contains 36 entries. Three appendices, which occupy half the book, provide detailed samples of screener questionnaires, discussion guides, and summary reports.

120. Goebert, Bonnie, with Herma M. Rosenthal. *Beyond Listening: Learning the Secret Language of Focus Groups*. New York: Wiley, 2002. 224p.

Writing from the perspective that "focus groups have more to do with concentrated and creative listening than with numbers and projects" (p. ix), Goebert's goal was to increase awareness of the importance of the dialogue that takes place between consumers and the products and services they prefer. The book is based on the author's personal experiences and impressions gained as a moderator of focus groups in the marketing environment. Among other topics, the chapters cover the rationale for conducting such research, the moderator's role, disappointments of the consumer, the marketing strategies of winning brands, and how marketers can better listen to what consumers and customers have to say and how they say it. Some possible trends for the new millennium are explored.

121. Langford, Barry E., Gerald Schoenfeld, and George Izzo. "Nominal Grouping Sessions vs Focus Groups." *Qualitative Market Research* 5, no. 1 (2002): 58–70.

The presentation is based on Langford's two previous studies, which indicate that the qualitative results produced by nominal grouping sessions (NGS) are "broad, deep, reliable and valid" (p. 58). In the NGS methodology, described as combining the best features of depth interviews, clinical focus groups, and the Delphi technique, only two or three questions are asked. The responses are then used to generate the topics to be discussed and ranked by level of importance by the same participants. The focus of the article is how the NGS procedure was used with a representative sample of 277 Floridian real estate appraisers, instructors, and brokers to determine their attitudes and opinions concerning qualifications, training, and personal attributes. In a detailed protocol, 66 questionnaire items were identified and rated, by consensus, by all the participants, resulting in a list of 13 overall competencies. Moderator probing and group interaction were common during the sessions. An important strength of NGS is that the researcher reports the actual results rather than an interpretation as is common in focus groups, and will eventually replace the latter as the qualitative method of choice. One limitation concerns the knowledge and skill level of the moderator. A table compares NGS and focus group procedures.

122. McQuarrie, Edward F. "The Focus Group." In *The Market Research Toolbox: A Concise Guide for Beginners*, 83–92. 2nd ed. Thousand Oaks, CA: Sage, 2006. 205p.

McQuarrie provides a pragmatic approach for the market researcher who wishes to conduct a focus group project. The focus group technique is defined as "a particular kind of group interview supported by a specialized infrastructure" (p. 83), the latter consisting of the facility, the market research vendor/client, and the moderator/facilitator of the sessions. Eight procedures are outlined for recruiting consumers, selecting the facility, choosing the moderator, conducting the sessions, analyzing the data, and preparing the report. The author estimates that most focus group projects cost between $15,000 and $72,000 (participant recruitment is the largest cost factor). Two detailed examples demonstrate the effective use of the technique in product evaluation. Among the advantages of focus groups are their ability to "produce surprise and a fresh perspective." The prime detractor is seen to be their reliance on small, nonscientifically selected samples.

123. Pearce, Michael. "Getting Full Value from Focus Group Research." *Ivey Business Journal* 63, no. 2 (Winter 1998): 72–76.

The focus group technique is particularly applicable during the early phases of a market research study and should be conducted when a subjective exploration of consumer thinking, attitudes, and behavior is desired. The market research manager should direct his or her attention to four critical issues: recruiting the participants, developing the discussion guide, selecting a moderator, and interpreting and reporting the findings. Since the results from focus group studies are not quantifiable, Pearce believes there is an "inappropriate tendency" to project their findings into policy. He calls this practice the "greatest misuse" by marketers and concludes that while the focus group is a valuable research tool, it generally must be used in conjunction with other data-gathering methods for resolving difficult market research questions.

124. Rook, Dennis W. "Focus Groups Fail to Connect Theory, Current Practice." *Marketing News* 37, no. 19 (September 15, 2003): 40–44.

It is Rook's opinion that, despite their tremendous economic success, focus groups fail to perform well in terms of cost and research yield, and "rarely" work in ways intended by the early practitioners of this qualitative data-gathering technique. Over time, marketing managers have strayed from the basic intent of focus groups, namely, the ability to influence and observe the group dynamics that have an impact on the perceptions, information processing, and decision making of consumers. To improve study reliability and validity, Rook suggests conducting longer sessions, reducing the number of questions asked, employing various projective methods, and selecting more heterogeneous samples—for example, those based on natural, existing, and accessible groups.

125. Rook, Dennis W. "Out-of-Focus Groups." *Marketing Research* 15, no. 2 (Summer 2003): 11–16.

Focus groups emerged from two fields: social psychology and psychotherapy. Rook argues that the practice of focus groups has strayed from its theoretical foundations, and in some cases, has become "little more than superficial, hurried, and expensive group surveys" (p. 16). He cites figures that indicate that there are now over 1,000 permanent research facilities, and that expenditures may exceed half a billion dollars annually in the United States. Rook personally has participated in over 250 focus group projects. Suggested solutions for improving focus group outcomes include the following: (1) take more time—perhaps two to four hours as practiced in Europe; (2) ask fewer questions, which would permit greater depth of coverage and more group interaction; (3) include physical stimuli to encourage responses (in marketing this may involve trying out or looking at the product); and (4) avoid "professional" respondents by diversifying the nature and source of the sample recruited for the focus group.

126. Turauskas, Linas, and Živile Vaitkūnienė. "Planning and Conducting Focus Group Discussions in Marketing Research." *Problems and Perspectives in Management* 2, no. 2 (2004): 304–8.

The advantages of the focus group method are summarized as well as its applicability to the market research field for collecting "rich empirical data covering verbal and nonverbal information" (p. 304). The authors review the key features of the methodology and describe several circumstances for which focus groups would be an appropriate data-gathering approach. An example of the method is provided in which three videotaped focus groups were conducted with 21 participants. The topic concerned a new client information service offered by a telecommunications company. The participants were able to contribute worthwhile suggestions. Focus groups are increasing in popularity and application by Lithuanian commercial and government companies.

127. Witthaus, Michele. "Group Therapy." *Marketing Week* 21, no. 46 (January 28, 1999): 43–47.

Witthaus begins the presentation by writing, "Individually unremarkable, the members of these groups [focus groups] come together to form a critical mass apparently invested with folk wisdom and highly prized insights" (p. 43). Six market researchers then discuss various aspects of conducting focus groups. Andrew Irving, managing director of Andrew Irving Associates, suggests asking participants simple questions about work, family, and children to help judge their level of confidence and articulation. Janine Braier, managing director of Define, encourages the use of an "ice-breaker" technique called the Name Game, in which participants provide their initial for the others to guess their name. Peter Knowles, marketing director for IML, uses automated methods (handsets) to complement traditional data-gathering approaches. Geoff Bayley, director of RDS Open Mind, recommends ways to deal with dominant personalities. Anna Thomas, research manager for Fast Marketing, emphasizes the need for a skilled moderator. Sean McHugh, a London-based entrepreneur, reports success with dividing groups by gender.

Consumers

128. Bristol, Terry, and Edward F. Fern. "The Effects of Interaction on Consumers' Attitudes in Focus Groups." *Psychology & Marketing* 20, no. 5 (May 2003): 433–54.

Three data collection techniques—focus groups, "individual self-administered interviews," and the nominal group technique (NGT)—were compared in order to determine which method would produce the most opinion change among consumers. (NGT is a highly structured form of group interviewing that restricts spontaneous interaction.) The authors hypothesized that, due to participant interaction, attitude shifting would be greatest in the focus group approach, with no difference between the latter two formats. In a behavioral laboratory setting, a group of undergraduate students attending a southeastern U.S. university were recruited and randomly assigned to one of the assessment conditions. The same moderator facilitated all of the group interviews. The topic considered was respondents' consumption of diet soft drinks. The greatest attitude shifts from previously held positions were found among the focus group participants, and more attitude "depolarization" was evident. The shifting occurred in the direction of more negativity in positions held, a condition attributed to the persuasiveness of the arguments. Caution is recommended when using focus groups to assess consumer attitudes.

129. Efken, Christine. "Keeping the Focus in Teen Focus Groups." *International Journal of Advertising & Marketing to Children* 3, no. 4 (July–September 2002): 21–28.

The challenges involved in conducting focus groups with people who are neither "big children" nor "small adults" are reviewed. Efken, associated with a qualitative market research firm in Chicago, observes that this segment of the population had over $250 billion in disposable income in the United States in the year 2000. Suggestions are offered for recruiting participants in this age category, including issues of gender, parental permission, race and ethnicity, group size, and length of the sessions. The chosen venue should be teen friendly. The moderator must establish rapport and trust with the group, be flexible, use visual stimuli whenever possible, and observe nonverbal cues. The author discusses four alternatives to traditional qualitative approaches: observational research, telephone focus groups, online bulletin board focus groups, and homework assignments.

130. Garrison, M. E. Betsy, Sarah H. Pierce, Pamela A. Monroe, Diane D. Sasser, Amy C. Shaffer, and Lydia B. Blalock. "Focus Group Discussions: Three Examples from Family and Consumer Science Research." *Family and Consumer Sciences Research Journal* 27, no. 4 (June 1999): 428–50.

The fundamentals of the focus group method are briefly reviewed—recruitment of participants and group composition, question development, interview protocol and logistics, and data analysis. To demonstrate the versatility of this qualitative approach, the authors discuss its applicability to three different projects within the field of family and consumer science. The first study examined the consumer behavior of 40 working female adolescents. Twelve 45- to 60-minute audiotaped focus groups were conducted with this group. A total of 16 adult males with low educational attainment participated in four 60-minute audiotaped focus groups for the second project. Study three involved 37 mothers of children in prekindergarten through fourth grade who participated in six 90-minute audio- and video-taped focus groups. The similarities and differences among the three examples are discussed in terms of group homogeneity, the number of questions asked, the age of the participants, the impact of incentives, and others. Three appendices contain the questions used for the three groups.

131. Geissler, Gary L., and George M. Zinkhan. "Consumer Perceptions of the World Wide Web: An Exploratory Study Using Focus Group Interviews." *Advances in Consumer Research* 25, no. 1 (1998): 386–92.

This 1998 article is one of the initial efforts to examine the potential impact of the Web on consumer behavior. Five two-hour audiotaped focus groups (three Web user groups, and two nonuser groups) were conducted with 43 participants who had been recruited via random telephone calls, newspaper advertisements, and flyers. All were over age 18 and had not recently been part of another study. The discussions took place in the conference room of the local public library and were transcribed. The focus group findings include the following: (1) consumers perceive more control with the Web than with other media; (2) those who had occasionally used the Web and become frustrated had more negative views than those who did not use it at all; (3) Web information is viewed as less trustworthy than other media formats; (4) Web use reduces television viewing and the placing of telephone calls; (5) the Web is viewed as better for comparison shopping than other media; and (6) Web purchases are more likely when items can be replaced or refunded, and when security assurances are available.

132. Hanks, Roma Stovall. "'Grandma, What Big Teeth You Have!': The Social Construction of Grandparenting in American Business and Academe." *Journal of Family Issues* 22, no. 5 (July 2001): 652–76.

Hanks writes from the perspective that "in the process of targeting grandparents as customers, businesses will construct an image of the American grandparent" (p. 653). The author reviews the popular images of grandparenting as well as those found in scholarly publications. Evidence of how business is eager to take part in the construction of knowledge about grandparenting is presented through a case study of strategic business philanthropy and a review of the academic literature. Part of the case study involved a qualitative approach (focus groups) and a quantitative approach (a newspaper survey of 180 respondents). Three focus groups were conducted with 20 predominately white female grandparents (ages 47 to 75) recruited from a sample of customers in three Gulf Coast cities. (Additional sessions were conducted with grandparents, grandchildren, academics, policymakers, media personnel, and business executives.) The results of the two approaches are discussed in terms of what matters most to the grandparents ("unconditional love" was most often cited as the greatest joy of grandparenting); their responsibilities; their concerns and hopes for the future; and the meanings they attach to their roles. Hanks discusses four types of business involvement that emerged from the initiative and relates them to the social construction of grandparenting by American business.

133. Kehoe, William, and John Lindgren. "Focus Groups in Global Marketing: Concept, Methodology and Implications." *Marketing Management Journal* 13, no. 2 (Fall 2003): 14–28.

The authors set the stage for using focus groups in global marketing by explaining that comments and reactions of consumers may not be "apparent or detected easily" in survey or experimental research. The need for global consumer feedback is expressed in the introduction, along with an outline of the origins of the methodology. Three types of focus groups are described: exploratory, clinical, and phenomenological. The exploratory format involves one person at a time interacting with the moderator, rather than interacting with the group. Clinical focus groups involve a moderator who does not interact but is instead an objective observer. In the phenomenological format, the moderator is a participant in the group and shares in the experiences of the group. A six-stage outline of focus group methodology is provided, including introduction, pre-focus, task-orientation, focus, conclusions, and debriefing. The authors cite cost effectiveness and time savings as major benefits of focus groups over other techniques, acknowledging that focus groups "complement" quantitative methodologies.

134. Schlosser, Ann, and Sharon Shavitt. "Effects of an Approaching Group Discussion on Product Responses." *Journal of Consumer Psychology* 8, no. 4 (1999): 377–406.

According to the authors, very little is known about the thought processes involved when consumers anticipate social interaction with others about a product, how they prepare or tailor their responses for group discussion, and how this translates into what they express in actual dialogue. Three experiments were conducted with 73, 143, and 107 undergraduates who were assigned to either group sessions or individual interviews. Extra credit was given for participation. In each study, the students were asked to read a fictitious restaurant review containing utilitarian information and social image information, and then to anticipate either group or individual discussion. Various types of cues regarding the information appropriate for discussion were manipulated across the studies. The results of each experiment are given in terms of the number of social image versus utilitarian thoughts, the importance of restaurant criteria, and attitude ratings. Although those students anticipating group discussion were found to be more responsive to appropriateness cues, their judgments regarding the restaurant were not influenced. The authors conclude that, when faced with an approaching discussion, people tailor their responses without changing their personal views.

135. Sheehy, Heather, in collaboration with Marc Legault and Derek Ireland. "Consumers and Biotechnology: A Synopsis of Survey and Focus Group Research." *Journal of Consumer Policy* 21 (1998): 359–86.

A mixed-method approach—one quantitative (surveys) and one qualitative (focus groups)—was used to determine consumers' knowledge about biotechnology, where there are gaps in their knowledge, and how the information they do have influences their perceptions and purchasing decisions. The authors report on three separate studies conducted by the Office of Consumer Affairs (OCA) of Industry Canada, and other federal agencies. The first OCA study used focus groups for pretesting a questionnaire for a national telephone survey (many respondents refused to participate or dropped out when they learned the topic of the survey). The other two studies employed focus groups to measure consumer attitudes, concerns, knowledge, and reactions to food and environmental application of biotechnology. The OCA also inserted two questions in the CROP (Centre de Recherchers sur L'Opinion Publique, Inc/Research Center on Public Opinion, Inc.) annual survey of sociocultural change in Canada. The research found that consumers "proceed very cautiously," feel "ill-prepared" to make informed decisions, express ethical and environmental concerns, and are especially confused about the risks and safety of genetically engineered products. The article concludes with a discussion of how the marketplace can respond to consumers' concerns. The "annex" provides examples of biotechnology applications.

136. Threlfall, K. Denise. "Using Focus Groups as a Consumer Research Tool." *Journal of Marketing Practice* 5, no. 4 (1999): 102–5.

When properly conducted, focus groups can be an "effective" strategy in marketing research for identifying attitudes, beliefs, and values. The author believes that the method is too often "abused and distorted" by researchers who have "hidden agenda[s] and outcome biases." Among the advantages are that focus groups offer speed and flexibility, in that the researcher can quickly explore participants' unconstrained views beyond structured interview questions. An unnatural environment, inability to generalize results, and "groupthink" are seen as limitations. Focus groups can assist in the triangulation process and can be employed in various phases of a research project.

137. Wrigley, Neil, Daniel Warm, Barrie Margetts, and Michelle Lowe. "The Leeds 'Food Deserts' Intervention Study: What the Focus Groups Reveal." *International Journal of Retail & Distribution Management* 32, no. 2 (2004): 123–36.

"Food deserts," a phrase coined in the late 1990s, refers to poor areas in British cities that have limited access to healthy affordable food. The introductory section of the article describes the setting and reviews previous research based on the use of diaries, questionnaires, and focus groups to understand food poverty in the United Kingdom. The "intervention" referred to in the title of the article concerns the opening of a new store. The focus group research conducted by the authors and reported here involves a determination of the changes found in the shopping behavior of the people selected (specifically travel changes and types of products chosen). Eight focus groups were formed, with eight participants per group, with age gradients in each (17–34, 35–54, and 55 years and older). Prior to the new Tesco store at Seacroft Green, alternate full-range major retailers were available, as well as limited-range budget retailers. The results of the focus groups indicated that 45 percent of participants had switched to the new store, that they were walking far less to get to the store, and that they were making more frequent trips. Little change was noted in terms of moving to a healthier diet.

Products

138. Allen, Theodore T., and Kristen M. Maybin. "Using Focus Group Data to Set New Product Prices." *Journal of Product & Brand Management* 13, no. 1 (2004): 15–24.

When no historical data for price setting is available, focus groups can be used to assist in recommending prices. One method discussed, called the Van Westendorp Pricing Method (developed by the Dutch economist Peter van Westendorp) consists of five steps. The authors propose a variation using the same technique, but which addresses personal uncertainty and sampling error, and maximizes the expected profit. The product in question was toothpaste gum. Allen and Maybin simulated the pricing decision making at Smith Kline Beecham, the manufacturer of "Aquafresh gum." Comparing the two approaches, it was found that the Van Westendorp "optimal" settings are "less than or equal to the ones that would be recommended from revenue and profit considerations under plausible conditions" (p. 22). The authors conclude that both methods can be useful, and that with a limited number of potential customers and a few questions, a recommended price can be achieved.

139. DiPofi, Jackie A., Michael S. LaTour, and Tony L. Henthorne. "The New Social Marketing Challenge to Promote Radon Testing." *Health Marketing Quarterly* 19, no. 1 (2001): 79–90.

As part of a larger project funded by the Environmental Protection Agency, this qualitative study was undertaken to determine people's perceptions of the threat of radon, an odorless, tasteless, and invisible gas. The Karst geological region, spanning parts of Alabama, Kentucky, and Tennessee, was selected for investigation due to the high levels of radiation found in area homes. The tenets of the Protection Motivation Theory (PMT) served as the theoretical framework for the research. According to the authors, PMT "offers a powerful explanation of how fear appeals are able to persuade consumers" (p. 81). To explore both adaptive and maladaptive behaviors, a series of focus groups were conducted with over 50 male and female blue- and white-collar residents who were representative of the targeted areas. The results are discussed in terms of participants' low awareness of and misconceptions about the threat of radon poisoning, the factors contributing to awareness level, recommendations, and subsequent actions taken. A "vast" amount of "valuable" information was retrieved by the focus group approach. Implications for the field of social marketing are discussed.

140. Kuhn, Klaus. "Problems and Benefits of Requirements Gathering with Focus Groups: A Case Study." *International Journal of Human-Computer Interaction* 12, nos. 3–4 (2000): 309–25.

Siemens AG, a multinational company, wanted to obtain early input on a home automation system. Part of the preparation leading to the final design was the use of focus groups for "requirements gathering." Kuhn identifies the following strengths of the approach: (1) a creative process is initiated that can have an impact on the design with "ideas, suggestions, and possibilities"—some of which may be beyond the scope of the project; (2) focus groups deliver data about the context in which a product is to be used that could not be generated via surveys or individual interviews; (3) the integration of representative opinions is not able to be generated through other means; and (4) this approach is helpful in apprising developers and policymakers of users' needs and usability issues in general. The limitations include the following: (1) scientific analysis of the data is not an option (notwithstanding transcribing and coding of the data); (2) moderators without knowledge of the relevant topic can lead to difficulties; and (3) focus groups are not useful for determining the best sequence of operation.

141. Schmidt, David B., Melanie M. Morrow, and Christy White. "Communicating the Benefits of Functional Foods." *Chemtech* 27, no. 12 (December 1997): 40–44.

Consumers, dieticians, and physicians were the audiences selected for focus group studies on functional foods, defined as foods having "benefits beyond basic nutrition," such as fiber-fortified cereals. Ten focus groups were conducted in five cities, with consumers from Boston and Richmond, and dieticians and physicians from Bethesda, Indianapolis, and Los Angeles. The age range was from 21 to 65, with two-thirds of the participants women. One of the goals was to establish a universal term that both consumers and health professionals would find appealing. "Functional foods" was preferred over other choices, with "nutraceuticals" receiving the least support. Consumers were very interested in learning more about functional foods. The U.S. Food and Drug Administration does not see the need to create a new category to include functional foods, believing that the existing categories of food can all be accommodated in one of the following: food, supplements, medical foods, or foods for special dietary use.

142. Seo, Sunhee, and Carol W. Shanklin. "Using Focus Groups to Determine Specific Attributes That Influence the Evaluation of Quality Food and Service Quality in Continuing Care Retirement Communities." *Journal of Foodservice Business Research* 8, no. 1 (2005): 35–51.

An evaluation of food and service quality was carried out in three retirement facilities located in three different cities in Kansas. The target population resided in independent living units of a Continuing Care Retirement Community (CCRC). To identify the specific quality and service attributes, eight one-hour audiotaped focus groups were conducted with 12 male and 33 female participants, who had been recruited by convenience sampling. A moderator experienced with CCRC residents asked a series of open-ended questions. The two most important attributes affecting food quality were flavor/taste in general and texture/tenderness of meat, while attributes affecting food service were appearance of staff and attentiveness of service. In addition to providing strategies for improvement, the results can be used to develop an assessment instrument and to benchmark satisfaction levels.

Organizations

143. Barber, Neil, and Emma Partridge. "Using Focus Groups Strategically for Organizational Success." *Best Practice Measurement Strategies* 1, no. 9 (November 2001): 10–15.

Two research consultants—Barber, of Maritz Research, and Partridge, of TRBI—share their experiences with focus groups conducted at two different venues. The authors provide the rationale for using focus groups in the business environment: They can help employees feel that their perspective is valuable and can help them accept change, and management teams can benefit by gaining an understanding of what motivates their employees. Care must be taken to ensure that participants' issues and ideas are translated into actions. Two case studies, one at British Gas and the other at a private bank, document how the effective use of employee focus groups led to simple but fundamental changes in the way the organizations were managed.

144. Brooks, Kit. "The Influence of Focus Group Feedback on the Three Organizational Levels of an International Retailer." *Journal of European Industrial Training* 26, nos. 2–4 (2002): 204–8.

As a consequence of disappointing holiday sales in two departments, corporate executives at Marco, a major international retailer, sought a more effective way to communicate with its 460 district managers, who received holiday sales information through catalogs and meetings. As part of a multimethod needs assessment approach, seven focus groups were conducted with 122 participants, who represented 38 district managers and 84 department managers in the United States. Anonymity was guaranteed. Brooks discusses the major themes that emerged from the sessions, primarily that all three organizational levels within the company (organizational, process, and individual/job) contributed to ineffective communication. Additional problems were also identified. As a result of the "powerful" information produced by the focus groups, changes were implemented at all levels.

145. Herndon, Sandra L. "Using Focus Group Interviews for Preliminary Investigation." In *Qualitative Research: Applications in Organizational Life*, edited by Sandra L. Herndon and Gary L. Kreps, 63–72. 2nd ed. Communication and Social Organization. Cresskill, NJ: Hampton Press, 2001.

The author defines and describes focus group interviewing, a qualitative data-gathering methodology, and assesses the benefits and limitations of the approach as a research tool in organizational communication. A detailed example demonstrates the use of focus group interviews in an organizational research project. The project involved a *Fortune* 500 company, Sciencetech, which sought to examine diversity in its managerial ranks. Five two-hour focus groups were conducted with 37 employees, who were segregated by race and gender. The primary use of the focus groups was to serve as the preliminary investigation on which to base a series of 32 individual interviews. The outcome is termed "highly valuable." Herndon briefly reviews several recent research applications and offers some practical advice for the conduct of focus groups in this field.

146. Hines, Tony. "An Evaluation of Two Qualitative Methods (Focus Group Interviews and Cognitive Maps) for Conducting Research into Entrepreneurial Decision Making." *Qualitative Market Research* 3, no. 1 (2000): 7–16.

Hines reviews two basic research paradigms, positivist and phenomenological, and offers suggestions for selecting the more appropriate approach for a given research project. Two qualitative methods—focus groups and cognitive mapping (a technique designed to identify cause and effect and explain causal effects)— were chosen to examine how owner-managers make decisions regarding future organizational strategies in two small companies: a clothing company with fewer than 50 employees and a publishing company with fewer than 10 employees. In separate two-hour sessions, the author moderated the focus group-mapping sessions with five clothing managers and four publishing managers. The selection of the combined approach in each of the cases is justified, and the utility of the two approaches for conducting research on small- and medium-sized enterprises is demonstrated.

Small and Medium Enterprises

147. Blackburn, Robert, and David Stokes. "Breaking Down the Barriers: Using Focus Groups to Research Small and Medium-Sized Enterprises." *International Small Business Journal* 19, no. 1 (2000): 44–67.

Focus group methodology was employed to elicit the "motivations, rationales, and experiences" of small- and medium-sized enterprise (SME) owners. To develop longer-term perspectives, the researchers adopted a longitudinal approach for collecting the desired data: five focus groups were held every six months with a core of the same participants drawn from a pool of SME owners. For the first round, meetings were held in London, Manchester, Reading, Kidderminster, and Glasgow. Subsequent rounds were held only in England. The discussion guide contained items relating to the current business climate, the primary challenges, the impact of government policies, and so forth. Incentives were offered. Blackburn and Stokes note that to date "the SBRC [Small Business Resource Center] has run twenty focus groups with over one hundred business owners" (p. 54). The method employed is viewed as an effective technique for "unearthing" personal attitudes and experiences.

148. Fallon, Grahame, and Reva Berman Brown. "Focusing on Focus Groups: Lessons from a Research Project Involving a Bangladeshi Community." *Qualitative Research* 2, no. 2 (2002): 195–208.

Fallon and Brown review the details of the focus group research process, and report on the use of the method in a research project involving small business and entrepreneurship in a Bangladeshi community located in a West Midlands city (U.K.). The study concerned the perceived education and training needs and requirements for career advice and guidance in order to help empower the group participants as well as the community as a whole. A purposive sampling frame was used to identify the target subgroups from which the participants were chosen (largely self-selected). Five local moderators, selected by community leaders, conducted the sessions in the language of the participants. The transcripts were subsequently translated into English and analyzed by means of content analysis. The authors discuss the negative features of the focus groups, specifically the difficulties with the selection of moderators, the nonpayment of moderators, and the "variable" quantity and quality of the study findings. The ethnic, community-based, data-gathering technique proved to be of "considerable value" for attaining the goals of the project.

149. Kilpatrick, Sue, and Rowena Bell. "Sharing the Driving Seat: Involving Everyone in a Family Business." *Rural Sociology* 10, no. 1 (2000): 5–13.

The authors report on the activities of Executive Link (EL), a farm management training program in Australia. The goal of the program is to help farm businesses, especially family businesses, learn how to better manage such challenges as globalization, low commodity prices, changing consumer preferences, and environmental demands. Kilpatrick and Bell explain the concept of whole team learning and explore the role of women in Australian farm businesses. The authors observed an EL meeting and then conducted a focus group with 15 volunteers. A semistructured interview guide was developed and administered to nine volunteers at their place of business. EL was found to be an "extremely effective" program.

150. Newby, Rick, Geoff Soutar, and John Watson. "Comparing Traditional Focus Groups with a Group Support Systems (GSS) Approach for Use in SME Research. (Small and Medium Enterprises)." *International Small Business Journal* 21, no. 4 (November 2003): 421–33.

Traditional focus groups are compared and contrasted with the Group Support Systems (GSS) approach in which computer technology is used within the focus group session. The setting used explored the goals of small and medium enterprise owner-operators. In the GSS format, up to 10 people are arranged around a table—each with their own computer (and all linked to a single central workstation). Responses to questions received from the facilitator are anonymous. The value of this process is to permit all ideas to surface, as well as to enable some quantitative analysis of responses to occur during the session. The GSS members were asked to input their ideas in response to each question prior to any discussion occurring, which had an impact on the flow of participant interaction. The authors recommend the GSS approach for gathering broad ideas but suggest that traditional focus groups are more appropriate if a deep understanding of a topic is desired. GSS avoids the cost of transcribing responses from audiotape.

151. Newby, Rick, John Watson, and David Woodliff. "Using Focus Groups in SME Research: The Case of Owner-Operator Objectives." *Journal of Developmental Entrepreneurship* 8, no. 3 (December 2003): 237–46.

The Australian authors addressed the question as to whether focus group research was appropriate for determining the objectives of small and medium enterprises (SMEs). Four focus groups were conducted with 31 SME owner-operators (11 female). Participants were selected from three sources: a Chamber of Commerce directory, retailers in a large shopping mall, and tenants in a business "incubator." One of the questions the researchers sought to address was whether there was a time element in the objectives of the owner-operators, namely, why they entered the business, why they stayed, and their future goals.

The authors maintain that the study findings indicate that focus group methodology is useful in SME research. Focus groups provide a range of views and a depth of understanding, and are also valuable for supporting other research and as a precursor for other types of research. The primary benefit is "to clarify that which is unclear" (p. 243), that is, to address the "somewhat ambiguous or imprecise." The researchers do not recommend using focus groups when an experienced moderator is unavailable.

152. Vernon, Jon, Stephen Essex, David Pinder, and Kaja Curry. "The 'Greening' of Tourism Micro-Businesses: Outcomes of Focus Group Investigations in South East Cornwall." *Business Strategy and the Environment* 12, no. 1 (January–February 2003): 49–69.

Focus group methods were used to obtain the perspectives of a group of owners of tourism microbusinesses (that is, those with fewer than 10 employees) in South East Cornwall (U.K.) regarding their awareness, knowledge, and barriers to adoption of sustainable tourism practices. Sustainable tourism refers to efforts to protect the environment's nonrewable physical and cultural resources in the process of tourism development. A series of five audiotaped focus groups were conducted with 34 business owners, who represented 25 diverse businesses and who might be expected to have different views. The principal researcher served as moderator, with the assistance of a note taker. Incentives were provided. The results reveal that the business owners possessed a limited awareness "of both their individual and collective impacts on the environment and the concept of environmental sustainability" (p. 65). Many of the owners transferred their responsibilities in this area to the tourists themselves. Costs were also a consideration. Focus group methodology is described as a "valuable" way to collect the needed information.

3.3 CARTOGRAPHY

153. Harrower, Mark, Alan MacEachren, and Amy L. Griffin. "Developing a Geographic Visualization Tool to Support Earth Science Learning." *Cartography and Geographic Information Science* 27, no. 4 (2000): 279–93.

The authors developed a geovisualization tool, the Earth Systems Visualizer (ESV), to help students learn about global weather. Two exploratory spatial data-analysis techniques, *temporal brushing* and *temporal focusing*, were evaluated in terms of whether interactive geovisualization tools would have an impact on problem-solving strategies (that is, would students be able to create hypotheses concerning Earth-science processes). Two 60-minute audiotaped focus groups were conducted, the first with six faculty and graduate students from the Penn State Department of Geography (the "expert" group), and the second with eight undergraduate students (the "novice" group). Each focus group had three sections: a five-minute introduction and demonstration of the ESV by the facilitator; 10 minutes for group members' use; and the group interview. Prescripted questions generated 5 to 10 minutes of discussion each. Two of the authors served as facilitators. The value of the group experience is said to be the "trigger effect," in which participants are stimulated by listening to others. The authors note that positive reactions in focus groups do not "clearly translate" into good performance with an interface.

154. Kessler, Fritz C. "Focus Groups as a Means of Qualitatively Assessing the U-Boat Narrative." *Cartographica* 37, no. 4 (Winter 2000): 33–60.

The U-Boat Narrative (UBN) is a data-exploration system that documents Germany's use of these submarines to disrupt Allied supply lines during World War II. A prototype of UBN contains two components: narratives, which provide the historical background through static maps, text, and pictures; and data exploration modules, which allow users to view an animation of the Allied ships sunk and damaged, as well as statistical and graphical representations. The major goals of the study were to ascertain the level of computer skill and prior knowledge of the conflict needed to effectively use the software, and to identify the strengths and weaknesses of the prototype. Three 60-minute focus groups were conducted with a total of 18 predominately male participants drawn from three categories: novices, historians, and cartographers. The author, who served as project designer, moderator, and analyst, asked participants to evaluate the UBN's overall appeal, interface design, and usefulness as a data-exploration tool. The results are discussed in terms of the preferences and dislikes expressed by the participants toward the different components of the UBN. The "valuable" comments derived from the narratives will be considered for UBN revisions.

155. Olson, Judy M., Lesha Broomes, Scott Drzyzga, Geoffrey Jiunn Der Duh, Lisa K. Dygert, Jill Hallden, Amy K. Lobben, Alison Philpotts, Ian Sims, and Jennifer Ware. "Teaching and Learning Focus Group Skills: A Classroom Example Evaluating Map Design." *Cartographic Perspectives* 31 (Fall 1998): 26–36.

A two-part process was used in a Michigan State University graduate cartography course ("Map Automation") to evaluate both a recently designed map of the campus and the classroom learning experience itself. The first part of the project involved a 75-minute videotaped focus group held during regular class time. The instructor moderated the discussion, which centered on a set of issues concerning the map: color, image, errors, design elements, authenticity, and strengths and weaknesses. Over 50 suggestions and comments were generated. Part 2 took place at the next class meeting. Students were asked to appraise the focus group experience, with the former subjects of the research—the students—becoming part of the research team. The preplanning stage and the components of the focus group method were explained to the students, who unanimously felt the session was "enlightening" with regard to map design and the qualitative approach undertaken to evaluate it. A copy of the report sent to the university's Cartography Center is found in the appendix.

3.4 COMMUNICATION

Advertising

156. Chapel, Gage, Kristin M. Peterson, and Roy Joseph. "Exploring Anti-Gang Advertisements: Focus Group Discussions with Gang Members and At-Risk Youth." *Journal of Applied Communication Research* 27, no. 3 (1999): 237–57.

Focus group interviewing was selected as the methodology of choice to (1) evaluate the effectiveness of several anti-gang television advertisements; and (2) provide information for creating new and more persuasive ads directed to a target audience of gang members and at-risk youth. Three separate focus groups were conducted with a total of 22 black, white, Hispanic, and mixed ethnicity males and females, ages 12 to 17, recruited from a family and youth services department in Nevada. All participants had committed felony offenses; some belonged to gangs or were associated with gang members. Seven anti-gang ads produced by KVVV, a Fox affiliate, were shown to each group, followed by six questions related to aspects of the content. The results of the study indicate the following: participants were willing to share their opinions with researchers; similar responses were produced independently by all three groups; participants served in various roles as respondents, critics, and creators; and, interestingly, there was incongruity between attitudes and behaviors.

157. Kenyon, Alexandra J. "Exploring Phenomenological Research: Pre-Testing Focus Group Techniques with Young People." *International Journal of Market Research* 46, no. 4 (Winter 2004): 427–41.

Two techniques—semistructured questioning and nondirective questioning— were pretested through the use of focus groups. The purposes of the pretest were to determine which questioning technique was more appropriate for stimulating the study hypothesis and to identify a suitable process for sampling homogeneous groups. Two audio- and videotaped focus groups were conducted with a purposive sample of male and female Year 12 students enrolled in a suburban school in Yorkshire. The discussion topic concerned how young people read and interpret alcohol advertisements. The students were classified into regular drinkers and nonregular drinkers. The two question formats were tested in separate groups. Nondirective questioning proved to be the better method for eliciting participation from this population.

158. Waiters, Elizabeth D., Andrew J. Treno, and Joel W. Grube. "Alcohol Advertising and Youth: A Focus-Group Analysis of What Young People Find Appealing in Alcohol Advertising." *Contemporary Drug Problems* 28 (Winter 2001): 695–718.

The purpose of the research was twofold: to examine what aspects of television alcohol advertisements were appealing to young viewers and to determine whether age and gender affected these choices. Six commercials were selected from a total of 68 different advertisements. As part of a larger study, a series of audiotaped focus groups were conducted with 97 ethnically diverse male and female participants recruited from six elementary, middle, and high schools located in four school districts in Santa Clara County, California (the county encompasses "Silicon Valley"). The focus groups consisted of 5 to 11 students each and were separated by gender. Participants were asked to name general television commercials and why they liked or disliked them. Following a showing of the six previously selected alcohol commercials, the students were again asked to identify their favorite and least favorite advertisements. In general, the students liked commercials featuring humor, animals, music, innovative technical aspects, and natural, bar, and party settings. Conversely, they disliked product-oriented commercials. Implications for advertisers are discussed.

Bibliography

159. Walden, Graham R. "Recent Books on Focus Group Interviewing and Mass Communication." *Communication Booknotes Quarterly* 37, no. 2 (Spring 2006): 76–93.

The article provides an overview of the literature on focus group interviewing as used in, and applied to, mass communication. In total, 28 entries are annotated, including 18 books, 9 book chapters, and a monograph by the American Statistical Association. Most of the works included are guides and handbooks. Featured are the major contributions from the past decade, including the six-volume set, the *Focus Group Kit*, by Richard A. Krueger and David L. Morgan (as well as a number of other contributors). The intended audiences for *Communication Booknotes Quarterly* (*CBQ*) are librarian subject specialists in mass communication and others interested in the recent literature, such as faculty members, journalists, and members of the general public. Entries from this *CBQ* article have been revised and can be found in this Scarecrow Press book.

Journalism

160. Willey, Susan. "Focus Groups Newsroom Style." In *Qualitative Research in Journalism: Taking It to the Streets*, edited by Sharon Hartin Iorio, 575–92. Mahwah, NJ: Lawrence Erlbaum, 2004.

The use of focus groups by journalists is described as being a little different from standard social scientific approaches. The purpose in this case is information gathering, and the technique may involve a variety of venues—such as backyard barbeques. The goal is to stimulate community conversations, which are carefully listened to as "reality checks." The author discusses academic focus groups, explains how journalism focus groups operate, and comments on the nature of "action research"—a technique aimed at implementing acquired knowledge for community use. Three examples are provided: the *Savannah Morning News*, involving group conversations that led to citizen action; the *Lawrence Journal-World*, involving neighborhood discussions and a town meeting; and the *Cincinnati Enquirer*, involving focus groups and community partnerships. Willey observes that journalists are employing modifications of the focus group model. These approaches are complementary to traditional quantitative methods such as polls and surveys, as well as other methods of newsgathering, for example, document research and individual interviews.

Technical Writing

161. Abbott, Christine, and Philip Eubanks. "How Academics and Practitioners Evaluate Technical Texts: A Focus Group Study." *Journal of Business and Technical Communication* 19, no. 2 (April 2005): 171–218.

Two key questions were evaluated, namely, what do academicians and practitioners consider to be good technical writing, and do they use similar or different measures for examining the same texts. The authors chose the focus group approach because they wanted to understand the reasoning behind participants' choices, as well as the expressions and explanations provided. Over a six-month period, six focus groups were conducted with 29 participants found via a request from appropriate listservers. There were three groups of academics (8 women, 4 men) and three groups of practitioners (12 women, 5 men). Each session lasted two hours, with one hour for discussion of two versions of an instruction manual, and one hour for discussion of two versions of a memo. The authors served as moderators—one for the manuals and one for the memos. Thematic classifications of remarks were established. The authors determined that academics' and practitioners' ways of evaluating texts have "much in common," with both using standard sets of concepts and values, and a similar set of metaphors and meta-analysis. The main difference was in the way they considered the memos, with the academics interested in structure and rules, and the practitioners in the workplace context.

162. de Jong, Menno, and Peter Jan Schellens. "Focus Groups or Individual Interviews? A Comparison of Text Evaluation Approaches." *Technical Communication* 45, no. 1 (February 1998): 77–88.

A Dutch government publication titled *Do You Know? Do You Care?* was designed to encourage young people to be moderate and responsible when consuming alcoholic beverages. The brochure was used to compare and contrast individual interviews versus focus group results in terms of evaluating the effectiveness of the document from the readers' point of view. Several 90-minute focus groups were conducted with 38 participants, with five to six members per group. There were 35 individual interviews conducted. Participants in both formats were asked to complete a background questionnaire and mark the document with pluses and minuses indicating what they liked and aspects that they reacted to negatively. The researchers found that for documents that have a persuasive function, such as technical marketing texts, safety instructions, or health education brochures, the focus group approach appears to be preferable because the participants paid more attention to the acceptability of the information.

163. Elling, Rien. "Revising Safety Instructions with Focus Groups." *Journal of Business and Technical Communication* 11, no. 4 (October 1997): 451–68.

Two approaches—focus groups and the "plus-minus" method—were used to evaluate a manual titled *Basic Safety Knowledge*. The text, designed for personnel in a large chemical company in the Netherlands, consisted of 36 modules dealing with various safety rules and safety risk information. The purposes of the research were to ascertain whether all workers understood the basic rules of safety, and to determine their attitudes, opinions, and behavior on the importance of the manual. In total, 12 two-hour focus groups were conducted with 32 participants recruited from different departments within the organization. The researcher served as moderator. A few days before the focus groups took place, participants received a copy of the manual and were asked to read it and mark the pages with plus or minus signs (indicating their agreement or disagreement with a statement). The annotated text was brought to the sessions and discussed. The combined techniques produced "valuable" information for revising or maintaining the text.

164. Eubanks, Philip, and Christine Abbott. "Using Focus Groups to Supplement the Assessment of Technical Communication Texts, Programs, and Courses." *Technical Communication Quarterly* 12, no. 1 (Winter 2003): 25–45.

The authors describe some of the key features of focus groups, review the historical background of this qualitative research paradigm, and explain why the method is "especially well suited" for technical communication assessment tasks. Six audiotaped focus groups were conducted with three groups of technical communication practitioners and three groups of college-level teachers in order to compare and contrast the values and concepts associated with good technical writing, as well as how they arrived at evaluations. The researchers served as co-moderators. Prior to the focus group discussions, each group was given two sets of technical texts (bogus documents) and asked to mark them with either pluses (good writing) or minuses (poor writing) and provide a summary comment. Eubanks and Abbott discuss the benefits and risks of using the methodology and its applicability for assessing programs and courses.

165. Lederman, Linda C., and Lea P. Stewart. "Using Focus Groups to Formulate Effective Language for Health Communication Messages: A Media Campaign to Raise Awareness of Domestic Violence on a College Campus." *Qualitative Research Reports in Communication* 4 (2003): 16–22.

Focus group interviewing was selected as the qualitative method of choice for use in the initial phase of a health communication campaign to identify and analyze audience perception potential messages. The topic under consideration was the increasing amount of violence in interpersonal relationships among college students. The venue for the study was a large public university that wished to heighten students' awareness of domestic violence and the campus programs where assistance could be sought. Six focus groups were conducted by trained male and female graduate students, matched by gender to the participants. The groups consisted of between seven and nine students, who were each paid $30 to participate. Sessions were audiotaped, transcribed, and analyzed by the constant comparison technique. The results are discussed in terms of the students' understanding of the term "domestic violence," their comprehension of four statements related to such abuse, and their reactions to a slogan describing the four statements.

Television

166. Adams, William J. "How People Watch Television as Investigated Using Focus Group Techniques." *Journal of Broadcasting & Electronic Media* 44, no. 1 (Winter 2000): 78–93.

The research was designed to address the issue of how and why people watch television. The author reviews the two "seemingly irreconcilable" audience behavior theories: passive receivers who have little or no concept of what is being presented, and active viewers, who link program selection to content and mood. To determine support for one theory over another, 12 90-minute focus groups were conducted with the following participants: 57 undergraduate students (ages 18 to 24), 22 graduate students (ages 25 to 43), and 14 individuals drawn from the community (age 44 plus). The trained moderators, mass communication graduate students, used the same core questions for all groups. Television viewing was found to be a "complicated mix" of the two basic theories of programming. Nearly all participants had a "strong liking" for television as a medium, but this was linked to specific programs and expected moods. Negative views were expressed toward the broadcast networks. The majority (80 percent) watch television out of habit or when they have time.

167. Allen, Craig. "Gender Breakthrough Fit for a Focus Group: The First Women Newscasters and Why They Arrived in Local TV News." *Journalism History* 28, no. 4 (Winter 2003): 155–61.

Allen dates the use of female television newscasters in this country to the early years of the 1970s, noting that males had dominated this format since the inception of television in the 1940s. The author writes from the perspective that it was audience research, rather than gender or societal factors, that contributed to the rise of women in broadcasting. Support for this view was obtained by the recent release of the papers and records of McHugh & Hoffman, the first (1962), and for many years the largest, news consulting organization in the United States. The firm served as advisor and tactician to stations in more than 100 cities. After McHugh & Hoffman was sold in 2000, its papers were made available to scholars. Among the documents examined, it was found that surveys and focus groups had been at the "core" of the firm's news consulting process. These surveys and focus groups indicated that viewers, who were 50 percent female, wanted female newscasters. As a result, 50 stations had hired women reporters by 1971. By the end of the decade, male-female anchor teams were active in the Top 100 markets, with future developments in single female anchoring on the way. Allen believes that without McHugh & Hoffman's opening the dialogue between broadcasters and the viewing public, the arrival of women to the broadcasting arena "would not have come when it did."

168. Southwell, Brian G., Stephanie H. Blake, and Alicia Torres. "Lessons on Focus Group Methodology from a Science Television News Project." *Technical Communication* 52, no. 2 (May 2005): 187–93.

The *Discoveries and Breakthroughs Inside Science* (DBIS), a project funded by the National Science Foundation and operated by the American Institute of Physics, is a syndicated science news service available to large local television stations. DBIS was designed to deliver technical communications from universities and research institutions regarding science, technology, engineering, and mathematics to the stations in order to provide the general public with information on current developments in these areas. As a first step in a multiple-year evaluation effort, nine one- to two-hour videotaped focus groups were conducted in three U.S. cities: Richmond, Virginia; Denver, Colorado; and Chicago, Illinois. Quota sampling was used to recruit the participants, who were each paid between $50 and $75. The authors discuss how they addressed—or failed to address—five previously outlined guidelines for conducting focus groups. The focus group experience brought the scientific community "a step closer to understanding scientific information as publics engage it" (p. 192).

3.5 DEMOGRAPHY

169. Knodel, John. "A Case for Nonanthropological Qualitative Methods for Demographers." *Population and Development Review* 23, no. 4 (December 1997): 847–54.

Survey work is discussed in relation to how follow-up focus group efforts can confirm and enhance questionnaire findings. The example provided covers the fertility histories of rural Thai women and how within a few months after giving birth they typically resume agricultural labor. The questionnaire findings were confirmed through focus group discussions. The focus groups also added the information that the mother's productivity was interrupted by child care because the mother needed to bring the child to the fields (rural Thai parents are largely responsible for early child care). The elaboration during the focus group session was credited for this realization. The focus group technique is noted to be the most commonly used qualitative data-collection approach in population research. Focused in-depth interviews are also discussed and compared with focus groups. Focus groups permit demographers to collect data in a number of communities in the same study, and aid in the comparative analysis of the data between different settings.

170. Knodel, John. "Using Qualitative Data for Understanding Old-Age Security and Fertility." In *The Methods and Uses of Anthropological Demography*, edited by Alaka Malwade Basu and Peter Aaby, 57–80. International Studies in Demography. Oxford: Clarendon Press, 1998.

In social demographic research, quantitative data and analysis have been the norm. Knodel presents evidence that the addition of qualitative techniques provides a better and more complete picture, stating that neither approach used alone will yield sufficient information. The basics of the focus group method are discussed. A case study of the old-age security motive in Thailand is offered as an example. From the mid 1960s to the 1991–1992 official survey, results show that fertility declined from between six and seven children per woman to a rate of 2.17, which is just below the replacement level. The role of the old-age security motive in fertility decision making is the subject of this study. Two sets of focus groups were drawn upon for the data, the first collected by the Institute for Population and Social Research, Mahidol University; the second was collected as part of the University of Michigan's Comparative Study of the Elderly in Asia. Focus groups were found to be useful for their ability to indicate how participants are interpreting questions and to demonstrate meanings understood, as compared with closed-ended survey questions where unintended interpretations may be drawn. Many examples from the focus group transcripts are provided, and some limitations of focus groups are discussed.

171. Wellner, Alison Stein. "The New Science of Focus Groups." *American Demographics* 25, no. 2 (March 2003): 29–33.

Wellner recounts how Jump Associates, a California-based research firm, went beyond the traditional focus group to help Target stores increase revenues 12 percent over the third quarter of 2001. This example is used to highlight the changes currently taking place in qualitative research—not only in response to critics of the technique but also to benefit from technological advances and new or newly applied research methodologies. Prominent among these are innovations borrowed from other disciplines: segmentation science, ethnography, and psychology. Segmentation scientists base participant recruitment on demographic and psychographic characteristics, as well as media usage and purchasing behavior. Ethnographic methods are used to provide more participant comfort in order to elicit more authentic responses. Advances in cognitive science, such as neuroimaging, can be used to enhance one-on-one interviews. In an inset the author notes that while spending for online quantitative research has increased, it has been negligible for qualitative research. However, online bulletin boards are proving useful.

3.6 EDUCATION

General Studies

172. Billig, Stephen M. *Educators' Guide to Collecting and Using Data: Conducting Focus Group Research.* Denver: RMC Research Corporation, 1999. 23p.

Qualitative techniques are appropriate when the objective is exploratory or when an in-depth understanding is desired. Focus groups are effective for encouraging interaction and eliciting a variety of insights. Billig leads the user through the stages of conducting a focus group project: design and planning; identifying and recruiting participants; locating a facility; selecting a moderator/facilitator and detailing her or his activities and level of involvement; and analyzing and reporting the results. The author observes that the primary objective of this "valuable" methodology is to obtain a range of views and gain insights into them.

173. Jayanthi, Madhavi, and Janet S. Nelson. *Savvy Decision Making: An Administrator's Guide to Using Focus Groups in Schools.* Thousand Oaks, CA: Corwin Press, 2002. 132p.

The authors have chosen a pragmatic approach to help the reader learn how to conduct a focus group in the educational environment. The discussion is organized around the sequential tasks involved in designing and carrying out this form of qualitative research—planning and decision making, recruiting the key players, conducting the sessions, and analyzing and reporting the data. Initially, Jayanthi and Nelson comment on the rationale for using focus groups (especially those for "high-stakes" decision making), the importance of clarifying the purpose of the project, and the benefits and limitations of the method. Accompanying the text are examples, worksheets, sample forms, checklists, and "FYI" boxes.

174. Tiberius, Richard. "Making Sense and Making Use of Feedback from Focus Groups." *New Directions for Teaching and Learning* no. 87 (Fall 2001): 63–75.

Tiberius writes from the perspective that focus group interviewing, when properly conducted, can yield "highly useful" feedback for teachers—at a reasonable cost in time and effort. The author compares and contrasts focus groups with student evaluations and questionnaires, noting that the former is "superior" for some aspects of teaching. The article is centered around seven topics: (1) the importance of writing good questions that will generate discussion; (2) how to summarize the discussion into succinctly stated themes, issues, or ideas; (3) the amount of transcription necessary for the project at hand; (4) how to communicate the summaries to the teacher; (5) the benefits of face-to-face conversation between teachers and students; (6) the appropriate uses of the complete transcript, for example, for classroom research and for the documentation of teaching skills for tenure or promotion; and (7) other classroom applications of the technique.

Adult/Lifelong Learning

175. Chioncel, N. E., R. G. W. van der Veen, D. Wildemeersch, and P. Jarvis. "The Validity and Reliability of Focus Groups as a Research Method in Adult Education." *International Journal of Lifelong Education* 22, no. 5 (September–October 2003): 495–517.

The theory and practice of focus groups as they are used in adult education research are examined. Three theoretical frameworks relating to qualitative research are described: a radical hermeneutic position, a moderate interpretative position, and a pragmatic realistic position. The authors selected the last perspective for analyzing the components of focus groups because it bridges the gap with positivist research, which links qualitative and quantitative approaches. Chioncel et al. report on their examination of four recent (1993–2002) European projects carried out in the field of adult education. A total of 32 countries participated, with all projects using focus groups as well as other research techniques. To assess reliability and validity of these projects, three different methodologies for collecting data were employed: questionnaires, in-depth interviews, and an expert panel composed of researchers from all four projects. Results are given in terms of both technical and sociopsychological problems found in focus group research.

176. Field, John. "Researching Lifelong Learning through Focus Groups." *Journal of Further and Higher Education* 24, no. 3 (2000): 323–35.

Focus groups, in addition to a variety of other techniques, were used in a study of Lifelong Learning in Scotland and Northern Ireland. (The present analysis is based largely on the Northern Ireland experience.) The purposes of the research were to examine patterns of education and training from youth to old age, and to explore the attitudes of people in senior positions having human resources backgrounds in a number of sectors such as health care, tourism/hospitality, and finance. A total of 10 focus groups were conducted with 66 participants. The discussion was organized around four questions asked by a member of the research team. Field describes the analytic phase as both "time consuming and complex" in that, on average, each 90-minute session produced approximately 8,000 words of text. Participant reaction to the paradoxical findings, and to each other, are discussed in detail. The focus groups conducted are viewed as productive and a "useful complement" to large-scale surveys and individual interviews.

177. Wilson, Valerie, and Lindsey Bagley. "Learning at a Distance: The Case of the Community Pharmacist." *International Journal of Lifelong Education* 18, no. 5 (September–October 1999): 355–69.

Two methods—one quantitative (a survey) and one qualitative (focus groups)—were used for a study designed to gather data on how busy professionals, in this case community pharmacists, use distance learning (such as workshops, study groups, computer-assisted learning, and videotapes) for continuing professional development. Phase one involved a mail questionnaire sent to a sample of over 1,000 registered pharmacists. In phase two, six focus groups (each containing six to eight pharmacists) were conducted with a random sample of males and females, owner-managers and employees, and high and low users. Overall, the response to distance learning was positive. Nonusers expressed less favorable opinions. A large number (64 percent) found the method to be time consuming. As a result of the assessment, changes were made to the content and presentation of learning materials.

Auxiliary Services

178. Bullock, Marcy, and Jennifer Jones. "Beyond Surveys: Using Focus Groups to Evaluate University Career Services." *Journal of Career Planning & Employment* 59, no. 4 (Summer 1999): 38–44.

Although surveys have traditionally been used to measure client satisfaction with career services, the authors believe that this approach often fails to "capture the nuances" of clients' opinions. To gain a deeper understanding of students' perspectives, career services practitioners at the College of Agriculture and Life

Sciences at North Carolina State University selected focus groups to evaluate university-sponsored workshops. Bullock and Jones describe the four-step preplanning process and discuss the qualities necessary for an effective facilitator, including the various participant personality types that must be managed. Suggestions are offered for postfocus group activities. In response to the comments gathered from the groups, the career center's staff introduced a number of enhancements to the program, such as Web-based services, faculty advisors, workshops, and mentors to assist the students.

179. Erwin, Lorna, and Penni Stewart. "Gendered Perspectives: A Focus-Group Study of How Undergraduate Women Negotiate Their Career Aspirations." *Qualitative Studies in Education* 10, no. 2 (1997): 207–20.

The authors explore the processes (influences, opportunities, and contingencies) that mediate the educational and career aspirations and decision making of women undergraduates. Focus group interviewing was selected as the qualitative method of choice to gain insight into the perspectives of 85 first-year female students attending an ethnically and racially diverse university located in a large Canadian city. Group size varied from two to seven participants. The students were asked to discuss a wide range of issues—from their expectations of higher education to the impact of parents, friends, and dating partners on their daily lives. The findings indicate that education and career options are still constrained by traditional conceptions of motherhood, and that, for most of the students, contradictions exist "between their ideal of gender egalitarianism and the practical concessions necessary to cope with existing gender practices" (p. 218).

Business

180. Hamilton, Diane M., Robert E. Pritchard, Carol N. Welsh, Gregory C. Potter, and Michael S. Saccucci. "The Effects of Using In-Class Focus Groups on Student Course Evaluations." *Journal of Education for Business* 77, no. 6 (July–August 2002): 329–33.

With the goal of improving students' level of satisfaction with a course titled Principles of Finance, a professor conducted focus groups with 45 students enrolled in two of four sections of the course. The professor quickly implemented two of the suggestions and explained to the students why he could not comply with the others. The two non-focus-group control sections of 49 students received the changes, but with minimum explanation. Another faculty member administered the Educational Testing Service's SIRII student evaluation forms to all four classes during the two-week period prior to final exams. Seven major sections of the SIRII were compared and analyzed. Higher evaluation ratings were given on 38 of the 40 instrument questions by the students who had participated in the focus groups. The authors conclude by discussing the presence of the Hawthorne

Effect (a concept dating to the 1920s and 1930s at the Hawthorne Works plant of Western Electric), which emphasizes open discussion, shared information, trust, and rapid implementation of suggested changes.

181. Selwyn, Neil, Neil Marriott, and Pru Marriott. "Net Gains or Net Pains? Business Students' Use of the Internet." *Higher Education Quarterly* 54, no. 2 (April 2000): 166–86.

The purpose of the study was to determine the students' use and nonuse of the Internet. Focus group interviews were conducted with business students in two institutions of higher education in the United Kingdom. One was a "traditional civic university" and the other a post-1992 former polytechnic. There were 18 audiotaped focus groups with a total of 77 students, who had already completed questionnaires on their use of information and computer technology at this university. Four basic themes emerged relating to the manner in which students were introduced to the Internet, the operational problems, the use of the material retrieved, and the social element of learning online. Approximately half the article presents group exchanges. Many students expressed a reluctance to use the Internet as a "fundamental" part of their studies. The discussion portion refers to operational anxieties and information overload expressed. Also considered was the role of the Internet as a "rival or absolute substitute" for libraries, textbooks, or classroom teaching.

Comparative

182. Dushku, Silvana. "Conducting Individual and Focus Group Interviews in Researching Albania." *TESOL Quarterly* 34, no. 4 (Winter 2000): 763–68.

The author discusses the special challenges encountered when conducting interview-based research in developing countries. This type of inquiry can be "complicated by economic, political, and social constraints on local contexts and on participants that result in emigration, turnover, workloads, and overall instability" (p. 763). Dushku reports on a study undertaken in Albania to evaluate three English-language aid programs at the university in Tirana. A multimethod data collection approach—questionnaires, individual interviews, and focus groups—was used to elicit the perspectives of program coordinators, English-language teaching (ELT) aid officers, university teachers, and education specialists. Almost all of the 30 key individuals involved in the three programs completed the questionnaires and granted individual interviews. The author then conducted three focus groups with 10 participants selected from the above categories. The purpose of the focus groups was to gain a more in-depth understanding of particular aspects of the topic and to provide triangulation of data. Dushku concludes that more "enthusiasm, expertise, and professional commitment" are required by the type of research as well as modifications to the approach.

183. Fentiman, Alicia, Andrew Hall, and Donald Bundy. "School Enrollment Patterns in Rural Ghana: A Comparative Study of the Impact of Location, Gender, Age and Health on Children's Access to Basic Schooling." *Comparative Education* 35, no. 3 (1999): 331–49.

The purpose of the research was to discuss the results of three censuses of school-age children (ages 6 to 15) in sub-Saharan Ghana. The authors focus on three rural school districts in the country, districts selected as being representative of cultural diversity as well as disparity between the disadvantaged north and the south. Statistics are provided on gross enrollment rates, issues related to age and gender, the classes where children drop out, and details about the children who never enrolled in school. Focus groups (and structured interviews) were conducted to examine the obstacles to completing a basic education (very few students in rural Ghana achieve this goal). To elicit a variety of perspectives, parents, teachers, enrolled and never-enrolled children, and dropouts were invited to participate. The focus group discussions identified a number of constraints to basic education: economics, health, location, gender, and the low value placed on education. Policy options are discussed.

184. Knodel, John. "The Closing of the Gender Gap in Schooling: The Case of Thailand." *Comparative Education* 33, no. 1 (1997): 61–86.

Knodel traces the development of formal education in Thailand, a country whose population is culturally and religiously (Buddhism) homogeneous. Although Thailand is experiencing a dramatic socioeconomic transformation, many people live in rural poverty-stricken areas, with low levels of primary education achievement. The country has a long-standing tradition of favoring the education of boys over girls. However, recent survey and census results indicate that this gender gap has narrowed, even though some preference for boys persists. To examine attitudes toward gender equality in terms of education, 15 audiotaped focus groups, with 7 to 11 participants each, were conducted in two rural districts. The mothers and fathers who participated represented particular targeted groups. Most of the discussion questions concerned the determinants and consequences of postprimary schooling. The transcripts were translated into English. The analysis reveals that parents' views regarding gender and education are "multidimensional" and "complex," and do not consistently favor one sex over the other. In some cases, parents thought it was more advantageous to favor girls at least as much as boys. Factors (largely socioeconomic) that serve to inhibit education for both sexes are discussed.

Elementary

185. Edmonson, Hank M., and Lyndal M. Bullock. "Youth with Aggressive and Violent Behaviors: Pieces of a Puzzle." *Preventing School Failure* 42, no. 3 (Spring 1998): 135–41.

The goal of the research was to gain a better understanding of the factors that contribute to aggression and violence among young students—from the students' own perspective via focus groups. The sample was drawn from youth placed in an inner-city elementary alternative setting due to disruptive behavior. One 45-minute audiotaped focus group was conducted with five ethnically diverse fourth- and fifth-grade male students. Following a short video, four major categories of questions were discussed, with much attention to developing a concept of violence. Four themes emerged that related to stealing, fighting, drugs, and gangs, with one student suggesting that these components "formed pieces of a puzzle." The students were "extremely willing" to share their views. The authors describe the focus groups as "efficient."

186. Sargent, Paul. "Real Men or Real Teachers?: Contradictions in the Lives of Men Elementary Teachers." *Men and Masculinities* 2, no. 4 (April 2000): 410–33.

The author observes that in the United States 88 percent of the elementary schoolteachers are women. In the local school board directory of teachers, from which this sample was drawn, only 2 percent of the K–3 teachers were men. Ethnographic and focus group interviews were conducted to determine the experiences of men who teach in the primary grades. Twenty-three men participated, with four involved in follow-up interviews, and six in two audiotaped focus groups. Most of the participants were white, between the ages of 25 and 55, middle class, married, and had an average of nine years' experience. The group composition was diverse: two African Americans, two of Asian decent, three Latinos, and three gays. The degree to which male teachers receive greater scrutiny is discussed in relation to how the teachers feel constrained to act versus the way they might prefer to express themselves. Division of labor and compensatory activities, such as rejection, defiance, and compensatory stances, are expressed.

Health

187. Dreachslin, Janice L. "Focus Groups as a Quality Improvement Technique: A Case Example from Health Administration Education." *Quality Assurance in Education* 7, no. 4 (1999): 224–32.

Due to the increasing numbers of health professionals pursuing lifelong learning on a part-time basis, an evaluation of the traditional curriculum and teaching practices is required. Dreachslin discusses the key features and "unique advantages" of focus group methodology and demonstrates its utility for assessing the satisfaction levels of adult learners about their educational experiences in a professional master's level management program. Two focus groups were conducted with 11 participants who were asked to discuss seven questions. As a result of student feedback, initiatives were developed to restructure the curriculum, and teaching quality is closely monitored on a continuous basis. The author discusses "group-think," a phenomenon produced by group interaction. To counteract possible bias, assessments from other stakeholders and data collection techniques are advised.

188. Kinsman, J., J. Nakiyingi, A. Kamali, L. Carpenter, M. Quigley, R. Pool, and J. Whitworth. "Evaluation of a Comprehensive School-Based AIDS Education Programme in Rural Masaka, Uganda." *Health Education Research* 16, no. 1 (2001): 85–100.

A mixed-method approach was used to assess a large school-based AIDS program in 18 parishes in Masaka, a rural district in southwestern Uganda. Nineteen activities were selected from a total of 53 outlined in a 1994 WHO/UNESCO (World Health Organization/United Nations Educational, Scientific and Cultural Organization) risky behavior reduction package. The program was implemented in 66 schools in the target area. The quantitative portion of the study involved questionnaires administered to 1,274 students from 20 intervention schools and 803 students from 11 control schools. From five randomly chosen intervention schools, 12 gender-separated audiotaped focus groups were conducted in the vernacular (Luganda) with 46 boys and 47 girls. The program evaluated had very little effect as evidenced by the triangulated analyses. The authors discuss the reasons for this failure and offer suggestions for remediation.

189. Porcellato, Lorna, Lindsey Dughill, and Jane Springett. "Using Focus Groups to Explore Children's Perceptions of Smoking: Reflections on Practice." *Health Education* 102, no. 6 (2002): 310–20.

The authors explore the appropriateness and feasibility of using focus group methodology for gathering information on children's perceptions of smoking. Twelve 40-minute audiotaped focus groups were conducted with 50 male and female second-grade students recruited from diverse school districts in Liverpool, U.K. An individual known to the children (but not their teacher) served as moderator. A visioning exercise was part of the protocol. The results indicate that (1) the children's responses were brief and simplistic, with some of a nonsensical nature; (2) negative attitudes toward smoking were evident in all groups; (3) group dynamics played an important role, but there was no evidence of overconformity; and (4) more moderator involvement was required than what is thought to be desirable when working with adults. In spite of significant methodological challenges, the focus groups were useful for "highlighting any universal perspectives and shared ideas" (p. 316), and that even young children are capable of participating in this data-gathering approach. An appendix provides the moderator's guide.

190. Wilson, Valerie. "Focus Groups: A Useful Qualitative Method for Educational Research?" *British Educational Research Journal* 23, no. 2 (April 1997): 209–24.

Wilson's stated goals are to review some of the salient points from the literature on focus group methodology; to discuss her personal experiences with the technique; and to "revisit" the concept in the light of those experiences. The author, associated with the Scottish Council for Research in Education in Edinburgh, recounts how a team of researchers at the council undertook a study of adults' perceptions of their lifestyle options for the purpose of informing initiatives in health education and promotion. Using a wide variety of respondents, 54 in-depth individual interviews were conducted, followed by seven focus groups moderated by the author and other researchers. The focus groups encouraged more open discussion of sensitive topics, allowed for deeper probing than the individual interviews, demonstrated a wider variety of discourse, and permitted the researchers to experience interaction with, and among, participants.

Higher Education

191. Archer, Louise, and Merryn Hutchings. "'Bettering Yourself'? Discourses of Risk, Cost and Benefit in Ethnically Diverse, Young Working Class Non-Participants' Constructions of Higher Education." *British Journal of Sociology of Education* 21, no. 4 (December 2000): 555–74.

The authors investigate the factors contributing to the decision-making processes of working-class individuals relative to their attendance at an institution of higher education. Archer and Hutchings write of the "persistent underrepresentation" of working-class students within British universities, and the implications and consequences for diversity in higher education, social class inequalities, and for the individuals themselves. To determine whether "official" perceptions regarding the value of higher education are "shared or contested" by this population, a qualitative method of inquiry was selected. A total of 14 focus groups were conducted with 109 male and female, ethnically diverse, working-class young people (ages 16 to 30) not enrolled in higher education (most were taking vocational education classes). The primary author (white), a white man, and another white woman moderated the focus groups. The results are discussed in terms of the participants' constructions of risks, costs, and personal, social, and economic benefits. The impact of social class inequality is considered.

192. Breen, Rosanna, Roger Lindsay, Alan Jenkins, and Pete Smith. "The Role of Information and Communication Technologies in a University Learning Environment." *Studies in Higher Education* 26, no. 1 (2001): 95–114.

At Oxford Brookes University in the United Kingdom, a study was undertaken to address a number of questions raised by information and communication technologies (ICTs). The overall study objectives were to determine PC ownership among the first-year students, how the computers and computing facilities were used, students' perception of ICT-based learning, and their attitudes toward

ICTs. The study used a questionnaire to determine how students incorporated computers in their learning process, diaries to record actual use, and focus groups for comparison, idea generation, and importance. Student selection was not systematic—posters were placed on campus. Ten focus groups, with four to six undergraduates per group, were conducted. A table shows the nationality, age range, computer experience level, and general area of study. The study data were independently analyzed. Tables indicate the number of minutes computers were used; the location, and in which software applications; definitions of terms used; and a full range of associated positives and negatives according to how the computes were utilized. The discussion considers perceived negatives associated with computers, including cost, competition for access, overcoming technophobia, and acquiring know-how.

193. Brenders, David A., Peter Hope, and Abraham Ninnan. "A Systemic, Student-Centered Study of University Service." *Research in Higher Education* 40, no. 6 (1999): 665–85.

Brenders, of DePaul University, and his Australian coauthors report the methodology and findings of the Student Focus Project, a six-month examination of university services (nonteaching) from the students' perspectives. From a pool of 768 undergraduate students at a large university in Brisbane, a sample of 145 first- through last-year students were randomly selected to represent such diverse groups as overseas students, part-time students, Aboriginal and Torres Strait Island students, and students with disabilities. In total, 24 two-hour audiotaped focus groups were moderated by the authors. The coding procedure revealed a number of themes, primarily a portrayal of the university as a "confused and malignant bureaucracy" (all 24 groups expressed this sentiment) and that information needed by these students was "fragmented" and "balkanized." The student focus group data are said to support several "intriguing generalizations and implications" relative to university services.

194. Caffarella, Rosemary S., and Bruce G. Barnett. "Teaching Doctoral Students to Become Scholarly Writers: The Importance of Giving and Receiving Critiques." *Studies in Higher Education* 25, no. 1 (March 2000): 39–52.

Three data collection approaches—focus groups, observations, and written and oral reflections—were used to elicit students' perceptions of the Scholarly Writing Project (SWP), a program designed to help improve writing skills (content, process, and critiquing) for dissertations and journal publications. The targeted population was 47 doctoral students from an educational leadership program offered at a U.S. university. The protocol called for 10 students to provide oral and written reactions to the SWP. A series of six audiotaped focus groups were conducted with 28 students (14 off-campus students responded by questionnaire). Males and females were nearly equally represented; most were Caucasian. The critiquing process (from peers and professors) was viewed as one of the most "influential" components of the SWP. The interview guide is found in the appendix.

195. Deem, Rosemary, and Kevin J. Brehony. "Doctoral Students' Access to Research Cultures—Are Some More Unequal than Others?" *Studies in Higher Education* 25, no. 2 (2000): 149–65.

Two qualitative approaches, individual interviews and focus group discussions, were used to examine the experiences of social science research students attending two universities in the United Kingdom. Three dimensions of culture were studied. Interviews were conducted with 26 male and female, full- and part-time doctoral students recruited by purposive sampling techniques. A range of social science disciplines and interdisciplinary areas were represented. Focus groups were conducted with some of the same interviewees plus 12 additional students. The results indicate that part-time and international students had the most difficulty in obtaining access to peer cultures, cultures related to research training, and academic research cultures. Among the groups involved, international students were found to be the most able to "enter and embrace" research training cultures. There was some evidence of gender differences. Implications for policy changes are discussed.

196. Freeman, Mark. "Video Conferencing: A Solution to the Multi-Campus Large Classes Problem?" *British Journal of Educational Technology* 29, no. 3 (1998): 197–210.

The outcomes of a videoconferencing trial (by two Australian companies) in an undergraduate lecture were evaluated by means of surveys, focus groups, interviews, videotapings, exam results, and diaries. The setting for the study was the University of Technology Sydney, an institution with over 23,000 students and multiple campuses. There were 250 students enrolled in one location and 80 in another for a business finance course. A total 25 students participated in three focus groups. Prior to the discussions, they were asked to write down their thoughts as to how the videoconferencing had affected their learning—both positively and negatively. A chart presents an analysis of these comments. In the concluding observations Freeman states that the students were positive about the equal treatment and access to experts and information, but they did not believe that lecturing, learning activities, and interactions were improved—in fact, the participants found them to be slow.

197. Goodfellow, Joy, and Jennifer Sumsion. "Transformative Pathways: Field-based Teacher Educators' Perceptions." *Journal of Education for Teaching* 26, no. 3 (2000): 245–57.

A study was undertaken to gain insight into field-based teacher educators' perceptions of their contribution to the personal-professional development of student teachers during their field experiences. The research sought to establish more effective partnerships between field-based and university-based personnel. A series of two-hour focus groups were conducted with 129 participants in 11 locations throughout the Sydney, Australia, metropolitan area. The discussion was facilitated by the authors. The three primary themes identified—wisdom, authenticity, and passion—provided the basis for the development of a conceptual representation for placement within a theoretical context. The focus groups are said to have "heightened" awareness of the value of field-based education.

198. Grant, Kevin, and Stuart Fitzgerald. "The Nexus between Teaching and Research: A Qualitative Study Using Two Focus Group [*sic*] on Academic Information Systems Teachers." *Electronic Journal of Business Research Methods* 3, no. 1 (2005): 37–56.

The purpose of the research undertaken for this article was to determine whether focus groups were useful for identifying the perceptions university staff have with respect to the nexus between teaching and research. The benefits and limitations of focus groups are explored, with the conclusion that, when used on their own, they are not appropriate. However, when viewed as part of multimethod design, they have merit for uncovering hidden issues and for providing insights into pressures, individual attitudes, roles, norms, and values on issues. Two focus groups, with seven participants each, met for up to 90 minutes in an audiotaped environment. Content analysis was employed. The authors found that the focus groups identified issues that would not have emerged via quantitative means, and that they assisted in the understanding of group language and coding. The group members had difficulty in reaching agreement as to the interpretation and understanding of key words and concepts, such as teaching, research, and scholarship.

199. Kezar, Adrianna. "Higher Education Research at the Millennium: Still Trees without Fruit?" *Review of Higher Education* 23, no. 4 (Summer 2000): 443–68.

It is the view of some writers that higher education is not generating appropriate, relevant, and meaningful research, and that a gap exists between researchers' and practitioners' perspectives as to what constitutes quality in terms of content, methodology, and format in higher education literature. To investigate the existence of such a gap, its nature, and strategies for bridging the gap, focus groups were conducted to generate questions for a subsequent survey. A total of 82 participants (practitioners, researchers, or combined status) were selected by stratified random sampling from registration lists of national higher education conferences. The 90-minute nonaudiotaped sessions were conducted over a three-year period at conference locations. Major themes were identified through a note-taker's summaries. Although there was general consensus among the practitioners and researchers that higher education literature was not "a source of important information," the two groups differed on many other issues. The author concludes that the subtitle metaphor "trees without fruit" is supported, but that "the traditional explanation and solutions may not be the best means for moving the field forward" (p. 464).

200. Morrow, Gloria Phillips, Deborah Burris-Kitchen, and Aghop Der-Karabe-tian. "Assessing Campus Climate of Cultural Diversity: A Focus on Focus Groups." *College Student Journal* 34, no. 4 (December 2000): 589–603.

The research project took place at the University of La Verne (ULV), a mid-size liberal arts university with about 1,000 undergraduates on the main campus (southern California). The purposes of the study were (1) to examine ethnic diversity-related issues with a quantitative measure (that is, surveys); (2) to assess student, faculty, staff, and senior management perceptions and opinions of the campus diversity climate with a qualitative approach (that is, focus groups); and (3) to demonstrate how information gathered from focus groups can complement the survey findings. Eight one- to two-hour focus groups were conducted with a total of 61 ethnically diverse (African American, Latino American, and European American) members from the above groups. Student research assistants moderated the sessions; some assistants were chosen to match the ethnicity of the participants. Discussions were audiotaped and transcribed, and thematic categories were identified. The focus group findings "confirmed and complemented" those generated by the surveys. Overall, participants' views were positive although perceptions and attitudes differed among the various ethnic groups represented.

201. Ottewill, Roger, and David Brown. "Student Participation in Educational Research: Experimenting with a Focus Group." *Journal of Further and Higher Education* 23, no. 3 (1999): 373–80.

Ottewill and Brown observe the lack of research on the contribution of focus groups to educational research in the United Kingdom. The authors report on a project, undertaken within the School of Business and Management at Sheffield Hallam University, to ascertain students' understanding of the terms and concepts presented in a first-year, resource-based learning project. Focus groups were selected for this task in order to involve students more directly in the research process, the goal of which was the construction of a survey questionnaire. Five students participated. Difficulties were experienced in a number of areas including recruitment, commitment, modus operandi, and role ambiguity and conflict. It is concluded that, if used with care, focus groups can add "considerable value" to educational research projects.

202. Panyan, Marion V., Sherry A. Hillman, and Annette M. Liggett. "The Role of Focus Groups in Evaluating and Revising Teacher Education Programs." *Teacher Education and Special Education* 20, no. 1 (Winter 1997): 37–46.

A mixed-method approach, quantitative (questionnaires) and qualitative (focus groups), was used to evaluate and revise the Collaborative Teaching Master's Program. The setting for the study was a private, independent Midwestern university with a student body of approximately 8,000. Demographic and specific course information was gathered by mail questionnaire. From 32 special education and regular education teachers, 19 were selected to participate in one of four 60-minute audiotaped focus groups. The sessions were moderated by two female faculty members, who used a semistructured interview guide. The participants identified a number of strengths and weaknesses of the program, leading the authors to conclude that focus group methodology "adds a degree of contextual nuance and enriches the analysis" (p. 45).

203. Quimet, Judith A., JoAnne C. Bunnage, Robert M. Carini, George D. Kuh, and John Kennedy. "Using Focus Groups, Expert Advice, and Cognitive Interviews to Establish the Validity of a College Student Survey." *Research in Higher Education* 45, no. 3 (May 2004): 233–50.

The technique of triangulation was employed to improve the design of *The College Student Report*, authored by the National Survey of Student Engagement (NSSE) in 1999. The NSSE survey measures student participation in various types of "fruitful" activities. The purpose of the research was to determine if instrument items and response options were clearly worded and easily interpreted, and if they accurately represented students' behaviors and perceptions. A total of 221 students from eight institutions of higher education took part in 35 sessions, all moderated by an NSSE staff member. Students were asked to identify and discuss ambiguous or confusing sections of the instrument. In the second stage, advice on the overall design was obtained from Don Dillman, "a widely recognized survey research expert." In the final stage, cognitive interviews were conducted with 38 undergraduates from Indiana University to ensure that the modifications from the previous stages had been appropriately incorporated into the survey. A comparison of the results from the three approaches, that is, triangulation, led to increased validity and reliability of the survey.

204. Whitney, Linda, Felipe Golez, Greta Nagel, and Consuelo Nieto. "Listening to Voices of Practicing Teachers to Examine the Effectiveness of a Teacher Education Program." *Action in Teacher Education* 23, no. 4 (Winter 2002): 69–76.

To assess the effectiveness of a fifth-year postgraduate teacher education program, the authors gathered feedback from former students who are now practitioners. Because a previous survey of 900 teachers produced some negative comments, more in-depth information was desired. Four audio- and video-taped focus groups (with 1 to 10 participants per group) were conducted with self-selected program graduates currently teaching in large urban schools that serve children of low socioeconomic status with diverse backgrounds—racially, ethnically, and linguistically. Emerging themes were identified, primarily by the constant comparison method. The authors discuss the changes that have been implemented in the teacher education program as a result of the focus groups, which they recommend should be "ongoing" to help maintain a two-way flow of ideas and information.

Immigrant

205. McLaughlin, H. James, Anna Liljestrom, Jae Hoon Lim, and Dawn Meyers. "LEARN: A Community Study about Latino Immigrants and Education." *Education and Urban Society* 34, no. 2 (February 2002): 212–32.

A mixed-method approach—focus group interviews (qualitative) and a survey (quantitative)—was used to generate data for a study of low achievement and high dropout rates among Latino students. The setting was a medium-sized city in Georgia, a state experiencing a rapid increase in immigration. As part of a school board task force to improve educational experiences for English learners, a school community project (LEARN) was undertaken. Focus groups were used to gain insight into the perceptions of various stakeholders: students, teachers, parents, principals, counselors, social workers, and support staff members. Eighteen 30- to 60-minute audiotaped focus groups were conducted with 74 participants from "higher impact" schools. All but seven interviews were conducted in English. The interview schedule was varied by the group. Surveys were then conducted with a larger number of respondents. The authors discuss the special challenges (primarily communication) encountered when examining this population. In general, they found that students from other countries are accustomed to a different classroom environment and that teachers must be aware of students' prior educational experiences and cultural models of schooling. Three appendices provide the interview protocols.

Learning Disabilities

206. Barr, Owen, Roy McConkey, and Jayne McConaghie. "Views of People with Learning Difficulties about Current and Future Accommodation: The Use of Focus Groups to Promote Discussion." *Disability & Society* 18, no. 5 (August 2003): 577–97.

As part of a larger planning project to assess future housing and support options for people with learning "difficulties" residing in Northern Ireland, six focus groups were conducted with 45 members of that population. The research goals were to determine what these individuals liked about their current accommodation, what they did not like, where they might like to live in the next five years, and the amenities they would value in the future. The composition of the groups included people living in various urban and rural settings, with parents or relatives, living alone, or residing in residential or nursing homes. In five of the six groups, one of the authors served as moderator, while another recorded the discussion in note form. Group size ranged from 4 to 11 participants (one session per participant). Confidentiality was ensured. It was found that participants valued social networks, the feeling of being included, reciprocal relationships, privacy, and security. Focus group methodology is viewed as a potentially valuable approach, in that the encouragement of interaction promotes more in-depth discussion.

207. Cambridge, Paul, and Michelle McCarthy. "User Focus Groups and Best Value in Services for People with Learning Disabilities." *Health and Social Care in the Community* 9, no. 6 (November 2001): 476–89.

"Best Value," described as "both a function and a process," is a 1998 government (U.K.) initiative designed to improve social services, including performance monitoring, national standards, partnerships, and consultation. Local authority and joint purchasers of services are responsible for implementation. Focus group methodology was selected over surveys to elicit user input concerning three aspects of the program: adult placement, outreach activities, and day support services. A total of six sessions were conducted with 48 participants of mixed gender, ethnicity, and age level. The results are discussed for each service type examined. In general, people with learning disabilities participated "well" or "very well" in the discussions, provided constructive and positive comments, and acknowledged the stigmas associated with their conditions. The focus groups were "particularly useful" for identifying areas in need of improvement.

Measurement

208. Chudowsky, Naomi, and Peter Behuniak. "Using Focus Groups to Examine the Consequential Aspect of Validity." *Educational Measurement* 17, no. 4 (Winter 1998): 28–38.

The Connecticut Academic Performance Test (CAPT) has been given to all Connecticut 10th-grade students every May since 1995. The test is not a minimum proficiency test but is instead intended to establish high goals for students. Focus groups were used to determine teacher concerns, differences in their views by type of school district, and the effectiveness of the group approach. Seven 90-minute audiotaped focus groups, with 10 to 12 teachers in each, were conducted and transcribed. The authors cite the positive elements of this methodology as compared with survey methods. These include the opportunity for unanticipated responses, the witnessing of emotional reactions, the gathering of anecdotal evidence, and the value of insights gained through participant interaction. Challenges include the limits of generalization of the results, the difficulty of gauging the true strengths of the issues raised, and the impact of peer pressure as an inhibiting factor.

Nutrition

209. Balch, George I., Kathleen Loughrey, Linda Weinberg, Deborah Lurie, and Ellen Eisner. "Probing Consumer Benefits and Barriers for the National 5 A Day Campaign: Focus Group Findings." *Journal of Nutrition Education* 29, no. 4 (July–August 1997): 178–83.

The purpose of the research was to gather insights into the perceived benefits and obstacles of the 5 A Day for Better Health, a national program designed to increase the number of daily servings of fruits and vegetables consumed by the American public. Eight two-hour audio- and videotaped focus groups (divided into "target" and "comparison" groups—the latter composed of people already meeting the daily quota) were conducted with a diverse group of 72 participants recruited by telephone from three cities: Philadelphia, Chicago, and Los Angeles. Target participants expressed little urgency for eating more fruits and vegetables and identified a number of barriers, such as time and inconvenience. Long-term benefits did not impact their consumption decisions. Nutrition educators are advised to offer "quick and easy" tips to help consumers make better food choices.

210. Keim, Kathryn S., Marilyn A. Swanson, Sandra E. Cann, and Altragracia Salinas. "Focus Group Methodology: Adapting the Process for Low-Income Adults and Children of Hispanic and Caucasian Ethnicity." *Family and Consumer Sciences Research Journal* 27, no. 4 (June 1999): 451–65.

The authors observe the increased use of focus group methodology by nutrition educators during the "exploratory, formative, or process evaluation phases" of projects or program development activities. A study is reported that demonstrates the utility of the method for nutrition education, the unique challenges encountered, and the "lessons learned" when conducting research with children and low-income, low-literacy groups. The following focus groups were conducted: five with 24 Hispanic adults; four with 21 Caucasian adults; and six each with Hispanic and Caucasian third-grade children. All participants lived in Idaho and were recruited through a variety of sources. Most of the sessions were audiotaped. The moderator and note taker were bilingual in Spanish and English. The questions concerned fruit and vegetable consumption. The authors recommend the use of incentives, an appropriate venue, a recruiter known to the target community, shorter sessions for children, and the Ethnograph program for analysis. Hispanic respondents were less verbal than their Caucasian counterparts.

211. Kempson, Kathryn, Debra Palmer Keenan, Puneeta Sonya Sadani, and Audrey Adler. "Maintaining Food Sufficiency: Coping Strategies Identified

by Limited-Resource Individuals versus Nutrition Educators." *Journal of Nutrition Education and Behavior* 35, no. 4 (July–August 2003): 179–88.

Kempson et al. examine the strategies that individuals with low incomes (for example, people eligible for public assistance programs) use to acquire and manage their food supplies to have enough food throughout the month for themselves and their families. To gain an understanding of the coping strategies used by these individuals, 11 90-minute audiotaped focus groups were conducted with 62 participants (ages 19 to 67) recruited from a variety of sources throughout the state of New Jersey. Each participant was paid $20. Two experienced research assistants performed the moderating tasks. The group identified 95 coping strategies, which were then compared to strategies previously reported by nutrition educators. There was an 83 percent agreement between the two lists. Among other practices, selling blood and food stamps were unique to participant groups. Implications for nutrition program planning and policymaking are discussed.

212. Reed, Debra B., Paula McCarron Meeks, Lan Nguyen, Evelina W. Cross, and M.E. Betsy Garrison. "Assessment of Nutrition Education Needs Related to Increasing Dietary Calcium Intake in Low-Income Vietnamese Mothers Using Focus Group Discussions." *Journal of Nutrition Education* 30, no. 3 (May–June 1998): 155–63.

The study was undertaken to assess the nutrition education needs related to dietary calcium intake of a group of Vietnamese women. Five 90-minute audio- and videotaped focus groups were conducted with 38 low-income Vietnamese mothers, ages 25 to 47. All were recruited through churches and church-related agencies in Baton Rouge and New Orleans, Louisiana. Thirteen of the women had resided in the United States for two years or less; 14 had lived in the United States for 11 or more years. Each participant was paid $15, and child care was provided. The Vietnamese member of the research team assisted with the recruitment and moderated the discussions, which were conducted in Vietnamese (most of the participants could not speak English fluently). Nonverbal activities were noted. After the moderator translated the videotape, the comments were transcribed and coded. The study identified participants' knowledge, attitudes, and misconceptions concerning the topic; barriers to recommended calcium intake; and preferred methods of receiving nutrition information. Culturally appropriate nutrition education programs should be developed for this population.

213. Verpy, Heidi, Chery Smith, and Marla Reicks. "Attitudes and Behaviors of Food Donors and Perceived Needs and Wants of Food Shelf Clients." *Journal of Nutrition Education and Behavior* 35, no. 1 (January–February 2003): 6–15.

The authors examined the decision-making process of individuals who donate to local food shelves and the perceived needs and wants of food shelf clientele. The convenience samples were drawn from the St. Paul/Minneapolis, Minnesota, metropolitan area. Five focus groups were conducted with 31 clients, representing a range of ethnic and age groups. Seven focus groups were conducted with a diverse group of 64 donors. All of the 60- to 90-minute sessions were audiotaped and led by trained moderators. The results indicate that food donations failed to meet the cultural, health, and nutritional requirements of the food shelf users. Donors were well-educated individuals who recognized the need to help feed hungry people in the community. Implications of the findings for nutrition educators are discussed.

Physical

214. Verner, M. Elizabeth, and Jennie A. Gilbert. "Focus Groups: Before Writing a Grant, Know Your Constituents' Needs and Desires; Widely Used in Politics and Marketing, Focus Groups Provide an Effective Means of Gathering Data in Other Settings, Too." *JOPERD—The Journal of Physical Education, Recreation & Dance* 77, no. 9 (November–December 2006): 46–51.

To collect data for the "Need for the Project" section of the Physical Education Program grant application/proposal, the authors selected focus group methodology to identify barriers to achieving state (Illinois) physical education standards, and to devise strategies to minimize or eliminate these barriers. Verner and Gilbert demonstrate how the four steps of the focus group process (planning, recruiting, moderating, and analyzing and reporting) were applicable to the grant proposal project. A two-hour focus group was conducted with fourth-, seventh-, and ninth-grade students, an administrator, and teachers. Two facilitators guided the discussion of two open-ended questions. An online, school-based, data-management and tracking system was determined to be the best way to help students meet physical education requirements.

Science

215. Booth, Kathryn M., and Brian W. James. "Interactive Learning in a Higher Education Level 1 Mechanics Module." *International Journal of Science Education* 23, no. 9 (2001): 955–67.

Current research is cited that supports the view that traditional higher education courses fail to promote an in-depth approach to learning for most students. In an attempt to encourage "deep" learning, the authors modified both the teaching method and the examination paper in a physics course at the University of Salford, U.K. Following changes to the module, assessments were made by means of an inventory, a questionnaire, a focus group, and lecturer input. The focus group was conducted with 10 self-selected students who were asked to consider three questions. A lecturer from another department facilitated the discussion. Improvement in deep learning was not detected. However, all involved "enjoyed" the experience.

216. Osborne, Jonathan, and Sue Collins. "Pupils' Views of the Role and Value of the Science Curriculum: A Focus-Group Study." *International Journal of Science Education* 23, no. 5 (2001): 441–67.

The authors observe the paucity of research that deals with students' own perceptions of their experiences with science education. To help fill the void about the future "form and function" of the school science curriculum and to document needs, attitudes, and expectations, data were sought from two groups of stakeholders—students and parents—followed by teachers' responses to those views (only student data are reported in this article). From 20 state schools in Leeds, Birmingham, and London, a sample of 16-year-old students was recruited. All had completed their compulsory education requirements. A total of 20 audiotaped focus groups were conducted with 144 pupils, who were divided by gender and whether or not they intended to pursue the study of science. Seven major themes emerged from the analysis, which was assisted by a grounded theory approach and NUD*IST. The focus groups were successful in identifying both positive and negative features of the science education curriculum. An appendix provides the interview questions.

Secondary

217. Denscombe, Martyn. "Social Conditions for Stress: Young People's Experience of Doing GCSEs." *British Educational Research Journal* 26, no. 3 (June 2000): 359–74.

Denscombe employed both a quantitative method (a survey) and two qualitative approaches (focus groups and individual interviews) to examine the level of mental stress experienced by students preparing for the required General Certificate of Secondary Education (GCSE). The 15- to 16-year-old participants were selected from 12 schools in the East Midlands of England. The first phase of the data collection process involved a survey with 1,648 young people. Twenty focus groups were then conducted with a subsample of 123 students, who were asked to discuss issues emanating from the survey. Ten semistructured interviews were undertaken with 20 students. The GCSE was identified as a prime source of anxiety, primarily due to pressure from teachers and parents as well as the internalized pressure to succeed. The exam was viewed as a turning point, a benchmark, in the lives of most students, who were also facing a wide range of challenges from other areas. Coping strategies are discussed.

218. Liu, Kristin Kline, Richard Spicuzza, and Ronald Erickson. "Focus Group Research on Minnesota's Implementation of Graduation Standards Testing." *Journal of Educational Research* 92, no. 5 (May–June 1999): 312–19.

The purposes of the study were (1) to examine the views and experiences of a group of teachers and administrators relative to the inclusion of limited English-proficient (LEP) students in the Minnesota Basic Standards tests; and (2) to gain an understanding of their needs and concerns for future test administrations. Two three-hour audiotaped focus groups were conducted with a sample of 23 Minnesota educators (testing coordinators, general classroom teachers, and English as a Second Language teachers) drawn from urban school districts and those outside the metropolitan area. The tapes and field notes served as the basis for analysis, which was accomplished by an inductive process and coding. Four primary themes emerged: the importance of LEP students' participation in large-scale assessments; the necessity to provide for testing accommodations; the need for clear communication among teachers, parents, and students; and the importance of not allowing testing to interfere with regular classroom instruction.

219. Szarkowicz, Diane Louise. "Exploring Focus Groups with Adolescent Students." *Academic Exchange Quarterly* 9, no. 3 (Fall 2005): 210–14.

The author compares and contrasts focus group methodology with other classroom-based qualitative data-collection techniques, such as direct observation, individual in-depth interviews, and document review. The advantages and limitations of focus groups are demonstrated in the context of a study designed to examine the strengths and areas of need in a senior high personal development program in Australia. Six one-hour audiotaped focus groups were conducted with 34 male and female culturally diverse students. The moderator was a teacher from another school. The focus groups provided a "flexible, efficient, and collaborative" approach for gathering the perspectives of the students. Limitations include time-consuming transcription of the dialogue, the problem of discussing sensitive topics, and the "more superficial" nature of the data produced.

220. Warrington, Molly, and Michael Younger. "Perspectives on the Gender Gap in English Secondary Schools." *Research Papers in Education* 14, no. 1 (1999): 51–77.

The authors focus on male underachievement in English secondary schools. They provide a background for the debates concerning this issue, offer explanations for the apparent gender gap in learning, and suggest some strategies for remediation. To examine this problem, three qualitative methods of inquiry were employed. As a first step, individual interviews were conducted with a selection of staff, and classroom observation was performed. Audiotaped focus groups were then conducted with Year 11 participants (ages 15 and 16), recruited from eight diverse schools in Suffolk, Cambridgeshire, and Lincolnshire. Three male and female moderators led the gender-separated "friendship" groups. The goal of the analysis was "to build up a picture sensitive to differences across schools, between boys and girls, and between high and low achievers" (p. 56). A variety of factors are seen to contribute to male underachievement. The students' own voices provided insight into some of these, such as the value of high expectations and praise.

221. Whitney, Linda. "Middle Level Teachers Using Focus Group Research." *Education* 126, no. 1 (Fall 2005): 3–9.

Eight graduate students (seven middle-school teachers and one sixth-grade teacher), enrolled in a master's level course taught by Whitney, planned and conducted focus groups incorporating various combinations of middle-school students, teachers, and administrators. Most of the topics explored some aspect of classroom instruction. The graduate students moderated the sessions, which were held at their respective schools. The discussions were audiotaped, or manual notes were taken. The graduate students perceived focus group methodology to be a positive, albeit underutilized, strategy for eliciting the perspectives and opinions of participants in the educational environment. High-achieving students were found to respond more quickly, and new teachers tended to be more reticent. Suggestions for improvement are provided.

222. Younger, Michael, Molly Warrington, and Jacquetta Williams. "The Gender Gap and Classroom Interactions: Reality and Rhetoric?" *British Journal of Sociology of Education* 20, no. 3 (September 1999): 325–41.

There is concern and debate over boys' educational underachievement in the United Kingdom. The authors investigated the role of teacher-student interaction in this situation, acknowledging that factors other than gender, such as ethnicity, social class, and parental educational backgrounds, are important in determining students' achievement levels. A multimethod data-collection approach was employed: focus groups, interviews, and direct observation. Eight schools, four selective and four comprehensive, were chosen to reflect different sizes and locations, but with similar teaching styles. In total, 48 focus groups were conducted with approximately 200 students in Year 11 of their education. Sessions were held in groups of four, separated by gender and ability level. Interviews were used to obtain the perspectives of the teaching staff. Teacher-student interaction data was gathered by classroom observation in four of the targeted schools. The analysis indicates that most teachers felt that they treated boys and girls equally. However, focus groups and observation suggest that this is "rarely achieved."

223. Yuen, Mantak. "Exploring Hong Kong Chinese Guidance Teachers' Positive Beliefs: A Focus Group Study." *International Journal for the Advancement of Counselling* 24 (2003): 169–82.

The research question is the following: "What are the positive beliefs about school counselling and guidance among the secondary school guidance teachers?" (p. 171). To inform this question, five focus groups were conducted with 24 secondary guidance teachers in Hong Kong. The participants were nominated to take part in the focus groups by colleagues or former supervisors. The author and a guidance teacher co-moderated the discussions. The participants were asked to describe examples of good counseling and guidance practices. The discussions were audiotaped, transcribed into Chinese, and analyzed by means of data reduction, data display, interpretation, and by drawing conclusions. Nearly all of the participants had positive beliefs, which are organized into five categories. In general, "[g]uidance is an ideal condition of care and concern in student-teacher relationship" (p.177). The implications of the findings for implementing a whole-school approach to guidance, through comprehensive guidance programs, are discussed.

Social Work

224. Sandel, Mark H., and Harriet L. Cohen. "Focus Group Effects on Field Practicum Preferences." *Educational Gerontology* 32, no. 3 (March 2006): 203–14.

The authors review a variety of academic and nonacademic factors that can influence how social work students choose an area of specialization within the discipline—specifically working with older persons. The social work program at a large state university in Texas undertook a study to determine if student observation of a focus group would have an impact on their field practicum preferences (a new methodological approach, according to the authors). Thirty advanced undergraduates served as participant observers of one focus group consisting of professional geriatric practitioners. Pre- and posttests were administered. The findings indicate that of the 14 field preferences offered, only the mean score of the aging category increased significantly. The "relatively quick and inexpensive" format served to replace students' negative attitudes with positive ones toward working with the dramatically increasing elderly population.

225. Saulnier, Christine Flynn. "Groups as Data Collection Method and Data Analysis Technique: Multiple Perspectives on Urban Social Work Education." *Small Group Research* 31, no. 5 (October 2000): 607–27.

In 1997, an ad hoc committee of faculty and administrators at Boston University's School of Social Work (BUSSW) began a two-year study to examine options for furthering the school's mission in an urban setting, and to elicit feedback on the ideas that had been generated from various constituency groups. Focus group interviewing was seen as the most promising method for meeting the goals of the research. Seven 90-minute focus groups were cofacilitated by the author and two other social workers trained in group techniques. A total of 57 individuals were selected from BUSSW teaching personnel and alumni, and community members. An "unusual" and "innovative" approach was taken with respect to data analysis: a committee addressed this task. HyperRESEARCH, a qualitative software package, assisted with analyzing transcript content. The coded data reports were then read and discussed by the committee (composed of the research team, faculty, and administrators). The use of interaction and group collaboration was seen to improve rigor in qualitative data analysis.

3.7 LAW

226. Ball, David. *How to Do Your Own Focus Groups: A Guide for Trial Attorneys.* South Bend, IN: National Institute for Trial Advocacy, 2001. 166p.

The focus group research discussed by Ball is exclusively for the purpose of determining how a group of laypeople will respond to a particular legal case, frequently those involving mock deliberations. As the subtitle states, this book is designed for attorneys, with additional use by trial consultants. Ball addresses every element—from when and where to conduct focus groups, to recruiting "focus-jurors," to questions relating to rooms and videorecording. Separate chapters are devoted to the preparations of the various statements, including those by the prosecution and defense. Issues surrounding the plaintiff or prosecution rebuttal are explored. Subsequent chapters deal with deliberative, focus-jurors, and verdict questions. The final substantive chapter addresses analysis, including the creation of good/bad lists of themes that focus-jurors weighed in favor and against the case in question. Half the book consists of appendices, including schedules, letters, forms, suggestions for selecting a trial consultant, debriefing methods, and what amounts to a glossary of alternative types of focus groups, such as debriefing, brainstorming, and "monster" (that is, hostile, intentionally selected to be unfavorable).

227. Castellblanch, Ramón, and Daniel J. Abrahamson. "What Focus Groups Suggest about Mental Health Parity Policymaking." *Professional Psychology Research and Practice* 34, no. 5 (October 2003): 540–47.

The authors provide the background for the development of Maryland's Mental Health Parity Law, a 1994 piece of legislation designed to regulate how health insurance benefit packages restrict coverage of mental health care. The law allowed insurers to deny payment "if treatments were not medically necessary or through a process of managed care" (p. 540). The purpose of the research was to gain insight into the impact of the parity law on the individuals it was intended to help—people with mental illness and their support networks. Five focus groups were conducted in late 1997 with a total of 45 African-American and white, male and female participants (patients, support givers, and mental health care professionals) recruited from two sites: Baltimore, Maryland, and Montgomery County, a large suburb of Washington, D.C. The constant comparison method was used for analysis. The law was seen as only part of the solution to improving access to services. Implications for policymakers are discussed.

228. Gorny, Stephen M. "Getting into Focus: Improving Trial Technique through Focus Groups." *Trial Lawyer* 23, no. 2 (March–April 2000): 111–17.

Instead of a full-scale mock trial, focus groups can be used to reduce courtroom shortcomings to the obvious benefit of clients. The focus groups need to be formed from individuals in the jurisdiction in which the case is to be tried. While the "verdict" that the focus group reaches may not be of significance to the actual trial, it is the videotaped deliberations and how the focus group members reached their conclusions that is of greatest benefit in terms of preparing for trial. Gorny outlines a dozen potential focus group objectives, including such elements as criticizing the opening statement, evaluating the style of presentation, and establishing favorable juror profiles. Procedural considerations are discussed, including the selection of the "jurors" (from 12 to 24 neutral individuals), the location, and the choice and role of the moderator. Debriefing after the conclusion of the focus group deliberation is stressed as an important step—one that can reveal blunt opinions necessary to refine trial preparations.

229. North Carolina Academy of Trail Lawyers. *Focusing on Focus Groups: Don't Try Your Case without One.* [Raleigh]: North Carolina Academy of Trial Lawyers, 2001. 1 vol.

This publication is the outgrowth of a one-day seminar sponsored by the North Carolina Academy of Trial Lawyers. The seminar was held on March 23, 2001, in Raleigh, North Carolina. The first paper, "Using Focus Groups to Prepare for Trial," was presented by Charlotte Wortz Morris. She writes that focus groups in the legal setting are referred to as a mock trial, trial simulation, or jury study, and are used for pretrial feedback. Although a focus group will not "guarantee" that the verdict reached will be the same as the trial outcome, an attorney will be better prepared for all phases of litigation. The second paper, by Bill Faison, is titled "The Nuts and Bolts of Do It Yourself Focus Groups." The author discusses the rationale for conducting a focus group in the legal environment, when the format would be appropriate, how to locate the moderator and participants, and how the information gathered will help gain insights into the merits of a client's case (and help profile possible jurors). The third paper, titled "Focus Groups: How They Help and How to Conduct Them Inexpensively," by Howard Twiggs and Don Strickland, details five uses for the method: to develop a theme for a case, to prepare plaintiffs and witnesses for trial, to evaluate the attorney's theory of the case, to determine damages, and to give the client a realistic view of damage awards. The authors conclude the following: "If you are not using focus groups, you are missing a great opportunity to improve your clients' cases. You will win more cases by using focus groups and the size of your settlements and verdicts will increase" (p. 10).

230. O'Connor, Amy. "Merchant of Mercy, Merchant of Death: How Values Advocacy Messages Influence Jury Deliberations." *Journal of Applied Communication Research* 34, no. 3 (August 2006): 263–84.

The core issue addressed by O'Connor was whether values advocacy messages [VAMs] could influence a jury's decision to reduce punitive damage awards. In this case the VAMs were generated by the 1999–2001 Philip Morris campaign called "Working to Make a Difference: The People of Philip Morris." Five focus groups were conducted with 37 female participants—all registered voters; between the ages of 25 and 49 with household incomes of $50,000 plus; college educated; and having two or more children (this profile was designed to be similar to the Philip Morris target audience as described in internal company documents). Thirty-four participants (91.5 percent) did not currently smoke cigarettes. The participants were shown seven television advertisements from the campaign. The focus group results indicated that the VAMs evoked "strong feelings among the majority of participants" (p. 273). Of the total, 30 to 40 percent were willing to reduce punitive damages based on the Philip Morris campaign. When asked to consider a different corporation using such messages, the number increased to 50–55 percent.

231. Oliver, Eric. "Testing, Testing." *Trial Diplomacy Journal* 21, no. 6 (November–December 1998): 399–409.

As a consultant, Oliver works with lawyers to improve their communication, persuasion, and interaction skills. This article is devoted to the benefits of pretrial focus groups. The author cites the value of practicing the components of a presentation that are likely to be troublesome or to experiment with a new or different approach. Some drawbacks of the focus group method are the following: members are paid; they are not under oath; the full case may not be heard; the moderator is not a judge; there are few procedural rules; witnesses do not appear; and the setting is usually dissimilar to the courtroom. The formation of values and beliefs or mind-sets are discussed. The mind-set reinforcing qualities of television newscasts are considered in the "Brainstorms" section. The tools utilized are important for trial lawyers, and include deletion, anchors, linkage, and editorializing. Oliver cites 13 factors for the lawyer to consider when determining how the message will be taken by the jury. One of the values of the focus group approach is that it can reveal any biases in the lawyer's demeanor.

232. Wenner, David A. "Preparing for Trial: An Uncommon Approach; The Trial Lawyer Can Use Focus Groups to Flag Potential Juror Reactions and

Prepare Effective Arguments for Trial." *Trial* 34, no. 1 (January 1998): 62–69.

Wenner, a practicing lawyer in Phoenix, Arizona, presents many ways that focus groups can be used to gauge potential juror reactions and help lawyers prepare their arguments. Focus groups are described as "a forum for reality testing." Issues for focus group examination include what the message is, the case and social themes, and utilization—using themes to aid in creating rapport between lawyer and jury. Others include the story, and employing the focus group as a "quest for meaning"—determining how the mock jury is constructing the story of the case being presented, and priming—the early presentation of positive themes. Testing how the focus group participants respond to message repetition, attribution of responsibility, defining causation, efforts to create empathy, the impact of visual information, and defense arguments are all covered by Wenner as valuable areas for the participants' reactions.

233. Wortz, Charlotte A. "Using Focus Group Research in Medical Negligence Cases." *Trial* 35, no. 5 (May 1999): 38–45.

A trial consultant or a self-trained lawyer can conduct focus groups to assist in the discovery phase and to prepare arguments for trial. The article begins with questions dealing with the issues and evidence in a medical negligence case. The questions that focus groups can answer range from jurors' perceptions of medical care, to issues related to award damages, to elective surgery, to inconsistencies in defense witnesses' testimony, and many others. Wortz continues by addressing specific aspects of medical negligence trials that she has been assisted with through the use of focus groups in the past five years. Areas covered are the opening statement; exhibits (she suggests employing simplified textbook definitions when preparing a glossary of perhaps no more than five scientific terms); standard of care; agency; record keeping; communication; catastrophic injury; themes; symptoms; and the need to provide the focus group with a balanced presentation.

3.8 LIBRARY SCIENCE

Administration

234. Ho, Jeannette, and Gwyneth H. Crowley. "User Perceptions of the 'Reliability' of Library Services at Texas A&M University: A Focus Group Study." *Journal of Academic Librarianship* 29, no. 2 (March 2003): 82–87.

The definition the authors are using for reliability is "the ability to perform a promised service dependably and accurately" (p. 82), as found in *Delivering Quality Service: Balancing Customer Perceptions and Expectations* by

Valerie A. Zeithaml, A. Parasuraman, and Leonard L. Berry, 1990. The authors conducted nine two-hour audiotaped focus groups with 51 participants: 28 graduate students (five groups) and 23 undergraduate students (four groups). The questions addressed participants' perceptions regarding locating books, interlibrary loans, circulation issues, signage and movement around the library, and using the online catalog called LibCat—both in the library and remotely. Refreshments and other incentives were provided to induce participation. The researchers found focus groups to be a useful approach for identifying areas in need of improvement, with the Texas A&M University Library making changes based on the observations of the students.

235. Williams, Sheryl, and Elizabeth Parang. "Using Focus Groups to Match User Expectations with Library Constraints." *Serials Librarian* 31, nos. 1–2 (1997): 335–39.

The authors report on a 1996 workshop based on the use of focus groups to elicit user input concerning a space planning project at the Leon S. McGoogan Library of Medicine at the University of Nebraska. Although the questions were written by the library staff, a consulting firm supplied a professional moderator and the transcription services. Data analysis and the final report were done in-house; a matrix was developed to facilitate analysis. Six focus groups were conducted with 12 to 15 participants in each session, a number subsequently viewed as too large. A neutral location was selected for the meetings. The use of better recording equipment would have reduced the incidences of unintelligible comments.

Bibliography

236. Walden, Graham R. "Focus Group Interviewing in the Library Literature: A Selective Annotated Bibliography 1996–2005." *Reference Services Review* 34, no. 2 (2006): 222–41.

The introduction to this article traces the development of the terminology associated with focus group methodology and considers the nature of qualitative research. A brief historical overview follows, noting the inception of the approach in the 1920s. An outline of the steps in conducting focus groups is presented, with sections on planning, recruiting the participants, conducting the discussion sessions, and analyzing and reporting the data. The annotated bibliography that follows includes library applications, primarily in the journal literature (21 articles, 1 book, and 3 book chapters), with sections on administration, catalog related, methodology, reference related, specific applications, and Internet. An examination of the publication dates reveals that the first five-year period covered in this article produced a higher number of entries (16) than the most recent five-year span (9), a marked reduction in the library-related focus group literature. Entries from this *Reference Services Review* article have been revised and can be found in this Scarecrow Press book.

Catalog Related

237. Connaway, Lynn Silipigni, Debra Wilcox Johnson, and Susan E. Searing. "Online Catalogs from the Users' Perspective: The Use of Focus Group Interviews." *College & Research Libraries* 58, no. 5 (September 1997): 403–20.

Focus groups for faculty and students were conducted at the University of Wisconsin-Madison to evaluate the strengths and weaknesses of the online catalog, referred to as the Network Library System (NLS). Recruiting for the groups was a challenge, with cash payment of $10 provided for the students who participated in the 90-minute sessions. There were 48 participants: 15 faculty, 14 graduate students, and 19 undergraduate students. Data analysis included both ethnographic and content analysis approaches. The participants' use of the NLS, as well as other catalogs, is documented, along with a review of positive and negative features of the catalog. The authors also summarize the pros and cons of using the focus group method.

238. Elhard, K. C., and Qiang Jin. "Shifting Focus: Assessing Cataloging Service through Focus Groups." *Library Collections, Acquisitions, and Technical Services* 28, no. 2 (2004): 196–204.

Focus group methodology was used by researchers at the library of the University of Illinois at Urbana-Champaign to assess cataloging services. Areas of interest were communication, use of the technical services Web page, problem solving, instances of confusion, what elements were deemed helpful, identification of unprovided services, and an open-ended question for additional comment. Costs were reduced by using an in-house moderator, by not recording the sessions (a total of six were held), and by having note takers record the discussions. The seven questions asked are reprinted in full, along with an analysis of the data. Overall, the researchers found that library personnel do not have a good grasp of the cataloging workflows and subprocesses. Solutions include the implementation of "outreach" projects, with catalogers available for visits to libraries. The authors suggest conducting an online survey as a follow-up tool.

Information Technology

239. Chase, Lynne, and Jaquelina Alvarez. "Internet Research: The Role of the Focus Group." *Library & Information Science Research* 22, no. 4 (2000): 357–69.

The traditional face-to-face focus group interview is compared and contrasted to the online focus group (OFG) format. One table displays the respective methodologies, with side-by-side comparisons, ranging from the interview guide to data analysis; another table presents the communication and dynamics of each technique. The authors observe that those "comfortable" with face-to-face communication will continue to be well served by the traditional approach. For individuals who prefer written communication, the online option may be more appropriate. Differences include the higher cost for face-to-face groups and the presence of body language, facial expression, and emotion in voice tone. With OFGs, the challenges of injecting probes and follow-up questions are noted, as well as the difficulty of staying focused. Group purpose may determine choice of format.

240. Crowley, Gwyneth H., Rob Leffel, Diana Ramirez, Judith L. Hart, and Tommy S. Armstrong II. "User Perceptions of the Library's Web Pages: A Focus Group Study at Texas A&M University." *Journal of Academic Librarianship* 28, no. 4 (July 2002): 205–10.

A brief overview of contemporary focus group research is presented, and the specifics of the methodology are provided. Researchers at Texas A&M University conducted focus groups to determine how the library's Web pages were perceived. A total of 26 participants (undergraduate and graduate students, teaching faculty, university staff, and library faculty) took part in the study. Analysis of the data indicated that "one-stop shopping" was preferred—meaning that all Web page links should be organized on a single page. Additionally, the focus group members liked having the most popular database at the top of the list, rather than positioned with other unfamiliar titles. It was reported that members had difficulty finding what they were looking for on the library's Web pages. Frequent changes to the pages is not considered favorably because consistency and predictability are desired characteristics. The participants noted that they preferred live assistance over online help screens. Many respondents found the Web pages to be intimidating, overwhelming, distracting, and too cluttered.

241. D'Esposito, J. E., and Gardner, R. M. "University Students' Perceptions of the Internet: An Exploratory Study." *Journal of Academic Librarianship* 25, no. 6 (1999): 456–61.

The present study was conducted at Monmouth University in West Long Branch, New Jersey, with both authors being librarians at the Guggenheim Memorial Library. Although recruitment of the student participants was clearly difficult, this problem was overcome by a professor granting extra credit for those who took part in the study. Two focus groups were held with a total of 14 undergraduate student participants. The location for the focus groups was the campus student center, with one of the researchers serving as moderator (this individual had received professional training as a facilitator). There are many findings reported concerning the general perception of the Internet, how it is used to complete assignments, its relationship to the library, comparisons of the resources of both, and how librarians are viewed in relationship to the Internet. One finding was that students were unlikely to ask a librarian for assistance with locating information on the Internet, but would have no hesitation to ask a computer lab assistant for help.

242. Leighton, H. Vernon, Joe Jackson, Kathryn Sullivan, and Russell F. Dennison. "Web Page Design and Successful Use: A Focus Group Study." *Internet Reference Services Quarterly* 8, no. 3 (2003): 17–27.

The research goal was to determine users' perceptions toward four Web page design elements: frames, link presentation, length and depth, and site index versus searchable site. A team from Winona State University Library, Minnesota, conducted two focus group sessions with a total of nine students and one faculty member. The results of the study indicate that students preferred (1) small frames in order to avoid additional scrolling; (2) hybrid links (a combination of a brief list of links followed by some list with annotations); (3) viewing a single screen; and (4) searches that lead directly to the information sought. Implications for future library Web page design are discussed.

243. Morrison, Heather. "Information Literacy Skills: An Exploratory Focus Group Study of Student Perceptions." *Research Strategies* 15, no. 1 (Winter 1997): 4–17.

The four "skills," as identified by the American Library Association, that an information literate individual can perform are the following: locating information, evaluating information, effectively using information, and recognizing a need for information. To explore the area of information literary, six undergraduate students plus one nonstudent participated in a single 90-minute focus group session, moderated by the author, at the Concordia University College of Alberta, in Edmonton, Canada. The session was audiotaped and transcribed. The transcript produced a 52-page document, which was subjected to a detailed content analysis. Focus group methodology demonstrated potential for gathering useful data, in particular hypothesis generation for future research.

244. Starkweather, Wendy M., and Camille Clark Wallin. "Faculty Response to Library Technology: Insights on Attitudes." *Library Trends* 47, no. 4 (Spring 1999): 640–68.

The authors were able to obtain the consulting services of a member of the university's (University of Nevada, Las Vegas) Marketing Department. This individual assisted in the development of the questions and conducted one pretest session, three focus group sessions, and six individual interviews. Names were selected from a list of faculty who had indicated in an earlier library survey that they would be willing to serve in a focus group. Through the use of screening questions, the faculty was divided into categories of information technology adopters: innovator and early, early and late, and laggards. In all, 31 faculty in the "early/late majority" were selected and took part in three 90-minute audio-taped focus groups (three from each of the other categories received individual interviews). Fourteen questions were presented for discussion. Each participant received a $25 check for use in the bookstore. The authors conclude that there may be fewer differences overall among the categories in the way in which faculty use library information technology, with late adopters simply preferring to wait until they need to actually use a new technology.

245. Thomsett-Scott, Beth C. "Web Site Usability with Remote Users: Formal Usability Studies and Focus Groups." *Journal of Library Administration* 45, nos. 3–4 (July–August 2006): 517–47.

Approximately two-thirds of this article addresses formal usability studies, with the stated goals of usability being "usefulness, effectiveness or ease of use, ability to learn, and attitude or satisfaction" (p. 519). Remote usability studies are reviewed, with the advantages and disadvantages considered. Formal usability studies are conducted on a one-on-one basis with actual users of the Web site. Details are provided on the equipment needed, the setting up and running of the study, debriefing, and poststudy questionnaires. In the rest of the article, the author discusses focus groups—in particular the strong points and limitations of remote focus groups, the implementation and conduct of online focus groups, the results of remote focus groups, and the analysis of the data. Thomsett-Scott concludes that remote focus groups provide "similar" information as face-to-face groups, and may in fact reduce the impact of such factors as dominant or shy participants, thereby generating an overall more balanced set of viewpoints on the Web site under consideration.

Methodology

246. Covey, Denise Troll. "Focus Groups." In *Usage and Usability Assessment: Library Practices and Concerns*, 15–23. CLIR Tools for Practitioners series. Washington, DC: Digital Library Federation, Council on Library and Information Resources, 2002.

Covey acknowledges that "much of the information" in this section is "taken" from B. A. Chadwick et al. (*Social Science Research Methods*. Englewood Cliffs, NJ: Prentice-Hall, 1984). The focus group methodology is defined. The "why" and "how" of library usage is considered, along with who uses the results and for what purpose. Difficulties of the format are reviewed, primarily the issue of unskilled moderators and the interpretation and use of focus group data.

247. Goulding, Anne. "Joking, Being Aggressive and Shutting People Up: The Use of Focus Groups in LIS Research." *Education for Information* 15, no. 4 (December 1997): 331–41.

Goulding observes the lack of use of focus group methodology for library and information research, particularly in the United Kingdom. Among the advantages of the technique are the naturalistic context, the ability of the moderator to assume an active or less active role, the capacity for spontaneous responses and interaction, and the ease of conduct. The author outlines the organizational elements of focus groups—planning, moderating, the conduct of the sessions, the participants, transcription, and data analysis. Six extended focus group exchanges, quoted directly (on one occasion for up to nine lines of dialogue among three participants), demonstrate key points of the discussion.

248. Hernon, Peter, and Ellen Altman. "Listening to Customers through Focus Group Interviews." In *Assessing Service Quality: Satisfying the Expectations of Library Customers*, 137–46. Chicago: American Library Association, 1998.

The authors review the strengths and weaknesses of focus group interviewing (described as "a type of case study application") and discuss its applicability and appropriateness for the library environment. An overview is provided that deals with the purpose of the interview, the composition of the group, and the duties of the moderator. In a section titled "Lost and Never-Gained Customers," suggestions are offered for determining the views of individuals, who are, at present, nonlibrary users. Focus group interviews may also be conducted with internal users to assess levels of service quality.

249. Shoaf, Eric C. "Using a Professional Moderator in Library Focus Group Research." *College & Research Libraries* 64, no. 2 (March 2003): 124–32.

The author is of the opinion that, among other reasons, librarians serving as focus group moderators may risk biasing the study results, especially in cases in which librarian expertise is low. Shoaf enunciates the rationale for retaining a professional marketing and opinion research firm to conduct the sessions and provide data analysis. To support this view, research undertaken at Brown University is reported. Although a User Needs Team of eight members was in charge of the project, professionals were hired to conduct the meetings, analyze the data, and prepare a report. Five focus groups were held over a three-week period to assess library users' (graduate students and faculty) needs, perceptions, and preferences. The final report received from the professional research company was "highly charged with negativity," a finding contrary to previously conducted print surveys that indicated that students were either satisfied or very satisfied with the library.

250. Verny, Roger, and Connie Van Fleet. "Case Study 2.2: Conducting Focus Groups." In *Library Evaluation: A Casebook and Can-Do Guide*, edited by Danny P. Wallace and Connie Van Fleet, 41–51. Englewood, CO: Libraries Unlimited, 2001.

The goals of the research were to evaluate the need for library and information science education in the state of Ohio, and to identify the role of the Kent State University School of Library and Information Science in providing appropriate education. Three focus group sessions were conducted by the State Library of Ohio with a total of 29 academic, special, public, and school librarians. The data gathered were used in conjunction with input from graduating students, alumni, the advisory council, and others, for strategic planning, curriculum revision, goal setting, and accreditation purposes. Focus groups are viewed as an effective and cost-efficient technique for gathering qualitative data.

251. Von Seggern, Marilyn, and Nancy J. Young. "The Focus Group Method in Libraries: Issues Relating to Process and Data Analysis." *Reference Services Review* 31, no. 3 (2003): 272–84.

The authors identify and discuss seven issues involved in planning a focus group project for a library setting. The research was untaken to evaluate the effectiveness of reference services in light of the rapidly changing electronic environment. Throughout the process, users of this qualitative approach are encouraged to seek advice from focus group experts. About a third of the article reports on how Ethnograph, a computer software program, facilitated data analysis. The software is designed to assist with a variety of tasks: sorting, coding, and classifying textual material by formatting the file into short lines and adding line numbers for subsequent coding. The appendix is a bibliography of 38 briefly annotated entries, of which 20 deal specifically with library settings.

Reference Related

252. Massey-Burzio, Virginia. "From the Other Side of the Reference Desk: A Focus Group Study." *Journal of Academic Librarianship* 24, no. 3 (May 1998): 208–15.

The site for the research was the Milton S. Eisenhower Library at Johns Hopkins University in Baltimore, Maryland. The goals were to examine library users' thought processes and behaviors as they seek information, and to determine if the library is addressing users' needs. To achieve this aim, the author conducted six focus groups with a total of 38 students and faculty representing a variety of academic departments. The study results indicate that the participants were uncomfortable asking questions of librarians, they mistakenly thought their library skills were adequate, and most were unaware of many library services and resources. Stronger liaison with library users is advocated.

253. Norlin, Elaina. "Reference Evaluation: A Three-Step Approach—Surveys, Unobtrusive Observations, and Focus Groups." *College & Research Libraries* 61, no. 6 (November 2000): 546–53.

A multimethod approach to data collection—surveys, unobtrusive observations, and focus groups—was used to determine if reference librarians and staff at the University of Arizona libraries were approachable, accurate, and attempted to promote information literacy. The research design, involving 100-plus students over a period of three semesters, called for (1) surveys to obtain demographic information and initial opinions of reference desk service; (2) observation worksheets to be completed immediately following a reference desk encounter; and (3) a one-hour focus group session with three to five students participating at a time. The overall results of the evaluation, deemed favorable and very meaningful, indicated that unobtrusive observation provided the most useful insights.

254. Rose, Pamela M., Kristin Stoklosa, and Sharon A. Gray. "A Focus Group Approach to Assessing Technostress at the Reference Desk." *Reference & User Services Quarterly* 37, no. 4 (Summer 1998): 311–17.

The focus group interviewing technique was used to determine if reference desk staff were experiencing anxiety due to the increasing number and complexity of automated systems in the library. The study took place at the Health Sciences Library at SUNY Buffalo in 1995. Two library staff members conducted the two-hour focus groups with eight nonreference (part-time) librarians and library school students working at the reference desk. The moderator was an "insider." The authors state that the methodology used was innovative and effective, and that the experience was viewed as positive by the participants. Of the eleven recommendations for decreasing staff anxiety that emerged from the study, three are related to technology.

255. Young, Nancy J., and Marilyn Von Seggern. "General Information Seeking in Changing Times: A Focus Group Study." *Reference & User Services Quarterly* 41, no. 2 (Winter 2001): 159–69.

Noting that little research exists on general information-seeking activities in the academic library setting, the authors used focus group methodology to determine if reference services were keeping pace with technological advances. Seven open-ended questions were asked during five sessions, with four of five held outside the library. A neutral moderator led three of the discussions. Thirty-three undergraduate students, graduate students, and faculty at the University of Idaho served as participants. The sessions were audiotaped, transcribed, and loaded into Ethnograph, a qualitative data-analysis software program designed to facilitate textual analysis. Young and Von Seggern discuss seven prominent themes that emerged from the data, as well as the implications for evaluating reference services.

Part III

Specific Applications

256. Curran, Charles, Stephen Bajjaly, Patricia Feehan, and Ann L. O'Neill. "Using Focus Groups to Gather Information for LIS Curriculum Review." *Journal of Education for Library and Information Science* 39, no. 3 (Summer 1998): 175–82.

A curriculum review at the College of Library and Information Science (LIS) at the University of South Carolina involved the use of focus groups (conducted by the authors). The goals of the evaluation were to determine what constituents—that is, employers of LIS program graduates—expect from new graduates, and if the core and elective courses meet expectations. The article addresses the choice of open-ended questions, participant selection, and session management. An analysis of the participants' observations is presented. The authors conclude by noting that changes occur over time, new needs are recognized, and perceptions are varied. The focus group "snapshot" was deemed a valuable assessment tool.

257. Frank, Polly. "Student Artists in the Library: An Investigation of How They Use General Academic Libraries for Their Creative Needs." *Journal of Academic Librarianship* 25, no. 6 (November 1999): 445–55.

Using a study population of 181 undergraduate visual art students attending 12 Minnesota institutions of higher education, 19 focus groups were conducted between 1995 and 1997. The purpose of the research was to identify the resources utilized by the students to support their creative endeavors, the search strategies involved, their views toward the library experience, and the reasons these views were held. A good portion of the article covers library browsing and why the students were motivated to use this option. Among the many findings are that while in the focus groups the students discussed asking a librarian for assistance, not many acknowledged that it was their practice to do so (preferring instead an art professor or another student).

258. Harris, Pam, and Pamela J. McKenzie. "What It Means to Be 'In-Between': A Focus Group Analysis of Barriers Faced by Children Aged 7 to 11 Using Public Libraries." *Canadian Journal of Information and Library Science* 28, no. 4 (2004): 3–25.

Harris and McKenzie write from the perspective that there is a gap in library service for children between the ages of 7 and 11, noting a paucity in the literature concerning what children in this age group actually do when they use the library. (The reasons for selecting the term "in-between" are explained.) The goal of the research was to ascertain how this clientele could be better served in using both computer- and print-based information sources in the library. The focus group approach was chosen to elicit the children's own perceptions and understandings of their information-seeking activities; to identify the search strategies the children "thought they had," and to investigate whether the library used these strategies to provide better service. Three 60-minute audiotaped focus groups were conducted with 20 boys and girls in the age group under consideration. The research took place in a southern Ontario city. Informed consent was obtained. Refreshments were served. The children identified a number of challenges, which fell into three categories: intellectual, physical, and administration access. Focus groups are seen as an "effective" way to explore the needs of library users in middle childhood.

259. Hughes-Hassell, Sandra, and Kay Bishop. "Using Focus Group Interviews to Improve Library Services for Youth." *Teacher Librarian* 32, no. 1 (October 2004): 8–12.

The authors define focus group interviews, describe the situations and settings where they can be appropriately used by librarians, and evaluate the benefits and limitations associated with the methodology. Nine steps for conducting focus groups are outlined and discussed: determine the goals of the project; select a moderator; identify and recruit participants; design effective questions; conduct and record the sessions; analyze the data; report the findings; and utilize the results for service evaluation, understanding an issue, decision making, and so forth. Bishop reports her use of approximately 20 focus groups of four to six students each to examine how the National Library Power initiative affected student learning at a Lincoln, Nebraska, middle school. Hughes-Hassell used focus groups to gather data from a group of teachers regarding development of the library collection.

260. Lin, Tom M. Y., Pin Luarn, and Yun Kuei Huang. "Effect of Internet Book Reviews on Purchase Intention: A Focus Group Study." *Journal of Academic Librarianship* 31, no. 5 (September 2005): 461–68.

The three authors from the National Taiwan University of Science and Technology used focus group interviews to consider what Internet book-review characteristics (such as number, length, positive or negative content, or order of appearance) had on consumer purchase intentions. The article provides a literature review on consumer purchase intentions related to these characteristics. Seven focus groups, consisting of six to eight members each, were conducted with 50 student participants. The focus group members considered two romance novels, and were then asked to discuss 21 questions (included in the article as appendix B). The discussion revealed the following: a large number of reviews had a direct impact on purchase intentions; length needed to be somewhere between brevity and verbosity; and negative reviews diminish the likelihood of purchase, especially when "fierce" or appearing prior to positive reviews. The participants were accepting of anonymous Internet book reviews.

3.9 POLITICAL SCIENCE

General Studies

261. Bartle, John. "Measuring Party Identification: An Exploratory Study with Focus Groups." *Electoral Studies* 22, no. 2 (June 2003): 217–37.

The purpose of the research was to determine the format that will assist voters to differentiate between their enduring party identification and their current political preference. Bartle determines that the question used by the British Election Study (BES) is inadequate, and proposes alternative question wording. The recruitment of participants and the conduct of the focus group sessions were managed by MORI (Market and Opinion Research International, a survey research organization located in Great Britain). The focus groups were held in three contrasting locations with varying levels of party identification. At the beginning of each session participants were asked to talk about the area where they lived. After 20 minutes, the three forms of the party identification question were read to the group. Participants were then asked to write down their responses, and group discussion followed. The author maintains that focus groups could have significant usefulness in question design. The focus groups validated the perceived difficulties with the BES question but were less conclusive about the form of the alternate question.

262. Glick, Joseph A. "Focus Groups in Political Campaigns." In *The Manship School Guide to Political Communication*, edited by David D. Perlmutter, 114–21. Baton Rouge, LA: Louisiana State University Press, 1999.

Focus groups can be used in political campaigns to devise strategy, to test strategic moves prior to communicating with the general public, and to assess "the likely impact of media and for fine-tuning the execution of campaign communications" (p. 118). Glick discusses the differences between focus groups and public opinion polls, the importance of an underlying framework of thinking versus mere opinion holding, and how focus groups can encourage participant disagreement that allows these frameworks for thinking to emerge. The critical role of the moderator in encouraging deeper discussion among participants is highlighted.

263. Heith, Diane J. "One for All: Using Focus Groups and Opinion Polls in the George H. W. Bush White House." *Congress & the Presidency* 30, no. 1 (Spring 2003): 81–94.

The uses of focus groups and public opinion polls during the presidency of George H. W. Bush are compared and contrasted. The author provides a brief history of how quantitative methods were employed by the White House to seek public attitudes on a wide variety of issues. Franklin Delano Roosevelt was the first president to use public opinion polls to determine public attitudes. Although

Truman and Eisenhower also used polls, it was to a lesser degree. The adminis-trations of Kennedy and Johnson emphasized polling, and subsequent presidents increased their use of the approach. This article addresses the manner in which focus groups were used by President Bush to define intangibles—to cover areas beyond the reach of polls. In particular, focus groups were used to identify and test themes and phrases, and to serve as aids in defining the message, as in the radio and television addresses prior to the Gulf War. Focus groups were used to consider the language of politics, and through the group dynamics, do, to some degree, represent a form of public discussion.

264. Manheim, Jarol B., Richard C. Rich, Lars Willnat, and Craig Leonard Brians. "Focus Group Methodologies." In *Empirical Political Analysis: Research Methods in Political Science*, 339–54. 6th ed. New York: Pearson Longman, 2006.

Within the context of a textbook on research methods in political science, Manheim et al. consider when to use focus groups, the benefits and drawbacks, how they are conducted and analyzed, and the value of combining the approach with other methodologies. The authors observe that focus groups can assist in understanding the "meanings people attach to responses and actions" (p. 352). The usefulness of the technique at various stages of both qualitative and quantita-tive research is highlighted, such as for purposes of question clarification and the possibility of finding new approaches. Additional applications include assisting with the design of measurement instruments, as well as in the analysis phase when attempting to interpret quantitative data. The preface implies that the work is aimed at both undergraduate and graduate students.

265. McKinney, Mitchell S., and Elizabeth R. Lamoureux. "Citizen Response to the 1996 Presidential Debates: Focusing on the Focus Groups." In *The Electronic Election: Perspectives on the 1996 Campaign Communication*, edited by Lynda Lee Kaid and Dianne G. Bystrom, 163–77. Mahwah, NJ: Lawrence Erlbaum, 1999.

The authors set the stage by explaining the history of U.S. presidential candi-dates' debates, beginning with the televised Kennedy-Nixon debate in 1960. As a means of determining voter response to the 1996 presidential debates between Clinton and Dole, 10 focus groups were conducted, with 6 of these following the first presidential debate and 4 sessions after the town hall debate. The typical group size was just over 10 participants (varying from 6 to 12). The participants revealed their perception of new information (very little). The issues raised, the questions asked, and the debate formats were evaluated. Citizens learned about the personality and image of candidates through the debates. The authors recom-mend that people from multiple locations be in the audience of the town hall model, rather than just from a single place.

266. Park, Hyun Soon, and Sejung Marina Choi. "Focus Group Interviews: The Internet as a Political Campaign Medium." *Public Relations Quarterly* 47, no. 4 (Winter 2002): 36–42.

Young voters' perceptions were explored through three focus groups involving 24 undergraduate students. There were two steps for each focus group. In the first, the students in a computer lab navigated two presidential candidates' Web sites for 30 minutes (in this case, George W. Bush and Al Gore in the 2000 election). Students were to record interesting and problematic elements from the Web sites. In the second step, the participants discussed their findings in another room. The one-hour sessions were videotaped, and a one-way mirror permitted unseen observation. The moderator and researchers met after each session to improve the questioning route. Areas of interest included interactivity, personalization, ease of navigation, variety of communication cues, and design features. Overall, Gore's site was preferred, largely due to user-friendly aspects, the ability to make viewers feel personally welcome, and invitations to become part of the campaign. Some students preferred the Bush site because it was "simpler," "serious," and "straightforward."

267. Perrin, Andrew J. "Political Microcultures: Linking Civic Life and Democratic Discourse." *Social Forces* 84, no. 2 (December 2005): 1049–82.

Using 20 focus groups composed of 137 participants from five types of civic organizations, Perrin views these "political microcultures" as places for political discourse that had an impact on the members' understanding of citizenship. Participants were each paid $35 and provided with refreshments. The author addresses the issue of selection bias. The following types of organizations, all located in southern Alameda County, California, were represented: Protestant churches, Catholic churches, labor unions, businesses (such as the local Chamber of Commerce), and organized sports groups. Each focus group consisted of members from one organization. Prior to the group discussions, participants completed a short questionnaire containing items about demographics, political ideas, and organizational affiliations. The focus groups were conducted within a four-month period. Perrin notes that the group context in which political discussion occurs has an independent effect on how it proceeds, and that the discussion is social and affects citizenship.

268. Wring, Dominic. "Focus Group Follies? Qualitative Research and British Labour Party Strategy." *Journal of Political Marketing* 5, no. 4 (2006): 71–97.

The use of focus groups by the British Labour Party—in particular by Tony Blair and preceding party leaders—is traced in this historical overview. The nature of focus group research as a tool for campaign strategy is explored. Beginning with their incorporation into party planning in the mid-1980s and through to their extensive use in the 1997 election and the advent of "new" Labour, focus groups have played an important role. In 1997, 300 preelection focus groups were conducted, with an additional 70 following the election. The focus groups, consisting of 6 to 10 people, were designed to determine the participants' values and attitudes. In the 1960s, depth interviewing was in vogue, followed by polling, with focus groups gaining popularity in the early 1980s. Selective use of focus group material became a tool in the development of Labour's new right, the so-called "modernisers," starting in the early 1990s and continuing for a decade. Polls failed to predict the outcome of the 1992 election, giving focus group research an advantage still pursued by politicians seeking data with authority.

Public Administration

269. Cohen, Joel. *Focus Groups: A Valuable Tool for Public Policy.* CRB Note, vol. 7, no. 1. Sacramento, CA: California State Library, California Research Bureau, 2000. 9p.

Four uses for focus groups in public policy are identified as the following: to gain an understanding of people' knowledge about the existence of services; to examine why they use a certain service; to assess views on proposed legislation, codes, and/or regulations; and to acquire insights on services and environments. Cohen identifies and describes eight guidelines for conducting a policy discussion focus group and provides an example of its use for a school safety and security issue. Twenty focus groups were conducted with students in second, sixth, eighth, and twelfth grades in five cities in California. The results produced insights useful as the basis for policy recommendations.

270. Davies, Anna R. "Where Do We Go from Here? Environmental Focus Groups and Planning Policy Formation." *Local Environment* 4, no. 3 (1999): 295–316.

Davies begins the presentation by writing that "focus groups have achieved a profile in the analysis of public values unparalleled since the emergence of national opinion polls" (p. 295). A case study is used (1) to demonstrate how interviews and focus groups informed a land-use planning project; and (2) to suggest potential problems such techniques may present when attempting to influence the development of planning policy. Davies is of the opinion that focus groups are both "undertheorized" (much of the literature concentrates only on methodology) and "underpracticed" (focus group results typically have little impact on policy). The case study involved two locations in the United Kingdom:

Luton, a densely populated urban area, and South Bedforshire, a predominately rural environment. A total of 34 individual interviews were conducted with a wide range of stakeholders—developers, landowners, politicians, and environmentalists. Twelve audiotaped focus group sessions involved 86 participants of mixed gender, age groups, and ethnicity, who were nonrepresentative of the environmental groups. The author served as recruiter, moderator, note taker, and analyst. The results indicate that the public's views on environmental issues were "consistently marginalized or excluded" from plans and policies of the planning policy community, perhaps leading to an "unjust devaluation" of the focus group method.

271. Halfacre, Angela C., Albert R. Matheny, and Walter A. Rosenbaum. "Regulating Contested Local Hazards: Is Constructive Dialogue Possible among Participants in Community Risk Management?" *Policy Studies Journal* 28, no. 3 (Autumn 2000): 648–67.

Focus groups were used to examine the connection between scientific uncertainty concerning environmental risks and the emergence of "mutual distrust" among key stakeholders—local populations, regulators, and technical experts. To identify the sources of miscommunication and distrust among these groups, the Consortium for Environment Risk Evaluation (CERE), an organization composed of universities and consulting firms, was charged by the U.S. Department of Energy to collect data on the cleanup of U.S. nuclear weapons facilities. In total, CERE conducted over 40 audiotaped focus groups with activists, nonactivists, and regulators. The settings were the Idaho National Engineering Laboratory, Oak Ridge, and Savannah River. Although uncertainty, distrust, and frustration were expressed, there was some understanding in each group that they should reach out to other key players, respect each others' dilemmas, and seek common ground. When the voices of activists and nonactivists united, the public sector had more credibility with government regulators.

272. Kahan, James P. "Focus Groups as a Tool for Policy Analysis." *Analyses of Social Issues and Public Policy* 1, no. 1 (December 2001): 129–46.

The author provides an overview of the development of focus groups, noting the earliest use by Robert K. Merton and his colleagues for audience research during World War II. Four case studies are presented: River Dike Strengthening in the Netherlands; Gays in the Military (USA); Training Quality Assurance in Blood Banking; and The Safety of Schiphol Airport (the Dutch national airport near Amsterdam). In 2001 Kahan was the research director at RAND Europe in Leiden, the Netherlands. The studies discussed were part of RAND Europe research. The second part of the article considers the methodological guidelines for policy analysis focus groups in terms of achieving both breadth and depth, recruiting, successful research team formation, and the gathering of qualitative (and a limited amount of quantitative) data from focus groups. The author concludes with comments on how the focus group participants became part of the policy-making process, and the value of stakeholder groups in furthering that process.

273. McCarron, Brendan. *The Focus Group Aide Memoire: A Guide for Anyone Interested in Managing, Designing and Running Focus Groups.* Saint Michael, Wiltshire, UK: McCarron Heal, 2000. 32 unnumbered pages.

The mechanics of designing and conducting focus groups are discussed for those working in the public sector. (Focus groups are described as a "hot" issue in the U.K. public sector.) McCarron defines the terms population, sample, representative, and "groupthink," and then moves on to identify eight stages in a typical focus group project sequence. The reader is cautioned about some inappropriate uses of the methodology, namely, for team building, brainstorming, decision making, or as a problem-solving vehicle. There are three appendices: checklists for the observer and note taker, a sample discussion guide and questions, and a checklist for conducting the focus group meeting.

274. Nwoye, May Ifeoma. "A Focus Group Discussion Approach to the Comparative Analysis of Private and Public Sector Enterprises in Nigeria." *Technovation* 22, no. 8 (August 2002): 525–34.

Nwoye observes the poor performance of public sector enterprises compared to their private sector counterparts in Nigeria. To explore reasons for this situation, a series of two-hour audiotaped focus groups were conducted with owners, managers, and employees from 10 public and private business enterprises located in selected Nigerian states. The author moderated the discussions. The participants were asked to evaluate and compare the two sectors on a number of factors: reasons for government involvement in public enterprises; goals and objectives; performance; managerial autonomy; financial autonomy and acceptability; managerial skills and morale; employee recruitment; and organizational design and structure. Based on the focus group findings, the author concludes that public sector enterprises can succeed with the reduction of interference from the government.

275. Waterton, Claire, and Brian Wynne. "Can Focus Groups Access Community Views?" In *Developing Focus Group Research: Politics, Theory and Practice*, edited by Rosaline S. Barbour and Jenny Kitzinger, 127–43. London: Sage, 1999.

The presentation is based on a case study regarding residents' attitudes toward possible developments in, and expansion of, the nuclear waste repository at Sellafield, a town near West Cumbria, in northwest England. Because opinion polls indicated mixed views between locals (a higher measure of support) and county or country residents, 12 focus groups were conducted with the locals to seek further information on community perspectives on health and safety risks of the facility. The outcome suggests that when people express attitudes about risks, it is in relation to their social context, during interaction, and as a process of negotiation of trust. The focus groups provided much counterevidence to the poll data, uncovering "a far richer sense of community views" (p. 127).

Public Opinion

276. Glynn, Carroll J., Susan Herbst, Garrett J. O'Keefe, Robert Y. Shapiro, and Mark Lindeman. "Methods for Studying Public Opinion." In *Public Opinion*, 73–115. 2nd ed. Boulder, CO: Westview Press, 2004.

The methods of opinion assessment referred to in the title are survey research, focus groups, experimental research, and content analysis of mass media. In the section titled "Focus Groups: Using Group Dynamics to Measure Public Opinion" (pp. 91–101), Glynn et al. describe the unique contributions of the technique, noting its usefulness in conjunction with participant observation, in-depth interviews, experimental methods, and surveys. When used as an adjunct to traditional approaches, focus groups can assist in avoiding oversimplification of complex cognitive, social, and political processes, and aid in examining the "fluidity and dynamics" of attitude and opinion formation. Focus groups also can be useful in the wording of survey questions and to develop hypotheses, which can then be tested via quantitative methods. Several examples of focus group research are provided.

277. Wilkinson, Sue, and Celia Kitzinger. "'Clinton Faces Nation': A Case Study in the Construction of Focus Group Data as Public Opinion." *Sociological Review* 48, no. 3 (August 2000): 408–24.

The authors examine the work of a focus group used by the *San Francisco Chronicle*. The focus group served as the basis for "illustrating the kinds of debates that will rage across the country in the coming months, which will be crucial in determining Clinton's fate" (p. 408). This quote is in reference to President Bill Clinton's 1998 grand jury testimony in the Monica Lewinsky case. The issue is whether the 10-member focus group could provide insight into the public opinion concerning Clinton as perceived across the entire country. The authors see the real issue as being how the journalist reaches representativeness and generalizability from the focus group findings. The way in which social scientists engage in the same process is outlined, noting that they tend to use fewer direct quotes and a smaller number of interactive extracts than recommended in the focus group literature. The authors view these findings as part of the "understanding of the rhetoric of persuasion."

3.10 PSYCHOLOGY

Assessment

278. Vogt, Dawne S., Daniel W. King, and Lynda A. King. "Focus Groups in Psychological Assessment: Enhancing Content Validity by Consulting Members of the Target Population." *Psychological Assessment* 16, no. 3 (2004): 231–43.

The authors lament the lack of articles appearing in the professional psychological literature that were informed by the use of focus group methodology for instrument development projects. For example, through a search of PsycINFO for the years 1967 through 2002, using the keywords "focus groups" and either "instrument" or "measure," only 23 scale construction studies were identified that were based on focus groups with members of the target population. The goals of the authors were to emphasize the importance of population consultation as part of content validation, and to demonstrate the potential of focus groups for multiple stages of questionnaire construction. An example of the last point is provided and discussed in the context of developing an instrument to assess an array of war-related stressors that would be valid for veterans of current military deployment. Six audiotaped focus groups, averaging seven self-selected veterans per group, were moderated by a member of the research team. The method tested "holds promise" for enhancing content validity.

Body Image

279. Grogan, Sarah, and Helen Richards. "Body Image: Focus Groups with Boys and Men." *Men and Masculinities* 4, no. 3 (January 2002): 219–32.

The two self-described "feminist women researchers" used focus groups to examine the body-image perceptions of boys and men. Five focus groups were conducted with four age categories: 8, 13, 16, and 19 to 25. Each group had four participants—with the 16-year-olds having two groups of four. The authors provide the background for their work and why they found that women proved to be more appropriate moderators for this study. How the boys and men felt about their bodies, their body shape, and related issues of exercise and diet were the substance of the questions asked. The results of the focus groups are divided into the following topics: the importance of being muscular; fear of being fat; exercise; social pressure; and power and self-confidence. Focus groups were found to be useful because the participants used "natural speech" when talking about their bodies and were responsive about their feelings. The work is described as exploratory, with the suggestion for replication and a wider group, both socially and ethnically.

Economic

280. Chilton, S. M., and W. G. Hutchinson. "Do Focus Groups Contribute Any-
     thing to the Contingent Valuation Process?" *Journal of Economic Psychol-
     ogy* 20, no. 4 (August 1999): 465–83.

The Contingent Valuation Method (CVM) is used within environmental economics to determine "an individual's willingness to pay (willingness to accept
compensation) for improvements (reductions) in the use and nonuse 'services'
flowing from environmental or other public goods" (p. 466). The authors explore
the applications of focus groups in CVM research and review the challenges
related to analysis. Focus groups can be used for developing surveys (including
pilot questionnaires), in postsurvey exercises, and as "feedback" groups. Two
techniques for focus group analysis are covered: grounded theory and content
analysis. The authors believe content analysis is the better approach. The study
considered used eight separate focus groups, and cross-group comparisons were
performed. The sessions were videotaped, thereby permitting verbal and nonverbal communication to be considered when evaluating the confidence level of
group members. The authors argue that the systematic generation of qualitative
data should provide for an increased use of such data in the CVM process.

Mental Health and Services

281. Coggan, Carolyn, Pam Patterson, and Jacqui Fill. "Suicide: Qualitative
     Data from Focus Group Interviews with Youth." *Social Science & Medicine*
     45, no. 10 (November 1997): 1563–70.

In New Zealand, suicide is the second leading cause of death among young
men and women between 15 and 24 (an average of 124 deaths per year, the
highest in the Western world). As part of a larger needs-assessment program,
the authors decided that focus groups were an appropriate methodology for
eliciting the views of this age group and designing intervention strategies. A
total of 140 young people from the Auckland region volunteered to participate
in the study. Twelve audiotaped focus groups were held. All sessions were
conducted by a young, experienced group facilitator. The discussions were
transcribed, coded, and analyzed. Three warning signs of a suicidal friend
were identified: personality changes, risk-taking behavior, and unusual actions.
In addition, the participants perceived suicide as a taboo subject, some took
drugs and/or alcohol, and most would try to cope by themselves or would turn
to peers or friends before accessing professional services. Family support was
vital, as were school counselors. Despite drawbacks, the focus groups provided
valuable insights into this problem.

282. Encandela, John A., Wynne S. Korr, Kathleen Hulton, Gary F. Koeske, W.
     Dean Klinkenberg, Laura L. Otto-Salaj, Anthony J. Silvestre, and Eric R.

Wright. "Mental Health Case Management as a Locus for HIV Prevention: Results from Case-Manager Focus Groups." *Journal of Behavioral Health Services & Research* 30, no. 4 (October–December 2003): 418–32.

The relatively high prevalence and incidence of HIV/AIDS among people with severe mental illness (SMI) is described as a "growing concern." Risk factors include low condom use, multiple sexual partners, exchanging sex for drugs, and substance abuse. The authors review some of the current HIV-prevention interventions that have been tested with this population, but observe that "little is known" about whether mental health providers are prepared to support these interventions. To inform this question, two pilot and six other audiotaped focus groups were conducted with 42 male and female participants—all mental health-care case managers recruited by purposive sampling from urban, small-town, and rural communities in western Pennsylvania. The experienced moderator was assisted by one or two observers/note takers. Atlas-ti, a qualitative software program, was used in the analysis. The case managers identified both barriers and strengths to providing HIV-prevention messages and services to their clients with SMI, who indicated that they had both the motivation and the interest to adopt these services.

283. Gilbert, Paul, and Jean Gilbert. "Entrapment and Arrested Fight and Flight in Depression: An Exploration Using Focus Groups." *Psychology and Psychotherapy* 76 (June 2003): 173–88.

The British authors describe the fight/flight phenomenon as a "basic evolved defense system" and discuss the consequences if these defenses become blocked, inhibited, or arrested. Individuals so afflicted can feel trapped, become chronically physiologically stressed, and experience anger and depression. To examine people's own perspectives of entrapment and arrested fight/flight, three focus groups were conducted with participants recruited from three sources: a psychiatric acute in-patient unit, a bipolar self-support group, and a self-help depression alliance. All were depressed or had been depressed at some time, as evidenced by the Beck Depression Inventory. To elicit a different view, a fourth focus group was conducted with five psychiatric nurses and one occupational therapist. A trained female moderator led the discussions. Results are given, by group, for the two open-ended questions asked. Also discussed are some methodological concerns of the study. The data generated are seen to support other research findings about the link between stress and depression.

284. Manoleas, Peter, Kurt Organista, Gisela Negron-Velasquez, and Kathleen McCormick. "Characteristics of Latino Mental Health Clinicians: A Preliminary Examination." *Community Mental Health Journal* 36, no. 4 (August 2000): 383–94.

A qualitative approach (focus groups) and a quantitative method (a survey) were chosen to examine the personal and professional characteristics related to the therapist that may have implications for the provision of culturally sensitive services to Latino clients. The authors review some prior literature on the pros and cons of ethnic matching. The first phase of this exploratory study involved two focus groups with 65 Latino therapists and administrators. All were recruited by means of convenience sampling from San Francisco Bay area mental health agencies that specialize in the treatment of Latinos. The participants discussed items from a previously designed questionnaire. The second phase of the study consisted of a mail survey conducted with a different sample of Latino therapists. The findings were consistent for both the qualitative and quantitative data collection approaches. Some significant differences were found in how the therapists treated Latino and non-Latino clients. The impact of spirituality and other factors on treatment are discussed.

285. Nabors, Laura A., Mark D. Weist, and Nancy A. Tashman. "Focus Groups: A Valuable Tool for Assessing Male and Female Adolescent Perceptions of School-Based Mental Health Services." *Journal of Gender, Culture, and Health* 4, no. 1 (1999): 39–48.

Focus groups were used to examine male and female students' assessments of the mental health services they were receiving and to determine if there were gender differences in response to the interview questions. Four focus groups were conducted with 24 females; two were conducted with 13 males. All participants were receiving mental health services in three inner-city high schools. The questions concerned positive and negative aspects of the program, barriers to treatment, and treatment outcomes. The dialogue was audiotaped and transcribed, and key themes were identified. The results provided information on ways to improve mental health services and develop model programs. Important gender differences were noted. Females tended to discuss relationships and interpersonal problems, while males emphasized the value of specific skills training. Focus groups are described as an "efficient, cost-effective" research tool.

286. Nabors, Laura A., Matthew W. Reynolds, and Mark D. Weist. "Qualitative Evaluation of a High School Mental Health Program." *Journal of Youth and Adolescence* 29, no. 1 (2000): 1–13.

Two data-collection approaches—focus groups and individual interviews—were used to assess the strengths, weaknesses, and outcomes of the expanded school mental health (ESMH) program. A total of 61 students (some currently receiving treatment) were recruited from three predominately African-American high schools located in Baltimore City, Maryland. Ten focus groups were conducted with these students; nine were conducted with 47 adults (teachers, parents, therapists, and others). Because of the difficulty of scheduling parents for group sessions, 28 were asked to complete 20-minute interviews, either in person or by telephone. Using identical questions for both formats, the primary author and assistants moderated the sessions and conducted the interviews. Detailed tables display the various stakeholder perceptions of the ESMH program. In general, positive outcomes for students were reported. The two methods are described as "effective" for attaining the goals of the research.

287. Nabors, Laura A., Vincent Ramos, and Mark D. Weist. "Use of Focus Groups as a Tool for Evaluating Programs for Children and Families." *Journal of Educational and Psychological Consultation* 12, no. 3 (2001): 243–56.

The authors delineate several primary uses of focus groups in the mental health field: for conducting needs assessments, for evaluating children's programs, and for monitoring program implementation. The method is viewed as an effective way to gather stakeholders' (for example, students, parents, teachers, clinicians, and administrators) perceptions of mental health programs for children and their families. The discussion is centered around the methodological issues associated with the focus group process: developing questions and probes; determining location, seating, and session length; obtaining the services of a moderator; recruiting participants; writing the introductory script; collecting the data; and analyzing and reporting the results. To ensure confidentiality, it is recommended that friends not be included in the same groups. Computer programs such as Ethnograph, NUD*IST, and HyperQual are helpful for searching for key words in transcripts. Examples from the authors' script are found in the appendix.

288. Rauktis, Mary E., Kathleen Feidler, and Judy Wood. "Focus Groups, Program Evaluation and the Mentally Ill: A Case Study." *Journal of Health & Social Policy* 10, no. 2 (1998): 75–92.

The purposes of the research were to evaluate the strengths and weaknesses of an existing mental health services program, determine what new services were needed, and gain insight into what clients feel would be useful elements. The provider was a nonprofit, local government agency serving the mentally ill, disabled, addicted, and homeless in Allegheny County, Pennsylvania. Seven 60- to 90-minute focus groups were conducted with a diverse group of 58 male and female, white and African-American, mentally ill participants. The trained moderators were county mental health office evaluators. The same seven questions were asked of each group. The authors detail some of the modifications to logistic procedures that had to be made when working with this population. Although some limitations are acknowledged, focus groups are described as a "flexible," "effective," and "valuable" tool for gathering the evaluative data sought. The group interaction captured nuances that surveys and individual interviews fail to convey.

289. Siegel, Carole, Ethel Davis-Chambers, Gary Haugland, Rheta Bank, Carmen Aponte, and Harriet McCombs. "Performance Measures of Cultural

Competency in Mental Health Organizations." *Administration and Policy in Mental Health* 28, no. 2 (November 2000): 91–106.

Cultural competency (CC) is defined as "the set of behaviors, attitudes and skills, policies and procedures that come together in a system, agency or individuals to enable mental health care givers to work effectively and efficiently in cross/multicultural situations" (p. 92). The incorporation of the principles of CC into mental health services is based on the premise that individuals receiving such services will have better clinical and social outcomes if her or his cultural background, language, and beliefs are recognized and respected. The authors trace the development of the concept and present a framework of CC taken from a national report that sought to guide the selection of a list of performance measures. Data were gathered from a variety of sources: document reviews, an expert panel, and focus groups, the last conducted with 134 consumers, family members, advocates, and providers. Latino Americans, African Americans, Pacific Islanders, and Native Americans were represented. Sessions took place in New York, Florida, South Carolina, South Dakota, and California. A wide range of indicators, measures for needs assessment, services, outcomes, and other factors were identified.

Mental Retardation

290. Fox, Peter, and Eric Emerson. "Socially Valid Outcomes of Intervention for People with MR and Challenging Behavior: Views of Different Stakeholders." *Journal of Positive Behavior Interventions* 3, no. 3 (Summer 2001): 183–89.

The authors observe that individuals with mental retardation (MR) face a wide range of lifestyle challenges. To gain insight into the perceived importance of potential outcomes by a variety of stakeholders, a two-stage study was undertaken. In the final stage, item generation, a series of 12 one-hour focus groups were conducted with 102 participants drawn from people with MR, parents, program and day-services managers, nurses, clinical psychologists, and others. The first author facilitated the sessions. Including 35 items from a literature review, a total of 331 positive outcomes were identified. In the second stage, 150 respondents from seven stakeholder groups rated the relative importance of 73 potential outcomes. The most important among these was the reduction in the severity of challenging behavior. Alternative outcomes considered the most important included increased friendships and relationships, changing others' perceptions, and empowerment.

291. Mactavish, Jennifer B., Michael J. Mahon, and Zana Marie Lutfiyya. "'I Can Speak for Myself': Involving Individuals with Intellectual Disabilities as Research Participants." *Mental Retardation* 38, no. 3 (June 2000): 216–27.

Two data-collection approaches—individual interviews and focus groups—were used to elicit participants' own perspectives for the Lifespan and Disability Project, the goal of which was to develop a life-span model of social interaction of individuals with intellectual disabilities. An interdisciplinary research team and a network of community partners (for example, service providers, caregivers, and policymakers) undertook the two-year qualitative study. Through a nomination process, 32 male and female individuals, ages 17 to 82, were selected from urban and rural settings in western Canada. Their level of disability ranged from mild to profound. The interviews were used to collect demographic data and build rapport. A total of eight 60- to 90-minute audiotaped focus groups were moderated by members of the research team. Following analysis, additional focus groups, composed of some of the original participants, were convened to verify the researchers' interpretations. The mixed-method paradigm is described as an "effective" way of gaining insights into this population.

Prison and Jail Intervention

292. Belknap, Joanne, Kristi Holsinger, and Melissa Dunn. "Understanding Incarcerated Girls: The Results of a Focus Group Study." *Prison Journal* 77, no. 4 (December 1997): 381–404.

The authors observe that, until recent years, the factors contributing to delinquency among females, and their experiences of incarceration, have been "largely ignored." At the same time, women are being incarcerated at "unprecedented rates." To gain a better understanding of this circumstance in the state of Ohio, 11 60- to 90-minute focus groups were conducted with two groups of participants: six sessions with 58 13- to 20-year-old delinquent girls and five sessions with 42 professionals who work with the girls (such as probation officer, teacher, court administrator, and social worker). Approximately 75 percent of the girls were African American and the rest were "Anglo." A professional moderator (with note takers and observers) facilitated the discussions. The findings indicate that many of the girls experienced serious problems both before and during institutionalization, such as lack of respect, neglect, and sexually abusive backgrounds. The professionals expressed their frustration with the juvenile justice system. Recommendations were submitted to the governor and the appropriate state agencies.

293. Linhorst, Donald M., Kevin Knight, J. Scott Johnston, and Myrna Trickey. "Situational Influences on the Implementation of a Prison-Based Therapeutic Community." *Prison Journal* 81, no. 4 (December 2001): 436–53.

A multimethod approach—focus groups, telephone interviews, and document reviews—was used to evaluate the effect of two "situational influences" (the enactment of a smoking ban and a change in treatment providers) on the implementation of therapeutic communities (TCs), a substance abuse treatment program for criminal offenders. Individual and group counseling as well as community work programs are offered by TCs. The setting for the assessment was an all-male, 650-bed, minimum-security prison in the state of Missouri. Three focus groups were conducted with a total of 15 key administrators and treatment program staff. Two members of the evaluation team served as moderator and note taker. Telephone interviews were then conducted with a number of the inmates 12 months after their release. Document reviews provided additional information. All stakeholders—inmates, former inmates, administrators, and counselors— responded negatively to the situational influences.

294. Miller, Sarah, Carly Sees, and Jennifer Brown. "Key Aspects of Psychological Change in Residents of a Prison Therapeutic Community: A Focus Group Approach." *Howard Journal* 45, no. 2 (May 2006): 116–28.

Therapeutic communities (TCs), part of the prison system in the United Kingdom, feature an informal atmosphere and regular meetings. The residents not only participate in running the community but also serve as auxiliary therapists. The present research investigates residents' perceptions about the key components of therapeutic change and whether focus groups could assist their exploration of change. Four 60- to 90-minute audiotaped focus groups were conducted with 27 male participants, ages 22 to 57, residing in one of the TCs at Her Majesty's Prison Dovegate. Participants were advised that they were "co-researchers"—not just the subjects of an experiment. Thus, the two moderators kept their involvement to a minimum and used a nondirective approach. Residents identified change as a variable and gradual process—one based on individual properties and characteristics. "Novel" insights were produced by the focus groups, which are described as an "especially productive" research method.

295. Swartz, James A., and Arthur J. Lurigio. "Final Thoughts on IMPACT: A Federally Funded, Jail-Based, Drug-User-Treatment Program." *Substance Use & Misuse* 34, no. 6 (1999): 887–906.

Swartz and Lurigio describe, discuss, and report on a study designed to evaluate the outcome of a jail-based, drug-user treatment program called IMPACT (Intensive Multi-phased Program of Assessment and Comprehensive Treatment). IMPACT was implemented in 1991 in the Cook County Jail in Illinois and provided treatment to more than 3,000 inmates. The five-year program featured shorter-term treatment (as compared to community- and prison-based therapeutic communities), involved a three-phase process, and embraced a range of therapeutic interventions—many based on the 12-step Alcoholics Anonymous treatment model. To examine the success of the program, the research team undertook an outcome evaluation with staff and IMPACT recipients, as well as a series of focus groups with former recipients. Participants from one community-based treatment program were asked to discuss their positive and negative views of IMPACT, and their experiences in making the transition to the community-based program. Based on the two assessment approaches, the authors suggest ways to improve the design and implementation of such treatment programs in the jail environment.

Quality of Life

296. Nicolson, Paula, and Pippa Anderson. "Quality of Life, Distress and Self-Esteem: A Focus Group Study of People with Chronic Bronchitis." *British Journal of Health Psychology* 8 (2003): 251–70.

Nicolson and Anderson examine the psychological, emotional, and social aspects of quality of life for individuals with chronic bronchitis. To gain insight into patients' perceptions and to identify key experiences of living with this disease, 20 participants were recruited from lists of general practitioners in two cities in the United Kingdom. Four audiotaped focus group sessions were facilitated by the researchers, who then used Mason's two-stage qualitative analysis procedure to identify themes and provide a more detailed interpretive conceptual analysis. Three major themes were identified: the physical effects of the disease, its impact on family and social relationships, and themes related to emotional reactions, life disruption, and self-esteem.

297. O'Neill, John, Barbara B. Small, and John Strachan. "The Use of Focus Groups within a Participatory Action Research Environment." In *Using Qualitative Methods in Psychology*, edited by Mary Kopala and Lisa A. Suzuki, 199–209. Thousand Oaks, CA: Sage, 1999.

Appearing in part 5, "Qualitative Methods in Action Research and Evaluation," this chapter addresses issues surrounding community employment and quality of life for "people with HIV/AIDS" (PWAs), and how the use of focus group methodology, as part of a participatory action research (PAR) model, assisted researchers in addressing these issues. The authors explain the organizational principles of the PAR framework, which requires consumers of research (in this case, counselors, supervisors, administrators, and clients) to participate actively throughout the research process to solve practical problems. In addition, the results need to have "direct implications for action and change" (p. 201). Four organizations in the state of New York took part in the project. In order to prepare a grant proposal and formulate hypotheses, a series of focus groups were conducted with a sample of PWAs to gain an understanding of the impact of their condition on their lives. The methodology "contributed greatly" to the total research effort and helped enact changes in the program.

Social

298. Burgoyne, Carole B., Brian Young, and Catherine M. Walker. "Deciding to Give to Charity: A Focus Group Study in the Context of the Household Economy." *Journal of Community & Applied Social Psychology* 15, no. 5 (2005): 383–405.

The authors describe the act of giving to charity as a "complex and neglected" topic in the psychological literature, noting that most research has tended to examine either donors' individual characteristics or those of households. The present paper investigates the interactive processes and behaviors between partners and within households that can influence giving. These processes include the presence of children, whether the financial decisions for the family are arrived at individually or jointly, and whether charitable giving is an integral part of household financial management. To inform this topic, six audiotaped focus groups were conducted with a diverse group of male and female participants ranging in age from 24 to 72. All but one were married or living with a partner. Two moderators led the discussions. Over 50,000 words were collected and analyzed with the assistance of the principles of grounded theory. The authors found that although charitable giving occupies a "more marginal position" than other expenditures, it follows patterns of money management already established in the household.

Vocational Rehabilitation

299. Conyers, Liza M. "Expanding Understanding of HIV/AIDS and Employment: Perspectives of Focus Groups." *Rehabilitation Counseling Bulletin* 48, no. 1 (Fall 2004): 5–18.

Conyers' research addresses three areas: the impact of HIV/AIDS, the motivation to work, and barriers to employment. To gain insight into these questions, five 90-minute audiotaped focus groups were conducted with 46 male and female, primarily African-American participants with HIV/AIDS diagnoses. All had been recruited by purposive sampling from a vocational rehabilitation program and community events in New York City, were at various stages of employment (and unemployment), and had different health insurance benefits. Each participant was paid $10 and assured of confidentiality. Members of the research team moderated the focus group sessions. The results are discussed in terms of the three questions that formed the basis for the study. Although the majority of participants experienced physical, emotional, and financial vulnerability, they wanted to work and were motivated to do so. Barriers to employment included a variety of psychosocial factors, loss of benefits, unstable health, and medical appointments. The research contributed to the expansion of an existing five-construct, six-process ecological model (Syzmanski and Hershenson, 1998). Implications for rehabilitation professionals are discussed.

3.11 SOCIOLOGY

Aging

300. Barrett, Julia, and Stuart Kirk. "Running Focus Groups with Elderly and Disabled Elderly Participants." *Applied Ergonomics* 31, no. 6 (December 2000): 621–29.

The authors describe the purpose of the paper as "methodological," concentrating on the issues and challenges that have implications for future research with elderly participants in focus groups. The study, based in the United Kingdom, sought to determine the needs of this population and their caregivers in terms of the information, advice, and products that would help make life easier (initially, the data were gathered for a publication on this topic but later were broadened to include a questionnaire prepared for a national survey). Three 90-minute focus groups were conducted with 16 elderly participants; the fourth focus group consisted of four caregivers. The moderators were also elderly. Despite prediscussion preparation, the participants experienced difficulties in sustaining attention, in responding to questions in a timely manner, and in retrieving items from memory. Suggestions are offered for ameliorating these problems, which are said to be magnified when interviewing the elderly—especially those with disabilities.

301. Davis-McFarland, Elise, Becki Trickey, Beth Reigart, Lilless Shilling, Karen Wager, and Valerie West. "Using Focus Groups to Identify Lifestyle and Health Issues in the Elderly." *Gerontology and Geriatrics Education* 18, no. 3 (1998): 33–50.

The purpose of the research was to collect preliminary data on lifestyles (such as leisure interests, safety concerns, finances, socialization, and spirituality), as well as the health education needs of a sample of older people residing in the community. Focus group methodology was selected to interview this population. Twenty-six males and females, active in senior citizen centers in Charleston, South Carolina, volunteered to participate in two of six focus group sessions conducted by four trained faculty facilitators, who were associated with the Allied Health Project. College students attended the sessions as observers. The interview schedule contained nine open-ended questions. Discussions were audiotaped, transcribed, and reviewed on a number of levels by several evaluators. The focus group methodology was successful for meeting the goals of the project: seven lifestyle themes were identified, and information was gathered to help design the health education needs assessment component of the Allied Health Project grant. The authors summarize by writing, "The benefits of using focus groups for gerontological research 'cannot be underestimated'" (p. 46). An appendix contains the facilitator's guide.

302. Fisk, Malcolm J. *Guide to Successful Personal Interviews and Focus Groups with Older People*. Occasional Papers on Housing 13. Stirling, England: University of Stirling, Housing Policy and Practice Unit, 2002. 26p.

The guide was written for three audiences: those responsible for the administration and management of social research projects, those experienced with interviewing who are increasingly encountering older people, and those new to the field. Fisk writes that the two data-collection methodologies—individual interviews and focus groups—have been considered together because of the characteristics common to both formats. The social researcher encounters numerous challenges in this area because older people tend to be marginalized due to restricted access environments and a variety of physical and/or sensory impairments. Individual interviews are compared and contrasted with focus groups, the latter seen as a type of individual interview. The author offers suggestions for establishing contact with respondents or participants and for dealing with the problems and ethical issues involved when conducting research with older populations.

303. Grundy, E., and A. Bowling. "Enhancing the Quality of Extended Life Years. Identification of the Oldest Old with a Very Good and Very Poor Quality of Life." *Aging & Mental Health* 3, no. 3 (1999): 199–212.

To obtain an overall, multifaceted indication of quality of life in very old age, the authors sought to identify what proportion of older people experienced multiple difficulties in various domains of life, what proportion had few or no problems, and how these distributions changed over time. Quality of life is defined in terms of the perceptions of physical, psychological, social, and environmental well-being. Two qualitative approaches—baseline face-to-face interviews (630 respondents) and reinterviews (2.5 to 3 years later with 253 respondents), and focus groups—were used to collect the data from men and women ages 85 and over residing in Hackney, a poor suburb of London. Two focus groups were then conducted with a sample of 26 individuals selected from the reinterviews. Five additional focus groups, consisting of 4 to 15 participants each, were held with nonsample members. Nine variables or domains were identified. The study demonstrates the great diversity among the elderly—even in the homogeneous area from which this sample was drawn.

304. Ingersoll-Dayton, Berit, and Chanpen Saengtienchai. "Respect for the Elderly in Asia: Stability and Change." *International Journal of Aging and Human Development* 48, no. 2 (1999): 113–30.

The goals of the research were the following: to examine the ways in which respect for the elderly is manifested in four Asian countries; to explore the extent to which respect has changed over time; and to determine the reasons for these changes. In total, 79 focus groups were conducted with a sample of elderly men and women and their adult children recruited from the Philippines, Singapore, Taiwan, and Thailand. In some of the countries, males and females were interviewed separately for fear that the former would dominate the discussions. The sessions were conducted in the native languages of the participants (sometimes mixed with English). Data were transcribed, translated into English, and transferred to Ethnograph for analysis. The focus group participants identified five distinct manifestations of respect: gestures and manners, tokens, customs and rituals, asking for advice, and obedience. The changing forms of respect noted are attributed to such factors as variations in family structure, education, income, and modernization.

305. Lees, Faith D., Phillip G. Clark, Claudio R. Nigg, and Phillip Newman. "Barriers to Exercise Behavior among Older Adults: A Focus-Group Study." *Journal of Aging and Physical Activity* 13, no. 1 (January 2005): 23–33.

Due to longer life expectancy, rapid population growth, and low exercise participation rates among people age 65 and older, the research sought to identify the factors impeding a more active lifestyle among this group. To inform this topic, six 60- to 90-minute audiotaped focus groups were conducted with 66 participants (57 women, 9 men) recruited from senior housing, senior centers, and swim clubs in Rhode Island. A trained moderator led six focus groups, three with exercisers and three with nonexercisers. Refreshments were served, and each participant received a $10 gift certificate. A total of 12 barriers were identified, with five of them—fear of injury/falling, inertia, time constraints, lack of motivation, and physical ailments—as the most significant. Three members of the exercise groups reported having no impediments to exercise. Implications for exercise intervention programs are discussed.

306. Mehta, Kalyana. "Respect Redefined: Focus Group Insights from Singapore." *International Journal of Aging and Human Development* 44, no. 3 (1997): 205–19.

The research was conducted as part of an international project to examine the social, economic, and health characteristics of the older population in four countries: Taiwan, Thailand, Philippines, and Singapore. For the present study, the author (University of Singapore) considers the meaning of the concept of respect in Singapore, a rapidly changing, highly industrialized Asian multicultural society. A total of 23 focus groups were conducted with 88 elderly individuals and adult children of Chinese, Indian, and Malayan ethnic backgrounds. The participants, recruited primarily through purposive sampling techniques, had varying levels of socioeconomic status. The results indicate that the meaning of respect has shifted—from a position of unquestioned obedience to one of courteous behavior—and that the degree of respect enjoyed by the elderly in the past has decreased. The impact of social change on the findings is discussed. Focus groups are described as an "effective and economical" way of attaining the goals of the research.

307. Powers, Charles B., and Patricia A. Wisocki. "An Examination of the Therapeutic Benefits of Focus Groups on Elderly Worriers." *International Journal of Aging and Human Development* 45, no. 2 (1997): 159–67.

The research was undertaken to determine if "self-designated" worriers, defined as people who reported spending at least 5 percent of the day worrying, experienced any therapeutic benefits from their participation in a focus group project. A total of 21 such individuals (20 women, 1 man), over the age of 70, were recruited from a variety of community sources, such as senior centers and churches. Nine seniors dropped out during the course of the study. Pretests were administered prior to participation in one of six 90-minute audiotaped focus groups conducted over a one-year period. The second author served as moderator. A posttest was administered one year later. Participants said they took part in the study because they wanted to better understand and deal with worry. A significant reduction in worry was evident from pre- to posttest. The experience was viewed as "positive" and "beneficial" by the majority of the seniors.

308. Rogers, Wendy A., Beth Meyer, Neff Walker, and Arthur D. Fisk. "Functional Limitations to Daily Living Tasks in the Aged: A Focus Group Analysis." *Human Factors* 40, no. 1 (March 1998): 111–25.

Focus groups were selected as the qualitative method of choice to gather data on the types of frustrations and difficulties experienced by active older adults in their everyday lives. Eight two-hour audiotaped focus groups were conducted with a heterogeneous sample of 59 males and females ranging in age from 65 to 80 (seven groups) and 80-plus (one group). Recruitment was through a variety of community sources. The same individual (plus assistants) served as moderator for the sessions. Participants' comments were coded along four dimensions, or contexts, in which constraints were faced. Each issue was further coded as to how it could be addressed by the appropriate human factors intervention, such as training, redesign, or some combination of the two. In-depth information was obtained about people's perceptions of their problems and their responses to them.

309. Zsembik, Barbara A., and Zobeida Bonilla. "Eldercare and the Changing Family in Puerto Rico." *Journal of Family Issues* 21, no. 5 (July 2000): 652–74.

The authors consider the challenges faced by older Puerto Ricans with respect to long-term care and quality-of-life needs, and assess the demographic and cultural factors impacting "attitudes, preferences, and expectations" for particular care options. Longer life expectancy, scarce resources, and changes in family structure (especially women's roles) have reduced the numbers of potential family caregivers, thereby increasing the demand for outside services. Two one-hour audiotaped focus groups were conducted with 17 male and female participants recruited by convenience sampling from a rural area in Cayey, Puerto Rico. The participants ranged in age from 50 to 92, but the majority were in their 60s. Each received $15 for participation. The second author, who grew up in rural Puerto Rico, conducted the discussions in Spanish. These were transcribed and coded. The participants identified a wide range of concerns about their future. They expressed the belief that traditional family care provisions are being "rewritten" to accommodate demographic and cultural changes. Focus groups and other qualitative methods are needed to evaluate informal care.

Alcoholism and Drug Abuse

310. Abrahamson, Maria. "Young Women's and Men's Different Worlds of Alcohol, Fear, and Violence in Focus Group Discussions with 18-Year-Olds in Stockholm." *Contemporary Drug Problems* 33, no. 1 (Spring 2006): 3–27.

To determine young men's and women's feelings and behaviors relative to alcohol, drugs, street violence, risks, and fear of assault by a stranger, as well as possible gender similarities and differences concerning these issues, a qualitative approach was undertaken. (The results of the group discussions on alcohol and violence are reported in this article.) Seven two- to three-hour audiotaped focus groups were conducted with 36 18-year-olds (22 girls, 14 boys) recruited by purposive snowball sampling from a suburb in Stockholm. To stimulate discussion, four brief excepts from relevant films were shown. Altogether the group discussions contained references to 13 episodes that dealt with situations involving both alcohol and street violence or fear of assault by strangers: 7 from the three all-female groups, 4 from the two all-male groups, and 2 from the three mixed-gender groups. The narratives and accounts of the participants are compared, contrasted, and discussed in terms of gender similarities and differences, the role of blame, parental and cultural influences, the nature of fear, and the relationship between alcohol and violence.

311. Campbell, Todd C., Christopher Daood, Lynn Catlin, and Alissa Abelson. "Integration of Research and Practice in Substance Use Disorder Treatment: Findings from Focus Groups of Clinicians, Researchers, Educators, Administrators, and Policy Makers." *Journal of Addictions & Offender Counseling* 26, no. 1 (October 2005): 4–14.

Campbell et al. review the impediments to integrating research and practice. Among these are researchers' reliance on statistical versus clinical significance; miscommunication between researchers and clinicians; information overload; supervisors' inadequate training and lack of experience; and reliance on efficacy trials versus effectiveness studies. The article concentrates on strategies for overcoming these barriers in the context of substance abuse treatment in the state of Wisconsin. Focus groups were selected as the method of choice for gaining insight into the perspectives of five key stakeholders: clinicians, researchers, educators, administrators, and policymakers. Five 1.5- to 2-hour audio- and videotaped focus groups were conducted with 37 male and female self-selected participants between the ages of 26 and 65. Campbell and Daood, with research assistants, moderated the discussions. The results of the analysis are discussed in terms of four general areas: definition of research, training/education, current integration, and future integration. Despite some progress, barriers remain. However, all of the groups expressed optimism.

312. Houghton, Stephen, Annemaree Carroll, and Peta Odgers. "Young Children, Adolescents and Alcohol—Part I: Exploring Knowledge and Awareness of Alcohol and Related Issues." *Journal of Child & Adolescent Substance Abuse* 7, no. 3 (1998): 1–29.

The authors observe the paucity of literature devoted to primary school-aged children and alcohol-related issues (most published research deals with adolescents). To fill this gap, from the students' own perspectives, 40 25-minute videotaped focus groups were conducted with 240 boys and girls attending primary school, and 24 40-minute videotaped focus groups were conducted with 192 high-school students. All participants were randomly selected from low-, middle-, and middle-high socioeconomic status areas of the metropolitan region of Perth, a large city in Western Australia. Informed consent was obtained. Six color slides were shown, which depicted adolescents in a variety of alcohol-related situations, and different types of alcoholic and nonalcoholic beverages were also shown. The 35 open-ended questions presented concerned knowledge, health risks, exposure, social image, and others. Nearly 75 percent of the primary school-aged children and almost all of the high-school students reported that they had tasted alcohol, with parents being the primary provider. Prevention/intervention education curriculum materials need to be developed for younger children.

313. Kloep, M., L. B. Hendry, J. E. Ingebrigtsen, A. Glendinning, and G. A. Espnes. "Young People in 'Drinking' Societies? Norwegian, Scottish and Swedish Adolescents' Perceptions of Alcohol Use." *Health Education Research* 16, no. 3 (2001): 279–91.

A multimethod approach was used to examine drinking behaviors and views about alcohol use among young people in rural areas of Norway, Sweden, and Scotland. A total of 4,000 students from these countries were selected to take part in a quantitative, school-based, self-administered survey. A subsample of these students then participated in one of the following qualitative methodologies: essays in Norway, an essay competition in Sweden, and focus groups in Scotland. Five focus groups were conducted in five geographically diverse locations with the following groups: 20 15- to 16-year-old girls, 18 15- to 16-year-old boys, 19 17- to 18-year-old girls, and 16 17- to 18-year-old boys. The study findings, discussed in relation to social and cultural differences, indicate that teenagers in Scotland drank most; those in Norway, the least. Beyond nationality, strong predictors of alcohol use were involvement with peers and participation in commercial leisure activities. Parental influence tended to reduce drinking.

314. Levy, Kira B., Kevin E. O'Grady, Eric D. Wish, and Amelia M. Arria. "An In-Depth Qualitative Examination of the Ecstasy Experience: Results of a Focus Group with Ecstasy-Using College Students." *Substance Use & Misuse*, 40, nos. 9–10 (2005): 1427–41.

The authors provide documentation of the increased use of ecstasy among college students in the United States. Ecstasy is defined as an illicit "club" drug—"a class of synthetic compounds that have various stimulant and hallucinogenic properties" (p. 1,427). To gain a greater understanding of why young people choose to use this drug, a qualitative study was undertaken. Four 60-minute focus groups were conducted with 30 male and female, predominately white college students, who acknowledged that they had used ecstasy at least once in their lives. This convenience sample of students was recruited from fliers posted on the campus of 35,000 students. There was one male-only group, one female-only group, and two mixed-gender groups. Each participant was paid $20. The moderator was a graduate student in clinical psychology. Ten topics were discussed: pill ingredients; mechanism of effects; reasons for starting ecstasy use; risky behaviors and drug use; sexual activity and ecstasy use; ecstasy and polysubstance use; perceived risks; and motivational factors promoting the discontinuance of use. The participants were "uniformly forthright and forthcoming" in their responses. The remainder of the presentation summarizes the discussions relative to each of the topic areas. The small size of the sample is noted as a limitation of the study. Implications for prevention and intervention programs are discussed.

315. Manfredi, Clara, Loretta Lacey, Richard Warnecke, and George Balch. "Method Effects in Survey and Focus Group Findings: Understanding Smoking Cessation in Low-SES African American Women." *Health Education & Behavior* 24, no. 6 (December 1997): 786–800.

Two basic research methods—one quantitative (a survey) and one qualitative (focus groups)—were compared to explore potential method effects in a study of the factors involved in smoking cessation. The authors write from the perspective that the use of multiple methods to gather data may "counterbalance" any bias produced by a single approach, and that "triangulation will produce some form of convergent validation of findings" (p. 786). However, the authors observe that the use of multiple methods may produce "divergent" as well as "convergent" results. The survey involved face-to-face interviews with 248 African-American women of low-socioeconomic status, between the ages of 18 and 39. All were current smokers and were at high risk for continued smoking. The survey instrument contained items on health beliefs and risks, level of motivation to stop smoking, and barriers to cessation. Three years later, eight two-hour videotaped focus groups were conducted with 54 women from the original study. The discussion guide was similar to the survey questionnaire. The two data-collection methods are compared and contrasted in terms of the types and quality of information generated, the strengths and limitations of each mode, and the inconsistencies in the data produced. It is concluded that, when considered together, the multiple findings complement, enhance, and explain each other. Implications for health education research are discussed.

316. Tsiboukli, Anna, and Kim Wolff. "Using Focus Group Interviews to Understand Staff Perceptions from Training in the Therapeutic Community Model." *Journal of Drug Education* 33, no. 2 (2003): 143–57.

Focus group methodology was selected to gain insight—from the perspectives of new staff members themselves—into the training and education needs required for working in therapeutic communities for drug users. The training program examined was part of a study delivered at KETHA, an organization providing outpatient and residential treatment from addiction to rehabilitation in Greece. Two two-hour audiotaped focus groups were conducted three weeks apart with seven predominately female participants. A senior staff member of the organization and an observer used an interview schedule that progressed from general to specific. Content analysis assisted in organizing the material. The participants identified a variety of issues concerning the training program, such as needed changes, the role of the therapist, and advantages and limitations. The participants described the focus groups as "a very good experience."

Children and Adolescents

317. Abrahamson, Maria. "Alcohol in Courtship Contexts: Focus-Group Interviews with Young Swedish Women and Men." *Contemporary Drug Problems* 31, no. 1 (Spring 2004): 3–29.

Focus groups were used to explore the vital role that alcohol plays in facilitating social and sexual interaction among young women and men, as well as the differences and similarities in their positions regarding drinking in a heterosexual courtship context. Nine three- to four-hour focus groups were conducted with a homogeneous sample of 54 males and females in their 20s, recruited from established networks in different parts of Sweden. For interviewing purposes the groups were separated by gender. Seven film excerpts portraying drinking in various settings were shown to stimulate discussion. All of the participants agreed that alcohol helped promote flirtation. However, clear differences appeared in the discussion of the "pick-up" situation, with the women believing that "it is possible to take sexual initiatives while being intoxicated" (p. 3), but self-restraint is also important. For the men, intoxication is "a means of daring to be open and natural with women" (p. 3). The author discusses the dilemmas and contradictions that emerged during the discussions and the impact of traditional and nontraditional gender identities on the study findings.

318. Charlesworth, Leanne Wood, and Mary K. Rodwell. "Focus Groups with Children: A Resource for Sexual Abuse Prevention Program Evaluation." *Child Abuse & Neglect* 21, no. 12 (December 1997): 1205–16.

Focus group methodology was used to assess children's understanding and perceptions of a sexual abuse prevention play. Through the use of a case study, Charlesworth and Rodwell describe the processes involved in the development and implementation of the project, noting the underutilization of the focus group approach in sexual abuse prevention research. The play was presented to elementary school children residing in a mid-Atlantic state. From three schools in the target area, a total of 72 children were selected and assigned to three 30-minute sessions (eight per group). (Teachers' and parents' perceptions were elicited separately.) Two adults moderated and audiotaped the discussions. The results indicate that most of the children liked the play, understood its salient messages, and were capable of articulating this understanding. The focus group method is described as "innovative" and conducive to the discovery of "unanticipated information."

319. Children's Charter Board. *Children's Focus Groups: Young People Voice Their Ideas and Concerns on Social Services in Michigan.* [Lansing]: State of Michigan, Family Independence Agency, 1997. 26p.

In order to gather opinions about their past experiences, a series of focus groups were conducted with a sample of children who had received community services in such areas as foster care, subsidized housing, homeless shelters, and substance abuse. A total of 75 children, ages 6 to 20, participated in 10 focus groups held at numerous locations throughout the state of Michigan. The moderators were experienced, and community leaders were present at four of the sessions. It was found that the young people interviewed expressed themselves very well and appreciated the opportunity to share their views. Participants' perspectives can assist in developing new programs or improving current services. Guidelines are provided for conducting effective focus groups.

320. Grover, Rachel L., and Douglas W. Nangle. "Adolescent Perceptions of Problematic Heterosocial Situations: A Focus Group Study." *Journal of Youth and Adolescence* 32, no. 2 (April 2003): 129–39.

The goal of the research was to develop a taxonomy of teen-identified problematic heterosocial situations. For this purpose, 10 one-hour, audiotaped, gender-separated focus groups were conducted with 58 primarily white male and female students. The sample was drawn from two high schools, one urban and one rural, in the state of Maine. Due to the sensitive nature of the topic, the two trained moderators were matched to the gender of the groups. The students were asked to discuss a variety of social situations involving other-sex interactions with peers or other individuals whom they found difficult. The transcription-based analysis revealed a wide range of problematic heterosocial situations, such as those occurring in these types of relationships: casual, friendship, romantic, work related, and abusive. Three of the nine themes centered around romantic and/or dating relationships. The presence of alcohol or drugs contributed to the difficulties experienced by many of the participants. The focus groups were "effective" for gathering adolescents' perspectives.

321. Large, Andrew, and Jamshid Beheshti. "Focus Groups with Children: Do They Work?" *Canadian Journal of Information and Library Science* 26, nos. 2–3 (June–September 2001): 77–89.

The research represents the final stage in a large-scale research project that was designed to investigate the information-seeking behavior of elementary school children in searching the Internet. Large and Beheshti used focus group methods with this population to elicit opinions on four Web-based portals designed for children: Ask Jeeves for Kids, KidsClick, Lycos Zone, and Yahooligans! Twenty-three children were divided into four single-sex focus groups and asked to use, compare, and evaluate the portals. Three of the one-hour sessions were held in a private home, and the fourth took place in a meeting room. The first-time moderator was trained by an experienced professional. Refreshments were served following the sessions. Each child readily shared her or his likes and dislikes and offered suggestions for improvements. There were possible signs of peer pressure, and some recommendations appeared to be influenced by gender. The authors believe it is necessary for Library and Information Science researchers to also try other techniques, such as contextual inquiry, technology immersion, participatory design, and, especially, cooperative inquiry when designing software for children.

322. Large, Andrew, Jamshid Beheshti, and Tarjin Rahman. "Design Criteria for Children's Web Portals: The Users Speak Out." *Journal of the American Society for Information Science and Technology* 53, no. 2 (2002): 79–94.

As a preliminary step to designing a test portal, focus groups were used to collect and evaluate user feedback regarding four childrens' Web portals: Ask Jeeves for Kids, KidsClick, Lycos Zone, and Yahooligans! Four 60-minute audiotaped focus group sessions were conducted with 23 young Web users, ages 10 to 13, in order to elicit their first impressions, the preferred and disliked features, and suggestions for improvements. (None of the children had previously used the portals selected for the study.) Based on the participants' comments, the authors discuss each portal in terms of four categories: portal goals, visual design, information architecture, and personalization. An ideal portal should be both educational and entertaining, be attractively designed, and provide keyword search facilities and browsable subject categories. All the children readily participated in the discussions with minimal prompting.

323. Mauthner, Melanie. "Methodological Aspects of Collecting Data from Children: Lessons from Three Research Projects." *Children & Society* 11 (1997): 16–28.

The discussion is based on three empirical studies conducted at the University of London. A variety of qualitative methodological approaches were utilized to gather the data. The first study dealt with healthy eating. It involved 29 children, ages 5 to 9, who attended a primary school in southern England. Participant observation, a self-completed food chart, and focus groups featuring structured activities were part of the protocol. Individual interviews were used for the second project on poverty and friendship. In the third study dealing with family communication and health, demographic interviews, a self-completion communication inventory, participant observation, and focus groups were employed to collect data from 26 families. Focus groups, combined with ethnography, are viewed as the "most appropriate" method for interviewing young children. The author discusses the special challenges involved when conducting research with this population, such as acquiring consent, obtaining access, negotiating privacy, ensuring confidentiality, and dealing with the unequal power relationships between adult researchers and children. Children should be "subjects rather than objects" of research.

324. Michell, Lynn. "Combining Focus Groups and Interviews: Telling How It Is; Telling How It Feels." In *Developing Focus Group Research: Politics, Theory and Practice*, edited by Rosaline S. Barbour and Jenny Kitzinger, 36–46. London: Sage, 1999.

Using data from her longitudinal study of teenage lifestyles—specifically how changing peer group structures influence health behaviors—the author demonstrates how it was necessary to supplement data generated by focus group discussions with that gathered by individual interviews. A total of 36 11-year-olds and 39 12-year-olds took part in 21 focus groups and 76 interviews. Ten months later these students were offered the choice of the two methodologies, a choice that resulted in 17 focus groups and 23 interviews. The differences between what the girls' revealed in focus groups as compared to interviews are noteworthy (more so for girls than for boys). Although the focus groups were successful at revealing information on peer group "pecking order," only individual interviews elicited experiences of bullying and victimization.

325. Morgan, Myfanwy, Sara Gibbs, Krista Maxwell, and Nicky Britten. "Hearing Children's Voices: Methodological Issues in Conducting Focus Groups with Children Ages 7–11 Years." *Qualitative Research* 2, no. 1 (2002): 5–20.

The research was designed to "complement" the largely medical view of children with asthma, and "to avoid reliance on parent- or teacher-based accounts" (p. 6). The emphasis is on how to conduct focus groups with children in order to best elicit their perspectives and experiences of living with the disease and its treatment. As part of a larger project undertaken in the United Kingdom, 11 audiotaped focus groups were conducted with a sample of 42 children (ages 7 to 11) drawn from an ethnically and socioeconomically diverse urban area. The authors discuss the methodological challenges involved in recruiting participants; maintaining a balance of power between researcher and participants; creating a conducive atmosphere; asking appropriate questions; managing group dynamics; and accessing children's meanings. Morgan et al. advocate the use of a variety of techniques, such as alternative personality, drawing activities, and role-playing scenarios to supplement the data gathered via focus groups.

326. Nelson-Gardell, Debra. "The Voices of Victims: Surviving Child Sexual Abuse." *Child and Adolescent Social Work Journal* 18, no. 6 (December 2001): 401–16.

The author reports that a wide-ranging electronic search of the scholarly literature published over a 10-year period failed to retrieve a single study that used child or adolescent informants. To obtain personal accounts from this population, five 60- to 90-minute audiotaped focus groups were conducted with 34 girls (ages 10 to 18) recruited from therapy groups in two southeastern states. All girls had experienced sexual abuse (penetration, fondling, and other sexual activities) at some point in their lives—sometimes with multiple offenders. For 18 of the girls, threats or actual violence had accompanied sexual abuse. Nelson-Gardell served as moderator, with others as note takers. Four themes emerged from the analysis, with the importance of "being believed" as the primary finding. According to the girls in this study, being believed was synonymous with being helped. The author believes that obtaining the perspectives of children and adolescents through focus groups can provide "unique and valuable" information and may have some therapeutic value as well. An appendix lists the study questions.

327. Reitsma-Street, Marge, Mechthild Maczewski, and Sheila Neysmith. "Promoting Engagement: An Organizational Study of Volunteers in Community Resource Centres for Children." *Children and Youth Services Review* 22, no. 8 (2000): 651–78.

Focus groups were conducted to gather data on why adults volunteer their time and energy to help others, as well as their perceptions of the organizational factors that foster or discourage meaningful volunteer work. The settings for the study were three Canadian multicultural community resource centers for children. A series of nine focus groups were conducted with 46 low-income male and female volunteers who closely represented the variety of clients served by each center. The data from the focus groups were combined with data gathered from other sources: calculations of volunteer hours, participant observation, and documents. It was found that volunteers valued engaging in relationship building, completing important tasks, and having a role in decision making. Organizational factors that promote volunteerism were found to be adequate financial resources, the support of paid staff, and opportunities for community governance.

328. Singh, Nirbhay N., Jeri Baker, Alan S.W. Winton, and Dawn K. Lewis. "Semantic Equivalence of Assessment Instruments across Cultures." *Journal of Child and Family Studies* 9, no. 2 (2000): 123–34.

The goal of the research was to highlight the need for better assessment instruments for children and adolescents with emotional and behavioral disorders. Numerous instruments have been developed from a middle-class Caucasian perspective and therefore may not be appropriate for multicultural populations. In addition to age, gender, and ethnicity/race, diversity may take many forms — nationality, language, religious beliefs, socioeconomic status, social class, sexual orientation, and others. To obtain feedback on the Youth Adjustment Indicator (YAI), a commonly used evaluation tool containing 23 behavioral items, four audiotaped focus groups were conducted with African-American and Caucasian parents of children with emotional and behavioral disorders. The participants were interviewed in separate racial groups by ethnically mixed moderators, who alternated groups. Different interpretations of the YAI were evident between and within ethnic groups.

Criminal Justice

329. Hardy, Mary, Cheryl Teruya, Douglas Longshore, and Yih-Ing Hser. "Initial Implementation of California's Substance Abuse and Crime Prevention Act: Findings from Focus Groups in Ten Counties." *Evaluation and Program Planning* 28, no. 2 (May 2005): 221–32.

In November 2000, the voters of California passed Proposition 36, which was enacted into law as the Substance Abuse and Crime Prevention Act (SACPA). The act mandated a large-scale shift in California's criminal justice policy: In lieu of incarceration, nonviolent drug-involved adult offenders could be sentenced to probation with community-based, court-monitored treatment. As part of a larger effort to assess the implementation issues that arose in the state's 58 counties during SACPA's first year, and to gain insight into stakeholders' experiences with and attitudes toward the law, focus group methods were selected to gather information in 10 counties. Ten 1.5- to 2.5-hour audiotaped focus groups (one per county) were conducted with 136 male and female participants. These included representatives of drug and alcohol program administration, probation, the courts, prosecutors, public defenders, parole officers, treatment providers, and others.

The authors discuss how they adapted a previously developed analytic framework (Winter 1990) to examine four interrelated sociopolitical processes involved in implementation: policy interpretation, target group behavior, agency and interagency practices, and street-level bureaucratic behavior. The focus groups helped inform the implementation progress. Some participants questioned the validity of focus groups and other qualitative methods.

330. Kakar, Suman. "Understanding the Causes of Disproportionate Minority Contact: Results of Focus Group Discussions." *Journal of Criminal Justice* 34, no. 4 (2006): 369–81.

A multimethod approach (official records, focus groups, and in-depth interviews) was used to explore the causes of disproportionate minority contact (DMC). This concept means that "a disproportionately large number of minority youth come into contact with the juvenile justice system in relation to their representation in the general population" (p. 370). These minority groups are African American, Native American, Asian American, Pacific Islander, Hispanic/Latino, or any other non-Caucasian group. Kakar provides a historical overview of DMC, including the federal legislation designed to reduce it. To elicit the perspectives of the multiple stakeholders involved, four 90-minute focus groups were conducted with 60 participants. Each group included representatives from law enforcement, juvenile justice, school personnel, families and communities, business, and community, faith-based, and grassroots organizations. Permission for audiotaping the sessions was not granted. Two researchers led the discussions. The causes of DMC, described as "multi-faceted and complex," are classified into six categories: system, social, family/parental, educational, individual, and economic. The author concludes that all sectors of society must work together to reduce DMC.

331. Kakar, Suman, Marie-Luise Friedemann, and Linda Peck. "Girls in Detention: The Results of Focus Group Discussion Interviews and Official Records Review." *Journal of Contemporary Criminal Justice* 18, no. 1 (February 2002): 57–73.

Two approaches—official records and focus group discussions—were used to explore the psychological, societal, familial, and economic risk factors associated with the rising rates of delinquency among young women, an underresearched area in the literature (most studies have focused on how boys enter the juvenile justice system). Three 90-minute focus groups were conducted with a convenience sample of 30 black, white, and Hispanic 12- to 18-year-old participants, all female residents in a County Regional Detention Center in South Florida. Two experienced researchers conducted the discussions in the center's cafeteria. Permission for audiotaping was not granted. The questions concerned the type, structure, male-female role, methods of discipline, award systems, and the emotional context of the girls' families. Significant delinquency risk factors were identified:

school discipline problems; childhood maltreatment, such as physical and sexual abuse; family and parental incarceration; alcohol and other substance abuse; and violence. An examination of 100 official intake records supported this finding. Effective prevention and intervention programs must recognize the importance of the family environment within which the girls live.

Disabilities, People with

332. Balch, George I., and Donna M. Mertens. "Focus Group Design and Group Dynamics: Lessons from Deaf and Hard of Hearing Participants." *American Journal of Evaluation* 20, no. 2 (Spring–Summer 1999): 265–77.

Focus groups were used to identify the "unaddressed" and "unanticipated" communication needs among deaf and hard-of-hearing individuals who have had experience with the U.S. court system (as a victim of a crime, a defendant, a witness, or for jury duty). A total of 32 such individuals (who were demographically diverse in other characteristics) were recruited and divided into five groups that were based on the degree of disability and other factors. An incentive of $50 was offered to each participant. The three-hour focus group sessions were conducted in four different cities, with the primary author serving as moderator and a deaf, signing social worker as co-moderator. Mertens was the "evaluator." The sessions were audio- and videotaped in centrally located market research focus group facilities. Balch and Mertens reflect on eight "lessons" learned from the study, the most important being that focus group methodology proved successful for identifying many experiences and unmet communication needs relating to hearing impairment. Advantages of the approach include group interaction, open-ended interviewing, observation by stakeholders, and time efficiency.

333. Chan, Simon K. K., and David W. K. Man. "Barriers to Returning to Work for People with Spinal Cord Injuries: A Focus Group Study." *Work* 25, no. 4 (2005): 325–32.

Chan and Man note the low rate of reemployment among Asians who have experienced spinal cord injuries (SCIs). Although there is a paucity of literature on this topic in Hong Kong, victims of SCIs report disillusionment, disappointment, and high stress associated with their work roles. Focus group methodology was selected to gain an understanding of participants' attitudes, feelings, beliefs, experiences, and reactions toward perceived job-related impediments. Three two-hour audiotaped focus groups were conducted with 16 participants, both employed and unemployed, recruited by purposive sampling. One of the researchers asked a series of open-ended questions that concerned some phase of the reemployment process. The focus group members identified a range of physical, psychological, and environmental barriers. Rehabilitation interventions are deemed necessary.

334. Crowe, Teresa V. "Using Focus Groups to Create Culturally Appropriate HIV Prevention Material for the Deaf Community." *Qualitative Social Work* 2, no. 3 (September 2003): 289–308.

Due to a number of factors, members of the deaf and hard-of-hearing (HOH) community are acknowledged to be at risk for HIV transmission. Three organizations—the Washington, D.C., Department of Health, the HIV and AIDS Administration, and Deaf-REACH (a D.C. community service center)—sponsored a study to assess information needs and develop prevention materials aimed at this population. Crowe, a hearing woman at Gallaudet University, reports on five focus groups conducted with 31 participants with different ethnicity, age, and educational backgrounds. All group members used American Sign Language (ASL) as their primary mode of communication. The moderator was fluent in ASL. Two certified interpreters recorded the data. Information needs were identified, and an HIV prevention poster and condom card were designed and evaluated. Although participants exhibited a lack of knowledge about HIV, discussions were "lively and energetic." Group dynamics served to "enhance" data quality. Crowe cautions that traditional educational and outreach programs may not address the unique cultural and linguistic requirements of deaf and HOH individuals.

335. Gilson, Stephen French, Elizabeth P. Cramer, and Elizabeth DePoy. "Redefining Abuse of Women with Disabilities: A Paradox of Limitation and Expansion." *Affilia* 16, no. 2 (Summer 2001): 220–35.

According to a national study, 62 percent of women, disabled or nondisabled, have experienced emotional, physical, or sexual abuse at some point in their lives. For disabled women the abuse may be longer in duration, performed by a greater number of perpetrators (including health-care workers and attendants), and take the form of sexual assault. These women have fewer options for escape or for resolving issues. To further examine the types of abuse and requirements for services and resources, the authors conducted two audiotaped focus groups at centers for independent living in a southeastern state. The first focus group was convened in an urban area with 10 self-selected women. The second, which took place in a rural setting, involved five women and one man. Some members of each group were professionals in the disability or medical services field. The sessions were facilitated by the authors and two graduate students. QSR NUD*IST and the principles of grounded theory assisted with analysis and coding. The findings indicate that although there were commonalities of abuse among disabled and nondisabled women, the former have "unique" experiences requiring specialized services.

336. Iacono, Teresa, Susan Balandin, and Linda Cupples. "Focus Group Discussions of Literacy Assessment and World Wide Web–Based Reading

Intervention." *AAC: Augmentative and Alternative Communication* 17, no. 1 (March 2001): 27–38.

The 13 Australian participants (4 women, 9 men) in the study were mostly persons with cerebral palsy, with several others having brain damage or a neurologic condition—all presenting with severe communication disorders and nonambulatory status. To gain insight into the perspectives of this group relative to a reading program, a series of one-hour focus groups followed a trial period of Web-based reading intervention. A note taker recorded the exchanges, which were transcribed and subjected to content analysis. The actual questions and response summaries are provided. The brainstorming of the program aided future strategies and helped to deal with such practical problems as scheduling, changing of appointments, and breakdowns in communication. The research process was enhanced by permitting the participants to air their views.

337. Raczka, Roman. "A Focus Group Enquiry into Stress Experienced by Staff Working with People with Challenging Behaviours." *Journal of Intellectual Disabilities* 9, no. 2 (June 2005): 167–77.

A total of 19 direct-care staff employed by three registered care homes in the United Kingdom participated in three 60-minute focus groups. The study was designed to collect information from these caregivers regarding their experiences with, and responses to, working with individuals presenting with learning disabilities. These individuals had a variety of significant "challenging" behaviors (such as physical aggression, self-injurious tendencies, and antisocial displays), often accompanied by mental health needs and sensory and physical disabilities. Analysis of the discussions identified four major themes—that is, areas of concern among the staff. Although the majority of the views expressed were negative, positive experiences and perceptions were also reported. Stress levels were high among the service providers. Raczka concludes that focus group interviewing is an "appropriate" method of inquiry.

338. Woodring, Jonathan C., Susan M. Foley, Gabriella Santoro Rado, Keith R. Brown, and Doris M. Hamner. "Focus Groups and Methodological Reflections: Conscientious Flexibility in the Field." *Journal of Disability Policy Studies* 16, no. 4 (Spring 2006): 248–58.

Focus group interviewing was selected as an initial component of a mixed-method, five-year longitudinal research project designed to elicit the perspectives of people with mental and/or physical disabilities with regard to how recent policy initiatives—specifically employment policies—affected their lives. Throughout, the authors emphasize the methodological design challenges they encountered and the thought processes necessary for resolving the dilemmas. A total of 58 ethnically diverse males and females who used federal income supports, vocational rehabilitation, and other disability services, were recruited from three cities: Atlanta, Newark, and New Orleans. Nine 90-minute audiotaped focus groups were conducted at the chosen sites. The special difficulties involved when interviewing people with disabilities include adjustments in physical accommodations, possible need for the use of American Sign Language interpreters, additional time requirements for answering questions, "groupthink," and ethical considerations. Smaller group size is recommended. Focus groups are seen as a "remarkably diverse and flexible" research method.

Ethnic Groups

339. Bradford, Lisa, Renée A. Meyers, and Kristine A. Kane. "Latino Expectations of Communicative Competence: A Focus Group Interview Study." *Communication Quarterly* 47, no. 1 (Winter 1999): 98–117.

The research extends the work of J. N. Martin et al. (1994) in three ways: (1) by using focus groups as the data collection approach; (2) by examining the comparative importance of Martin's behavioral categories for different contexts; and (3) by identifying additional behaviors. Communicative competence was explored in four contexts: intracultural-social, intracultural-task, intercultural-social, and intercultural-task. Five videotaped focus groups were conducted with 18 male and female Latino students recruited from a Midwestern university. Group assignment was based on the level of acculturation. The sessions were moderated by two Latinos, one from each gender. Four questions and four scenarios representing different contexts were presented for discussion. Overall support was found for seven of Martin et al.'s eight behavioral categories, and additional behaviors were identified. Focus groups are seen as a "promising venue" for continuing research with this population due to the technique's compatibility with Latino values (such as *simpatia* and deference to power) and communication style preferences.

340. Jonsson, Inger M., Lillemor R-M. Hallberg, and Inga-Britt Gustafsson. "Cultural Foodways in Sweden: Repeated Focus Group Interviews with Somalian Women." *International Journal of Consumer Studies* 26, no. 4 (December 2002): 328–39.

The goal of the research was to gain insight into what "feeding the family" means to Somalian women residing in Sweden. This "small but distinctive" population of about 20,000 men, women, and children immigrated to Sweden in the 1990s and encountered an unusual number of barriers to assimilation in the host country. The authors address issues surrounding the food choices presented to this group outside their homes (for example, in child care, schools, and hospitals), in contrast to their own preferences based on cultural identity and traditions. Using a longitudinal design, two rounds of focus groups were conducted with a sample of Somalian women recruited by Somalian "gatekeepers": six initial focus groups had 33 participants, followed by four focus groups with 24 participants. A moderator with an assistant well known in refugee and immigration groups facilitated the discussions. The principles of grounded theory assisted analysis. Factors both within the family and beyond were found to influence food choice and traditions. The women interviewed struggled with cultural identity, a matter primarily decided by the husband.

341. Madriz, Esther I. "Using Focus Groups with Lower Socioeconomic Status Latina Women." *Qualitative Inquiry* 4, no. 1 (March 1998): 114–28.

To gain insight into women's perspectives on how the fear of crime has an impact on their everyday lives, 10 focus groups were conducted with a sample of women residing in New York City and northern New Jersey. The use of focus groups is framed within the context of feminist methodologies. The author discusses the special challenges, especially culturally oriented ones, encountered when attempting to locate and select lower socioeconomic status Latina women, noting that conventional recruitment strategies are inadequate for this population. Personal networking is advocated. Madriz, a Latina, believes that matching the researcher's race and ethnicity to that of the participants enhances rapport and reduces "distance" between researcher and respondents. Language issues are discussed, and the importance of group homogeneity is stressed. Focus groups are seen to provide a "provocative and unique" way of listening to the voices of an often marginalized and oppressed group of women.

342. Matei, Sorin, and Sandra J. Ball-Rokeach. "Real and Virtual Social Ties: Connection in the Everyday Lives of Seven Ethnic Neighborhoods." *American Behavioral Scientist* 45, no. 3 (November 2001): 550–64.

The connection between online and offline social ties in seven Los Angeles ethnically marked residential areas is the subject of this study. The multimethod approach included telephone and mail surveys, a media census, focus groups, mental mapping, and structured interviews. The primary technique utilized was a random telephone survey in selected neighborhoods. In total, 115 Internet-connected telephone survey respondents and their children were offered the opportunity to participate in focus groups and a mail survey. The focus groups highlighted how Internet social relations are part of the lives of each participant within her or his family and community. The findings indicate that online connections linked respondents of similar ethnicity or countries of origin, and that new online social connections are mostly within the ethnic group. The authors propose that the greater the degree of belonging to real communities, the higher the likelihood for interaction online. The data generated by this study surveyed only one ethnicity per study area, with the suggestion that future research sample multiple ethnicities.

148

Part III

343. Mayeda, David Tokiharu, Meda Chesney-Lind, and Jennifer Koo. "Talking Story with Hawaii's Youth: Confronting Violent and Sexualized Perceptions of Ethnicity and Gender." *Youth & Society* 33, no. 1 (September 2001): 99–128.

The research goals were to explore how at-risk adolescents living in Hawaii establish their ethnic and gender identities within various social environments and to investigate possible links to delinquency and violence. The authors observe that Hawaii has one of the most ethnically diverse populations in the nation, with many young people coming from economically and culturally marginalized backgrounds. In addition, boys of certain ethnicities have a tendency to derive their self-concept (and even their self-worth) from engaging in delinquent behavior. Girls engage in such behavior as a reaction to being "ignored in and/or abused by" mainstream institutions. To gather the required data, the researchers used the "talking story," a phrase referring to "easygoing conversation" in Hawaii—in this case, focus groups. A total of 58 ethnically diverse male and female adolescents, recruited from agencies in Oahu, participated in 13 75-minute audiotaped sessions. (Two individual interviews were also conducted.) The moderators were of mixed ethnicity and in their mid-20s. Two free movie passes were offered. The authors conclude that, in addition to gender and ethnic issues, theoretical frameworks must incorporate interethnic violence, sexual exploitation, immigration patterns, and social and class constraints.

344. Nevid, Jeffrey S., and Nelly L. Sta. Maria. "Multicultural Issues in Qualitative Research." *Psychology & Marketing* 16, no. 4 (July 1999): 305–25.

The purpose of the presentation was to highlight some of the special challenges encountered when conducting qualitative research—especially focus groups—with minority participants or within minority communities. (Focus group methodology is noted as one of the most commonly used forms of the qualitative approach.) Investigators are advised that an appreciation of and a sensitivity to cultural differences and traditions is required when working with individuals of different racial and ethnic backgrounds. The authors discuss the issues of commonality and homogeneity among group members, as well as the merits of matching moderators to participants along racial/ethnic lines. Moderators need to be fluent in the language of the participants. Single-gender versus mixed-gender interviewing is evaluated, as is the impact of anonymity, the disclosure of personal information, cultural mistrust and suspicion, and differences in beliefs and values. A "major hurdle" is seen to be the recruitment of sufficient numbers of research participants. Most of the examples provided are from studies dealing with African Americans, Asians, Hispanics, and Native Americans.

345. Pérez, Miguel A., Helda L. Pinzon, and Raffy R. Luquis. "Focus Groups among Latino Farmworker Populations: Recommendations for Implementation." *Migrationworld* 26, no. 3 (1998): 19–23.

The authors review the key features of the focus group process within the context of a study of a sample of Latino farmworkers (mushroom industry) in the state of Pennsylvania. To validate several hypotheses concerning HIV and AIDS, 12 90-minute audiotaped focus groups were conducted with men living in camps for migrant farmworkers. The authors and an assistant moderated the sessions. The following are among the recommendations offered for interviewing this population: (1) involve community leaders in the project; (2) consider the ethnicity of the participants; (3) limit group composition to four to eight members; (4) match the gender and ethnicity of the moderator to the participants; (5) use the language of the migrants (usually Spanish); and (6) hold the sessions within the local community.

346. Swain, Carol M., Kyra R. Greene, and Christine Min Wotipka. "Understanding Racial Polarization on Affirmative Action: The View from Focus Groups." In *Color Lines: Affirmative Action, Immigration, and Civil Rights Options for America*, edited by John David Skrentny, 214–37. Chicago: University of Chicago Press, 2001.

The focus groups utilized for this study were formed in 1995, with six groups comprised of 10 to 12 members each. Two locations were selected for data collection. The first was in Edison, New Jersey, and consisted of separate groups of African Americans, Euro-Americans, and Latinos. The other location was New York City, with a second group of African Americans, a second group of Euro-Americans, and a group of Asian Americans. Each two-hour session was led by a moderator of the same race or ethnicity as the participants. Professional firms were commissioned to conduct the sessions. The results indicate that African Americans did not define affirmative action in terms of preferential treatment and perceived quotas differently from the other groups. Although African Americans viewed quotas as a "potentially harmful restriction," they did not oppose them, believing that the practice ensured at least a minimum level of protection against discrimination. The authors found a "striking difference in the greater support" of affirmative action by Asian Americans than by Latinos. Latinos "adamantly disapproved" of the harm done to minorities by affirmative action, whereas Asian Americans agreed that it had "little to do with them." The authors maintain that no consensus on affirmative action policies has been reached in the United States, and that part of the problem is a lack of a shared language and understanding.

Marriage and the Family

347. Adams, Jerome F., and Peter E. Maynard. "Evaluating Training Needs for Home-Based Family Therapy: A Focus Group Approach." *American Journal of Family Therapy* 28, no. 1 (2000): 41–52.

Focus group interviewing was used to gather information for possible revisions to the training curricula offered by Marriage and Family Therapy, a home-based services program. Two rounds of focus group discussions were carried out with a group of 12 student trainees, therapists, and supervisors. The research team, consisting of two senior faculty members and three graduate students, developed the interview guide for round one. Eight topic areas considered necessary for home-based practice were identified. For the second round, a rating scale was mailed to the same participants (except for one supervisor), who subsequently were asked to discuss the rankings. The research team moderated both rounds and analyzed the data with the constant comparison method. The authors discuss the results for the eight areas in which training programs and agencies might improve students' preparation for home-based care. Participants expressed a high level of satisfaction with the experience. Focus groups are "highly recommended" as a technique for assessing training needs.

348. Ansay, Sylvia J., Daniel F. Perkins, and Colonel John Nelson. "Interpreting Outcomes: Using Focus Groups in Evaluation Research." *Family Relations* 53, no. 3 (April 2004): 310–16.

The research goal was to examine the role that stakeholders' (in this case military parents) perspectives play in program outcomes. To evaluate the effectiveness of the Youth Action Program (YAP), a prevention program initiated for the U.S. Department of Defense and funded by the U.S. Air Force for military dependent adolescents at risk, the researchers conducted a two-hour focus group session with 19 families (both parents and children) whose children had completed either the one-year or the 18-month program. One member of the evaluation team moderated the discussions, which were audiotaped, transcribed, and analyzed. A narrative approach to data analysis, that is, "combining theme analysis with a systematic interpretive approach" (p. 310), was used. The results indicate that parents were unanimous in reporting favorable social and academic outcomes as well as improved parent and child relationships as a result of the YAP experience. The authors conclude that focus groups "provide a dynamic means to portray programs in action" (p. 316), thereby benefiting evaluators, program staff, policymakers, and administrators.

349. Carolan, Marsha T., Guiti Bagherinia, Rumaya Juhari, Jackie Himelright, and Monica Mouton-Sanders. "Contemporary Muslim Families: Research and Practice." *Contemporary Family Therapy* 22, no. 1 (March 2000): 67–79.

The authors observed the cultural and individual diversity within Muslim families living in the United States. These families include immigrants from the Middle East, Asia, and Africa, as well as African Americans who have converted to Islam. The research was undertaken to help family professionals work more effectively with this clientele and to more fully understand the influence of religious beliefs on daily practices. Two qualitative research approaches—focus groups and interviews—were used to gather the data from a convenience sample of approximately 40 Muslims residing in a Midwestern metropolitan area. In phase one of the study, five audiotaped focus groups were conducted, four with women and one with men. Ten interviews with couples were conducted in the second phase (with different individuals from the focus groups). Members of the research team served as moderators. The findings indicate an emphasis on gender respect rather than on gender equality, the importance of family and extended family, and the dominance of Islam in daily life. Most participants said they would choose a professional who was Muslim.

350. Glaser, Karen. "Consensual Unions in Two Costa Rican Communities: An Analysis Using Focus Group Methodology." *Journal of Comparative Family Studies* 30, no. 1 (Winter 1999): 57–77.

Latin American countries have a high incidence of consensual unions, defined as "a union in which couples share a household without being formally married" (p. 57). Glaser hypothesized that a woman's status, reflected by her relationships with men, influences her choice of union—consensual or legal. Two ethnically and culturally diverse Costa Rican communities were selected for the research because they have the highest frequency of informal unions in this country. Eight 60-minute audiotaped focus groups (with an average of five participants per group) were conducted with a sample of men and women representative of both types of unions. The discussions centered around their motivations, decisions, and expectations that affect union choice and if these factors affect family planning activities. The results indicate that although informal unions are less stable, they are "desirable alternatives to marriage." Men yield greater authority in both situations. The implications for fertility are discussed.

351. Hill, Miriam R., and Volker Thomas. "Strategies for Racial Identity Development: Narratives of Black and White Women in Interracial Partner Relationships." *Family Relations* 49, no. 2 (April 2000): 193–200.

A multimethod approach (individual interviews, questionnaires, a focus group, and a research journal) was used to generate questions to be examined in future studies. The purpose of the study was to investigate how women involved in interracial (black/white) heterosexual relationships described, retrospectively, how they had been active in shaping the development of their racial identity over the course of that relationship. To place the study in context, the authors review three theoretical frameworks for understanding the concept: racial identity development, social constructionism, and feminism. In order to elicit "thick" descriptions of racial identity development from the participants' own perspectives, women in interracial relationships were recruited through posters and snowball sampling techniques. In total, three white women and three black women completed questionnaires and received individual interviews. The audiotaped focus group was conducted with four white women and one black woman. The authors employed grounded theory to assist analysis, and triangulation to enhance validity. The results indicate that although all of the women interviewed had experienced racism, they used various strategies—blocking, transforming, and generating—"to empower themselves to self identity."

352. Michaels, Marcia L. "The Stepfamily Enrichment Program: A Preliminary Evaluation Using Focus Groups." *American Journal of Family Therapy* 28, no. 1 (January–March 2000): 61–73.

The author writes that although the stepfamily is becoming one of the most prevalent family forms, evidence indicates that this type of arrangement is at higher risk for dysfunction than the "intact" family. Early interventions that target remarried couples have been shown to be crucial for successful stepfamily formation. A pilot study was undertaken to evaluate the Stepfamily Enrichment Program, which was designed to help such families negotiate this process. Eight remarried couples were recruited: three were simple stepfamilies, five were complex. All of the couples had children at home. None had serious relationship problems. A five-week multicouple intervention took place in two locations: a large metropolitan area and a college town. Following these meetings, one audiotaped focus group, led by a therapist with moderator training, was convened to discuss the program. Positive behavior and attitude changes were reported by the couples. Suggestions are made for program modifications.

353. Piercy, Fred P., and Katherine M. Hertlein. "Focus Groups in Family Therapy Research." In *Research Methods in Family Therapy*, edited by Douglas H. Sprenkle and Fred P. Piercy, 85–99. 2nd ed. New York: Guilford Press, 2005.

The presentation is divided into two parts: methodology and discussion. The methodology section covers general issues such as research purposes and questions (five examples of family-therapy-related focus group research questions are listed); sampling and selection procedures (it is advised that the size of the group reflect participants' level of involvement in an issue); data-collection procedures (the activities of the moderator and the nature of the questions and interview guide); data analysis (with discussion of content analysis); and reporting the results (three models are described). In the discussion section the authors comment on the advantages and disadvantages of the focus group method, consider some of the "unique" ethical issues, and offer advice on how to enhance the reliability and validity of a project. Family therapy researchers can use the technique as a needs assessment tool, to identify and understand problems, and to evaluate existing services.

354. Sanchez, Laura, Steven L. Nock, James D. Wright, and Constance T. Gager. "Setting the Clock Forward or Back? Covenant Marriage and the 'Divorce Revolution.'" *Journal of Family Issues* 23, no. 1 (January 2002): 91–120.

Focus groups were utilized to elicit people's perspectives concerning marriage, divorce, and legal reform. Central to the discussion are two types of marriage: the traditional, with standard no-fault divorce provisions, and the covenant, a newer form whose key provision is that divorce requires proof of fault. Covenant marriage was first enacted in 1997 in the state of Louisiana, with Arizona and Arkansas following soon after (at least 20 other states are considering similar legislation). In total, three focus groups were conducted with approximately 36 Louisiana residents, who were selected to represent a range of views: covenant married couples, feminist activists, and poor women living in public housing. Although all stakeholder groups expressed concern about the effects of divorce on children, there were major disagreements as to whether family life is in decline and whether the institution of marriage is suffering. The pros and cons of covenant marriage and the political ramifications of this type of union are discussed.

355. Savaya, Rivka, and Orna Cohen. "A Qualitative cum Quantitative Approach to Construct Definition in a Minority Population: Reasons for Divorce among Israeli-Arab Women." *Journal of Sociology & Social Welfare* 25, no. 4 (December 1998): 157–79.

A multimethod research approach, qualitative and quantitative, was used to explore the reasons for divorce among Israeli-Arab women, a population that has experienced a rise in divorce rates over the past few decades (nearly doubling between the 1960s and the mid-1990s). The authors (Tel Aviv University) review the aspects of Israeli-Arab culture that might contribute to this dramatic increase. The setting for the study was the town of Jaffa. To gain an understanding of women's motives for divorce, two qualitative methods were undertaken: four face-to-face interviews and one two-hour focus group involving five divorced women. The discussions were in Arabic, which was later translated into Hebrew. A total of 36 statements of reasons for divorce were generated. W. M. Trochim's concept mapping, a quantitative technique, was then used to identify and group the relevant variables. The combined methodologies contributed to the design of a culturally sensitive research instrument appropriate for non-Western women. High levels of physical violence, sexual torment, emotional abuse, and/or mental illness or addiction prompted these women to end their marriages.

356. Spencer, Renee, Judith V. Jordan, and Jenny Sazama. "Growth-Promoting Relationships between Youth and Adults: A Focus Group Study." *Families in Society* 85, no. 3 (July–September 2004): 354–62.

Using a relational-cultural theory as a framework, the authors explore the factors that contribute to growth-fostering relationships between adults and young people, and the role of listening in these relationships. Seven 60- to 90-minute audiotaped focus groups were conducted with 91 male and female children and adolescents (ages 7 to 18) who had been recruited through after-school and school-based programs and church youth groups in a large metropolitan area in the northeastern United States. The groups were ethnically and socioeconomically diverse. A minimum of one adult and one youth leader facilitated the sessions. The thematic analysis highlighted the high value the participants placed on respect, mutuality, and authenticity in their relationships with adults as well as their desire to spend time and have fun with adults. Barriers to relationship building and the importance of caring adults are discussed. An appendix provides the question guide.

357. Umaña-Taylor, Adriana J., and Mayra Y. Bámaca. "Conducting Focus Groups with Latino Populations: Lessons from the Field." *Family Relations* 53, no. 3 (April 2004): 261–72.

The authors describe the published scholarship on Latino families as "limited." To investigate how Latino parents transmit their culture to their adolescent children, a focus group project was undertaken with a total of 119 Colombian, Guatemalan, Mexican, and Puerto Rican mothers. Umaña-Taylor and Bámaca discuss the special design considerations required when working with this population, beginning with the social characteristics of the group, such as homogeneity, age, social class, and, especially, language. The social characteristics of the moderator and note taker are also critical to a successful group experience. Community organizations and agencies, word-of-mouth, advertisements, and face-to-face contact were helpful for gaining access to Latino populations. The likelihood of participation was increased by reminder calls, compensation, evening meetings, child care, and assistance with transportation. Confidentiality assurances and hospitality were important to the participants. Among the recommendations are that the research team should be diverse, and that at least two individuals be involved in the transcription/translation process.

Sex and Sexual Behavior

358. Allen, Louisa. "Managing Masculinity: Young Men's Identity Work in Focus Groups." *Qualitative Research* 5, no. 1 (2005): 35–57.

Male sexuality, or rather the "talk" about sexuality by heterosexual males in a focus group setting, is the subject of the article. Allen refers to the "management of their own sexual identities" and "what they reveal and conceal about their sexual selves" (p. 35) as shown in the responses. A total of four focus groups were conducted with 20 teenagers (ages 17 to 19), with 4 to 10 participants per group. Two of the groups were all male, one group had one female, and the remaining group had an equal number of each gender. The author, who served as facilitator, suggests that focus groups of young people can reflect the inner workings of the peer group. Considerable discussion is devoted to the impact of the facilitator's gender (female) on the all-male groups. Allen notes that despite her efforts to avoid eliciting "hyper-masculine identity," her presence did not curb expressions of masculinity (as, for example, through the objectification of a woman by referring to her as a "chick," a term designed to demote her status).

359. Bakopanos, Christine, and Sandra M. Gifford. "The Changing Ties That Bind: Issues Surrounding Sexuality and Health for Greek Parents and Their Australian-Born Sons and Daughters." *Journal of Family Issues* 22, no. 3 (April 2001): 358–85.

The research was part of a larger three-part multistage qualitative and quantitative study carried out over a four-year period in Melbourne, Australia. The three parts of the study were the Non-English-Speaking-Background Women's Sexual Health Project; the Men, Culture and Sexual Health Project; and the Greek Parent Project. Each project had two stages. The first stage involved individual interviews and/or focus groups; a questionnaire was administered in the second stage. In this article the authors report on the Greek component of the qualitative stage. The purpose was to examine family context of second-generation adult children and their parents with regard to sexual behavior and expectations, changing gender roles, and health issues. The protocol called for individual interviews with 37 young adult Greek Australian men and women and seven Greek parents. Two same-gender and two mixed-gender audiotaped focus groups were conducted with 25 parents. Both the interviews and the focus group sessions were conducted in Greek, translated, and transcribed. The results are discussed in terms of the issues previously mentioned and the need for prevention strategies for sexually transmitted diseases (STDs) and HIV/AIDS.

360. Cameron, Kenzie A., Laura F. Salazar, Jay M. Bernhardt, Nan Burgess-Whitman, Gina M. Wingood, and Ralph J. DiClemente. "Adolescents' Experience with Sex on the Web: Results from Online Focus Groups." *Journal of Adolescence* 28, no. 4 (August 2005): 535–40.

The purpose of the research was to gain insight into Internet users' experiences with, exposure to, and perceptions of two types of Web sites: sexually oriented Web sites (SOWs) and sexually explicit Web sites (SEWs). Four 60- to 90-minute Web-based focus groups were conducted with 40 male and female adolescents (ages 14 to 17) stratified by age and gender. All were regular online users who were recruited from responders to online surveys for Harris Interactive, a market research company. The interview protocol was similar to an online chat room: the moderator asked the key questions and the participants posted comments and responded to the moderator and to other participants. Anonymity was ensured. Each online user received $40 for participation. High levels of exposure to the SOWs and the SEWs were reported, some intentional, some unsolicited. Gender differences were pronounced. Participants perceived no impact on themselves from exposure to the SEWs.

361. Crossley, Michele L. "The 'Armistead' Project: An Exploration of Gay Men, Sexual Practices, Community Health Promotion and Issues of Empowerment." *Journal of Community & Applied Social Psychology* 11 (2001): 111–23.

The "Armistead" Project, a government-funded health promotion project conducted in the northwest of England, was designed "to provide gay men with information and opportunities to develop the personal and social skills required to live healthier lifestyles, including practising safer sex" (p. 114). The evaluation of the project called for a triangulated approach—in this case, the use of a variety of qualitative and quantitative methodologies to enhance validity. These included an analysis of project documents, ethnographic work, in-depth interviews with key informants, semistructured interviews with agency representatives and clients, and a focus group involving six clients recruited from "The Lesbian and Gay Forum" in Merseyside, Liverpool. Letters of invitation had been sent to 45 members of the group. Crossley considers the areas of agreement and conflict among empowerment, safer sex, and government-funded health promotion programs operated at the community level.

362. Farquhar, Clare, with Rita Das. "Are Focus Groups Suitable for 'Sensitive' Topics?" In *Developing Focus Group Research: Politics, Theory and Practice*, edited by Rosaline S. Barbour and Jenny Kitzinger, 47–63. London: Sage, 1999.

The "sensitive" topic referred to in the title is lesbian sexual health. The presentation is based on two previous research projects carried out (separately) by Farquhar and Das, who conducted a total of 32 focus group discussions in six different cities across Scotland and England. All but one of the discussions took place with existing lesbian groups that were located through listings in gay and lesbian publications. The discussion is centered on the following questions: Are focus groups an appropriate methodology for this environment? How can access be gained to a sensitive population? How can the sessions be conducted to produce the best data? What is the impact of sensitive topics on group interaction? The authors conclude that the success of research in the area depends "to a great extent" on the nature of the research question under investigation.

363. Frith, Hannah. "Focusing on Sex: Using Focus Groups in Sex Research." *Sexualities* 3, no. 3 (August 2000): 275–97.

Frith reviews the literature on sex research and focus groups, and highlights three key advantages of this qualitative method for sexuality researchers. Foremost, focus groups are suitable for exploratory research into underinvestigated topics, the perspectives and experiences of a range of individuals can be collected simultaneously, and issues of importance to participants can be identified in a time-efficient manner. A second major benefit is that focus groups can assist researchers in gaining insight into the language and vocabulary typically used by participants when they discuss their sexual attitudes and activities. This information is valuable for developing questionnaire items. Finally, focus groups provide an environment conducive to the discussion of sensitive issues through (1) shared experiences; (2) agreement, which can contribute to elaboration; and (3) disagreement, which may require participants to defend their views and provide further information.

364. Fullilove, Mindy Thompson, and Robert E. Fullilove III. "Stigma as an Obstacle to AIDS Action: The Case of the African American Community." *American Behavioral Scientist* 42, no. 7 (April 1999): 1113–25.

The results of a 1996 study of AIDS attitudes among 51 African-American clergypeople in the New York City area indicated the presence of stigma toward homosexuality. The current study explored three issues: the extent of homophobia in African-American churches and the African-American community, the importance of the church in the community, and the impact of stigma on the gay population. The study protocol involved a secondary analysis of transcripts from 12 focus groups conducted by five different investigators in San Francisco, New York, and Washington, D.C. The focus groups took place over an eight-year period (1988–1995). The article focuses on gay men and Protestants, the dominant religion in the African-American community. Stigmatizing attitudes toward homosexuals were found to be common in various segments of the African-American community and its churches, thereby impeding effective AIDS prevention programs.

365. Harrison, Lyn. "Representing Sexual Hegemony: Focus Groups and Governmentality." In *Researching Youth*, edited by Julie McLeod and Karen Malone, 21–30. Hobart, Tasmania: Australian Clearinghouse for Youth Studies, 2000.

The article begins with an overview of the strengths and weaknesses of focus groups. Some strengths are the usefulness of the approach when resources are limited, and the restriction to the interviewer's control, which frees participants to interact. The author devotes four times the space to cover the limitations, starting with the "unnatural" social setting of the focus group. In this study focus groups were formed with young male students, with particular attention to the transcript of 16-year-old young men from a rural town in Victoria, Australia. The research concerned sexuality in schools—in particular, the strong social and psychological investment that the young men have to present themselves as heterosexual, and how maintaining this norm is critical in group situations. Comparisons are made with research conducted with young women, in which the participants acknowledge contradictions and uncertainties in relations and are willing to talk about sexuality, stereotypes, and gender expectations.

366. Kitzinger, Jenny, and Clare Farquhar. "The Analytical Potential of 'Sensitive Moments' in Focus Group Discussions." In *Developing Focus Group Research: Politics, Theory and Practice*, edited by Rosaline S. Barbour and Jenny Kitzinger, 156–72. London: Sage, 1999.

The discussion is based on five previous research projects that used 146 focus groups to investigate the impact of sensitive topics—in this case sex, sexual identity, and/or sexual violence—on group dynamics. "Sensitive moments" can take the form of explicit comments, shock, defensiveness, and awkwardness, and, paradoxically, can occur when participants are feeling comfortable in a group setting. The authors demonstrate how focus groups can "unpack the social construction of sensitive issues, uncover different layers of discourse and illuminate group taboos and the routine silencing of certain views and experiences" (pp. 156–57). Two points are emphasized: the researcher should have prior experience in conducting qualitative work, and the interviewing style of the moderator is crucial. The implications of sensitive moments for subsequent analysis are discussed.

367. O'Sullivan, Lucia F., Heino F. L. Meyer-Bahlburg, and Beverly S. Watkins. "Mother-Daughter Communication about Sex among Urban African American and Latino Families." *Journal of Adolescent Research* 16, no. 3 (May 2001): 269–92.

The authors observe that, in spite of younger adolescent girls' heightened risk of STDs, HIV, and pregnancy, "little is known" about their sexual behavior and how they communicate with their parents concerning sexually related topics. To examine communication issues from the perspectives of mothers and daughters, a convenience sample was recruited from the inner-city neighborhoods of Washington Heights and Upper Harlem in New York City. Twenty-two 90-minute audiotaped focus groups were conducted, separately, with 72 mothers and 72 daughters. The daughters ranged in age from 6 to 13. Ten of the groups involved Latinas; African-American participants made up the rest. The sessions were conducted in Spanish or English by female moderators, matched to the ethnicity of the participants. Analysis was facilitated by the principles of grounded theory. Mothers and daughters were found to adapt "relatively antagonistic" positions, leading the authors to conclude that other close contacts may provide better sex education for these girls.

368. Oswald, Ramona Faith. "A Member of the Wedding? Heterosexism and Family Ritual." *Journal of Social and Personal Relationships* 17, no. 3 (2000): 349–68.

The author, a self-described lesbian, used feminist critical science to investigate how gay, lesbian, bisexual, and transgender (GLBT) people experienced interpersonal dynamics at weddings. Nine 2.5-hour audiotaped focus groups were conducted with 45 GLBTs in Minneapolis-St. Paul, Minnesota. Flyers, newspaper and Internet postings, and word-of-mouth recruitment techniques were utilized. The race, religion, class, and to what degree the participants were "out" on a 1 to 6 scale, are identified. Refreshments were served prior to the meetings. The results indicate that GLBT people had a "sense of emptiness and unfairness" at weddings, which led them to question and/or avoid participation in these family rituals. Heterosexism is defined as "a dynamic whereby heterosexuality was elevated while GLBT identities and relationships were hidden or devalued" (p. 355). Examples of this are presented in relation to wedding invitations, clothing, the wedding party, religion, family portraits, the bouquet and garter-throwing, dancing, silencing, and the pressure to marry.

369. Överlien, Carolina, Karin Aronsson, and Margareta Hydén. "The Focus Group Interview as an In-Depth Method? Young Women Talking about Sexuality." *International Journal of Social Research Methodology* 8, no. 4 (October 2005): 331–44.

The purpose of the research was to determine the suitability of focus group methodology for gathering data from troubled young women about "high-involvement" (that is, sensitive) topics, such as drug abuse, relationships, and sexuality. As part of larger study, 11 young women, ages 15 to 20, were recruited from an all-female youth detention home in Sweden. Each displayed psychosocial problems of some type. Five one-hour audiotaped focus group sessions were conducted by the primary author. The discussions took place at a kitchen table in the detention home. A semistructured interview schedule and, especially, articles from popular magazines helped promote conversation and elicit responses. The researchers found focus group interviewing to be an appropriate methodology for researching sensitive topics (contrary to the traditional belief that the method is designed for low-involvement topics and mainstream populations). In comparison to other available data collection approaches, the discussions generated "deeper" insights and were "less intrusive" due to the voluntary nature of the project.

370. Pritchard, Annette, Nigel J. Morgan, Diane Sedgley, Elizabeth Khan, and Andrew Jenkins. "Sexuality and Holiday Choices: Conversations with Gay and Lesbian Tourists." *Leisure Studies* 19 (2000): 267–82.

The travel motivations of gay and lesbian tourists were studied through the use of focus groups and in-depth interviews. The authors examined the impact of homosexuality on tourist choices, with a second objective of including conversations with lesbian tourists (the perception is that there is a bias toward gay men in tourism research). Four two-hour audiotaped focus groups were conducted with 32 gay and lesbian residents of Wales and the Netherlands. The groups were equally divided by gender. Face-to-face interviews were conducted with six gays and four lesbians from the same locations. Additionally, there were 60-minute interviews with two specialist gay tour operators in the United Kingdom. Although a minority of the participants reported that sexuality was not important to their holiday choice, the majority had the opposite response. Motivations included the desire to relax, escape, and for self-fulfillment, with safety and escape cited most frequently. The authors conclude that homosexuality is a "significant influence" on travel choices.

371. Seal, David Wyatt, Laura M. Bogart, and Anke A. Ehrhardt. "Small Group Dynamics: The Utility of Focus Group Discussions as a Research Method." *Group Dynamics* 2, no. 4 (December 1998): 253–66.

The authors review some empirical studies that compare focus group discussions with other qualitative and quantitative data collection methods, noting the differences and similarities. Two formats, focus groups and individual interviews, are compared in the present research in order to explore four sensitive topics related to intimate and sexual relationships. For the individual interviews a convenience sample of 44 heterosexually active men of mixed ethnicity, ages 18 to 43, were recruited from social groups and STD health clinics. Subsequently, the men were offered the opportunity to discuss the same topics in an audiotaped focus group. Similar conclusions were obtained for the two methods. The individual interviews generated "a greater range and richness-depth of themes" (p. 261)—an advantage "offset by the insights produced by the dynamic interactions of the group setting" (p. 261). Three appendices provide information on the interview topics, the coding scheme employed, and how to conduct focus group research.

372. Steele, Jeanne Rogge. "Teenage Sexuality and Media Practice: Factoring in the Influences of Family, Friends, and School." *Journal of Sex Research* 36, no. 4 (November 1999): 331–41.

Four data-gathering approaches—focus groups, media journals, bedroom tours, and one-on-one in-depth interviews—were used to examine this question: "How do mass media images and messages about love, sex and relationships interact with what teens learn about sexuality at home, in school, and from their friends?" (p. 331). For the first step of the inquiry, a total of 51 male and female middle- and high-school students residing in a southeastern town of about 40,000 participated in eight 60- to 90-minute focus group discussions that were based on sexually related topics. A subset of these teens then took part in the other three protocols. The bedroom tours involved the researcher accompanying the teens on self-narrated visits to their bedrooms to get them to talk about the significance of favorite possessions. The teens were paid an additional $20 for the room tours. NUD*IST assisted with coding the 30-plus hours of audiotaped transcripts from the focus groups. Data generated from the multimethod qualitative study suggest that media practices are influenced in "important" ways by student ethnicity, gender, class status, and developmental level. The role of teens' sense of identity (of themselves and others) on media choice and application to everyday living is discussed.

Social Work

373. Bullock, Karen, Sarah A. McGraw, Karen Blank, and Elizabeth H. Bradley. "What Matters to Older African Americans Facing End-of-Life Decisions? A Focus Group Study." *Journal of Social Work in End-of-Life & Palliative Care* 1, no. 3 (2005): 1–19.

This research was part of a larger study (28 90-minute audiotaped focus groups conducted with a total of 196 participants) designed to investigate quality of care of dying persons in the state of Connecticut. A trained moderator facilitated the racially homogeneous groups. The questions concerned participants' end-of-life beliefs, attitudes, and preferences. Analysis of the transcripts from two of the above focus groups served as the basis for the present article. These focus groups were conducted with 22 moderately low to low-income African Americans (15 females, 7 males) having a median age of 64. The data were organized and analyzed by the use of NUD*IST 4 and the constant comparison method. The participants identified five major themes: spirituality, burden on family, trust, health insurance coverage, and cultural concerns. Recommendations are given for social work practitioners.

374. Chernesky, Roslyn H., and Beth Grube. "Examining the HIV/AIDS Case Management Process." *Health & Social Work* 25, no. 4 (November 2000): 243–53.

Due to the passage of the Ryan White Comprehensive AIDS Resources Emergency (CARE) Act of 1990, there has been a proliferation of case management programs in the United States. To provide empirically based information and new insights concerning one such program in a tri-county region in New York State, chart reviews, focus groups, and a case manager time study served as the data collection approaches. Two 2.5-hour audiotaped focus groups were conducted with 17 case managers, and 9 program supervisors participated in a similarly designed but separate group session. Most of the participants were white women with advanced degrees. The focus group discussions centered on the eight major themes that had been identified by the chart reviews. The authors performed the moderator duties and data content analysis. Case management is viewed as an essential service for vulnerable patients who tend to present in crisis. Focus groups helped contribute to a "more accurate and richer" picture of HIV/AIDS to case management.

375. Chung, Irene. "Creative Use of Focus Groups: Providing Healing and Support to NYC Chinatown Residents after the 9/11 Attacks." *Social Work with Groups* 26, no. 4 (2003): 3–19.

A series of focus groups were conducted as part of a research study to assess the mental health needs of three groups of people residing in New York City's

Chinatown, a community located approximately 10 blocks from Ground Zero. Following the September 11, 2001, terrorist attacks, "unprecedented and extended" disruptions occurred in all phases of daily life—businesses, schools, and civic activities. To respond to these "overwhelming" emotional needs, the author moderated 17 sessions with three generations of Asian Americans: children, dislocated workers, and the elderly (with 6 to 10 participants in each session). These focus groups were the first and only opportunity since 9/11 that the participants had to share their traumatic experiences in a group environment. Chung discusses the healing value of the mutual aid group process—despite variations in cultural background and communication style of those involved. The author concludes that focus groups are "effective and therapeutic with ethnic minority clients in many respects" (p. 18) and are a testimonial to the "healing power" of group dynamics.

376. Cohen, Harriet L., Mark H. Sandel, Cecilia L. Thomas, and Thomas R. Barton. "Using Focus Groups as an Educational Methodology: Deconstructing Stereotypes and Social Work Practice Misconceptions Concerning Aging and Older Adults." *Educational Gerontology* 30, no..4 (April 2004): 329–46.

Some of the "more prevailing" myths and negative stereotypes regarding older people fall into five major categories: physiological changes, cognition changes, social functioning, sexual capacity, and a variety of psychological factors. The authors review prior studies that support the view that college students—in this case, social work students at a large Texas state university—hold these negative attitudes toward older adults. To better prepare students for their social work careers, two 90-minute focus groups were conducted with 15 service providers who work with older adults. A total of 30 students attended as observers. Students, faculty, and service providers later convened to discuss the outcomes. For a separate but related focus group project, a different cohort of 15 students met with 30 older adults who had recently moved into an affordable older adult community. The purpose was to expose the students to the experiences of this population. The use of focus groups served to dispel the students' negative attitudes and replace them with more positive and accurate information about older adults.

377. Cohen, Marcia B., and Kendra J. Garrett. "Breaking the Rules: A Group Work Perspective on Focus Group Research." *British Journal of Social Work* 29, no. 3 (1999): 359–72.

The authors suggest that, when appropriate, social work facilitators should use their knowledge of group dynamics, their research skills, and other attributes to modify the traditional rules governing the conduct of focus groups. This observation is based on the primary author's qualitative study of client/worker relationships in five transient and permanent residential mental health programs in the northeastern United States. The first focus group was conducted with 10 homeless men and women with dual diagnoses of mental illness and substance abuse; the second involved three women with similar diagnoses. To accommodate the various socioemotional needs of the participants, the authors made changes to the existing guidelines found in the literature. These include being flexible (rescheduling meetings), holding sessions in a natural setting, using preexisting groups, considering sensitive topics, and assembling smaller groups.

378. Dane, Barbara. "Child Welfare Workers: An Innovative Approach for Interacting with Secondary Trauma." *Journal of Social Work Education* 36, no. 1 (Winter 2000): 27–38.

Prior literature indicates that child welfare workers (CWWs) experience high levels of burnout, which is exhibited as anxiety, depression, irritation, sleep disturbances, and low job satisfaction. This study investigates burnout resulting from this group's exposure to trauma victims and perpetrators, and their subsequent psychological reactions. Focus groups were selected as the most appropriate data-gathering approach to inform a training model to help these workers. Two 3.5-hour audiotaped focus groups were cofacilitated by the author and an assistant. A total of 10 CWWs were recruited from child welfare agencies located in a diverse metropolitan area. The majority of the participants were African American, female, Catholic, and single. A predesigned interview schedule guided the discussions. Content analysis and the constant comparison process assisted analysis. The participants reported feelings of sadness and loneliness. All had developed coping strategies, foremost, spiritual beliefs. Based on the focus group findings, the author developed and tested a two-day training model.

379. Doel, Mark. "Difficult Behavior in Groups." *Groupwork* 14, no. 1 (2004): 80–100.

The author reports his experiences with assisting three support teams facilitate discussions in a Children's Services Department in the English Midlands. Three focus groups were convened over a two-day period with 22 ethnically diverse, largely female group workers to consider this question: "What aspects of group work would you like the training to focus on?" The participants were asked to discuss and prioritize six topics that had gained the broadest support: purpose and planning, co-working, groupwork techniques, difficult behaviors, subgroups, and evaluation. Difficult behavior was identified as one of the most urgent concerns. The rest of the article concerns this problem, with nine themes emerging from the discussions. The focus group methodology is described as "very effective."

380. Ejaz, Farida K., David M. Bass, Georgia J. Anetzberger, and Kamla Nagpaul. "Evaluating the Ohio Elder Abuse and Domestic Violence in Late Life Screening Tools and Referral Protocol." *Journal of Elder Abuse & Neglect* 13, no. 2 (Fall 2001): 39–57.

A multimethod approach—qualitative and quantitative—was used to develop, refine, and disseminate screening tools and referral protocols on elder abuse and domestic violence in the state of Ohio. For the initial step in the evaluation process, focus groups were conducted to review and discuss the draft documents. The first focus group of 10 key informants, all professionals in the field, were "interviewed over the telephone." A focus group was held in a rural county with 29 community representatives. The final group involved 14 participants recruited from an urban area, who represented a variety of social services agencies and organizations. The fourth source of qualitative data was provided by experts in a roundtable environment. In the second year, numerous quantitative methods were employed with 160 practitioners. Key findings from both methodologies are discussed. The final version of the document was produced for use by service providers and practitioners.

381. Freedman, Ruth I., and Nancy Capobianco Boyer. "The Power to Choose: Supports for Families Caring for Individuals with Developmental Disabilities." *Health & Social Work* 25, no. 1 (February 2000): 59–68.

As part of a larger study, three cities in the state of Massachusetts were selected for the assessment: Boston, Springfield, and Worcester. Three two-hour audio-taped focus groups were conducted with 31 black, white, Hispanic, and Asian individuals (21 mothers, 8 fathers, and 2 significant others), who represented 26 families with children having a variety of developmental disabilities. All but two of the children lived at home with their families. Among the key themes that emerged from the analysis are the following: the positive types of assistance programs that were deemed valuable; the importance of parental choice of services; the obstacles and barriers they encountered in seeking help; unmet needs; and recommendations for change. Suggestions are given as to how social workers and health-care professionals can contribute to the well-being of these children and their families.

382. Gibbs, Jewelle Taylor. "Gangs as Alternative Transitional Structures: Adaptations to Racial and Social Marginality in Los Angeles and London." *Journal of Multicultural Social Work* 8, nos. 1–2 (2000): 71–99.

The research protocol called for a combined qualitative-quantitative design to examine the experiences, opinions, and behaviors of a sample of black gang members recruited from agencies and organizations in London and Los Angeles. In the first stage of the project, 10 focus groups were conducted in London with 86 Afro-Caribbean males and females (ages 15 to 30). In Los Angeles, 17 focus groups were conducted with 144 African-American youth with similar demographics. In the second stage, 36 youths in London and 32 in Los Angeles took part in individual interviews. All focus group sessions were audiotaped and moderated by the author and an African-American female assistant. Quantitative data were obtained from official government and social agency records, which were used to cross-validate the respondent-provided information. The results are discussed in terms of (1) the popularity of gangs; (2) the factors fostering gang formation, such as racial minority status, low-socioeconomic status, and institutional discrimination; and (3) the reasons why African-American youth choose to become gang members, for example, group identity, surrogate family, social status, and self-esteem.

383. Gibbs, Jewelle Taylor, and Teiahsha Bankhead-Greene. "Issues of Conducting Qualitative Research in an Inner-City Community: A Case Study of Black Youth in Post–Rodney King Los Angeles." *Journal of Multicultural Social Work* 6, nos. 1–2 (1997): 41–57.

A multimethod research strategy—qualitative (focus groups and individual interviews) and quantitative (statistical data, social agency reports, and scholarly articles)—was used to investigate the long-term impact of the Rodney King police brutality case. Both the verdict and the subsequent riots that took place in South Central Los Angeles and beyond had a profound effect on black youth. The study sought to determine the attitudes, behaviors, and experiences of this group in four institutional settings: education, employment, criminal justice, and health care. Seventeen 1.5- to 2-hour audiotaped focus groups were conducted with a diverse sample of 144 males and females recruited from various agencies and institutions serving the African-American community. (Focus groups were also used with agency personnel in previous phases of the project.) The individual interviews involved 32 young people. Multiple perspectives were obtained. The authors discuss eight major challenges encountered when attempting research in an inner-city environment and suggest specific techniques to address each challenge.

384. Gilbert, M. Carlean. "Spirituality in Social Work Groups: Practitioners Speak Out." *Social Work with Groups* 22, no. 4 (2000): 67–84.

Gilbert writes from the perspective that religious and spiritual aspects of the social work profession have been "largely neglected." This void is attributed to a variety of factors: spiritual beliefs and values can conflict with professional ethics; there exists a tradition of separation between church and state; and Freudian thinking about religion still influences clinical practice. To examine the inclusion of spirituality in social group work practice and education, the focus group approach was selected to elicit clinicians' attitudes, concerns, behaviors, and beliefs regarding this topic. A total of 14 purposely selected participants were recruited. All had in-depth experience in various aspects of group work: interpersonal, support, cognitive-behavioral, multifamily, and psychoeducational. Two 90-minute audiotaped focus groups were moderated by the author, who used a grounded theory approach to analyze the data. The participants "unanimously and strongly" recommended that spiritual content be part of the educational curriculum for this profession. Further, they felt that spiritual issues should be incorporated in the holistic treatment of their clients. An in-depth discussion of the implications of the findings for practice, research, and education follows.

385. Kapp, Stephen A., and Jennifer Propp. "Client Satisfaction Methods: Input from Parents with Children in Foster Care." *Child and Adolescent Social Work Journal* 19, no. 3 (June 2002): 227–45.

Focus group methodology was selected as the qualitative method of choice for examining the viewpoints of parents of children in foster care, described as a "neglected" area in the social work literature. The primary purpose of the research was to determine the most effective methods for designing an instrument for gathering client satisfaction data. Eight 1.5- to 2-hour audiotaped focus groups were conducted with 47 parents recruited from four different areas in a Midwestern state that has privatized its foster care services. The parents were diverse in terms of age, gender, race, and socioeconomic status. Each participant received a $50 honorarium. Analysis was assisted by NUD*IST and the constant comparison method. The parents interviewed provided a "wealth of information" with regard to their preferred method of data collection (telephone surveys were favored over mail questionnaires) and their perceived treatment as consumers.

386. Linhorst, Donald M. "A Review of the Use and Potential of Focus Groups in Social Work Research." *Qualitative Social Work* 1, no. 2 (June 2002): 208–28.

This bibliographic essay includes nearly five pages of references on the use of focus groups in social work research (as well as some citations from the general focus group literature to provide a context for the discussion). A computerized search of *Social Work Abstracts* retrieved 65 articles in professional journals. Of the total, 13 pre-2000 articles and 20 post-2000 articles were selected for review (30 of the studies took place in the United States). Linhorst's article is based on three sources of information: the general citations mentioned above, additional sources specific to social work, and four articles written by the author, in which he conducted 51 focus groups with over 400 participants. In the section titled "The Use of Focus Groups in Social Work Research," the references are divided by question topic: (1) "What research topics can focus groups address?" (2) "What populations are appropriate to include in focus groups?" (3) "Can focus groups be integrated with other qualitative or quantitative research methods?" (4) "What consequences do focus groups have for participants?" (5) "What ethical issues arise when using focus groups?" The author concludes that social work research can contribute to the further development of the methodology due to the wide range of topics involved, the diverse and vulnerable populations the profession serves, and the professional emphasis on empowerment.

387. Linhorst, Donald M., Gary Hamilton, Eric Young, and Anne Eckert. "Opportunities and Barriers to Empowering People with Severe Mental Illness through Participation in Treatment Planning." *Social Work* 47, no. 4 (October 2002): 425–34.

Empowerment, as related to the mentally ill, is defined as "having decision-making power, a range of options from which to choose, and access to information" (p. 427). Linhorst discusses the barriers to empowerment and the conditions that must be present for empowerment to take place through treatment planning. Data were collected through two qualitative approaches: document review (standards, mission statements, and policy and program materials) and focus groups. The setting for the study was a public psychiatric hospital located in the state of Missouri. Seventeen 30- to 60-minute focus groups were conducted with 72 patients (of 208) living at the long-term facility. The protocol then called for 15 focus groups to be held with 114 staff (of 389), who represented a range of management levels. Staff were excluded from the patient groups, and separate interviews were held with professional clinical staff, paraprofessional clinical staff, middle managers, and upper management. The facility under consideration was found to "embrace" the components of empowerment. Six factors, both psychological and organizational, were identified as maximizing patients' involvement in their own treatment.

388. Loneck, Barry, and Bruce Way. "Using a Focus Group of Clinicians to Develop a Research Project on Therapeutic Process for Clients with Dual Diagnoses." *Social Work* 42, no. 1 (January 1997): 107–11.

The input of social work practitioners/clinicians was sought to increase their involvement and interest in the development of research projects. The topic under consideration was the referral process of patients with dual diagnoses of mental illness and substance abuse, who are first seen in a psychiatric emergency room. Following treatment, patients are normally referred to other services in the community for follow-up. To elicit responses as to what leads to a successful referral, two audiotaped focus groups were conducted with 12 participants (psychologists, social workers, case workers, and addictions counselors). The focus groups were an "effective" means of informing the research process.

389. Marcenko, Maureen O., and Linda Samost. "Living with HIV/AIDS: The Voices of HIV-Positive Mothers." *Social Work* 44, no. 1 (January 1999): 36–45.

The research was undertaken to investigate the strategies HIV-positive mothers draw on to cope with the disease, to manage their parenting responsibilities, and to deal with concerns about the future. To elicit the women's own perspectives on this topic, a series of six two-hour audiotaped focus groups were conducted with

40 participants recruited from a variety of sites (homes, apartments, streets, and shelters) in the city of Philadelphia. A Caucasian female and an African-American male served as cofacilitators. A $25 honorarium, lunch, and transportation were provided. The issues identified were classified into the following: individual and family, organizations and providers, and policy and community. Also considered is whether these system levels provided needed resources or added additional stress. Implications for provider services improvements are discussed.

390. Orel, Nancy A. "Gay, Lesbian, and Bisexual Elders: Expressed Needs and Concerns across Focus Groups." *Journal of Gerontological Social Work* 43, nos. 2–3 (2004): 57–77.

Orel observes that the identification of the needs and concerns of the increasing numbers of gay, lesbian, and bisexual (GLB) seniors in the United States has largely been ignored in the research literature and by most institutions in our society. With the goal of developing a needs assessment instrument that would identify these areas of concern, two qualitative methods—focus groups and in-depth interviews—were used to gain insight from members of older GLB populations. Three 1.5- to 2-hour focus groups were conducted with an ethnically diverse group of 26 self-identified GLBs (ages 65 to 84) recruited from two Midwestern states. The author served as moderator. The content analysis revealed seven major areas of concern: physical health, legal rights, housing, spirituality, family, mental health, and social networks. Orel discusses the similarities between these areas and those identified by older heterosexuals, and the differences between the concerns of "outed" versus "closeted" GLBs. Implications for social workers are discussed.

391. Pearlmutter, Sue, and Elizabeth E. Bartle. "Supporting the Move from Welfare to Work: What Women Say." *Affilia* 15, no. 2 (Summer 2000): 153–72.

The authors describe the implementation of the Temporary Assistance to Needy Families (TANF) program as a "complex and arduous task" for social workers. The "controversial" legislation imposed time limits and assistance from welfare workers as conditions for exiting the welfare system. The goals of the research were to elicit the perceptions, knowledge, and understanding of welfare participants—those most affected by the changes to this program—and to determine how these people view the impact of the changes on their daily lives. Two large urban areas with significant TANF recipients were selected for the study. In Cuyahoga County, Ohio, two focus groups were conducted with 38 welfare recipients, primarily African-American women. In Los Angeles County, California, three focus groups were conducted with 15 individuals with similar demographics. The discussion topics concerned various aspects of welfare, subsidized child care, living-wage jobs, employment programs, support services, and relationships with welfare workers. The focus group participants were found to be confused by the program changes. Most agreed they were not receiving the support needed.

392. Scharlach, Andrew E., Roxanne Kellam, Natasha Ong, Aeran Baskin, Cara Goldstein, and Patrick J. Fox. "Cultural Attitudes and Caregiver Service Use: Lessons from Focus Groups with Racially and Ethnically Diverse Family Caregivers." *Journal of Gerontological Social Work* 47, nos. 1–2 (March–April 2006): 133–56.

Prior literature indicates the underutilization of formal and informal social supports by ethnic minority caregivers. To gain a greater understanding of the failure of this population to take advantage of available services, a qualitative study was undertaken. Eight two-hour audiotaped focus groups were conducted with 76 participants who had been recruited through a variety of community organizations in Sacramento, the San Francisco Bay Area, Los Angeles, and three areas in Southern California. A variety of racial and ethnic populations were represented: African American, Chinese, Filipino, Korean, Native American, Hispanic, Russian, and Vietnamese. The participants ranged in age from their early 20s to their early 70s, were primarily female, and were providing care to an elderly parent. The moderators were graduate students, staff, and faculty members from the University of California at Berkeley and California State University San Bernardino, and were matched to the language, ethnicity, and cultural backgrounds of the participants. The results are discussed in terms of the three "common cross-cultural constructs": familism, group identity, and attitudinal and structural barriers to service use. Implications for community-centered caregiver support services are discussed.

393. Stewart, Sally. "'A Tapestry of Voices': Using Elder Focus Groups to Guide Applied Research Practice." *Journal of Gerontological Social Work* 42, no. 1 (2003): 77–88.

The primary research question reads as follows: "What kinds of things should be researched that would result in making your life better?" A total of 15 audiotaped focus groups were conducted over a four-month period with a sample of elderly participants recruited from two very large and ethnically diverse "satellite" communities of Greater Toronto. The special challenges encountered in working with older populations included poor eyesight and frail voices that could not be heard clearly on the tape. Further, it was sometimes necessary to interview the caregivers in an attempt to represent those with cognitive impairments. The major themes identified will be used to guide research initiatives. The focus group experience was viewed as a "validating" one by many of the older people and their caregivers. Stewart writes that the discussions were "very valuable in offering participants an opportunity to increase self-worth through self-determination" (p. 83).

Some limitations of the method for researching this population are considered, and implications for health and human services professionals are discussed.

394. Templeman, Sharon B., and Lynda Mitchell. "Challenging the One-Size-Fits-All Myth: Findings and Solutions from a Statewide Focus Group of Rural Social Workers." *Child Welfare* 81, no. 5 (September–October 2002): 757–72.

Templeman and Mitchell write from the perspective that (1) rural youth have unique requirements; (2) there is an "inappropriate transfer" of urban child welfare models and policies to those residing in rural communities; and (3) interventions for rural populations must be different from urban approaches. Rural children are generally poor, less educated, experience long-term poverty, have limited access to human services, and are affected by geographical isolation. The authors selected focus groups to examine the economic, social, and geographical factors affecting rural families, as well as their attitudes toward receiving assistance. One focus group was conducted with approximately 50 social workers, social work students, and allied helping professionals attending a social work conference in Texas. The group was able to identify unique differences, strengths and assets, barriers to success, and needed changes to programs that target rural families. Implications of the study for Texas legislators, policymakers, and other leaders are discussed.

395. Tickamyer, Ann R., Debra A. Henderson, Julie Anne White, and Barry L. Tadlock. "Voices of Welfare Reform: Bureaucratic Rationality versus the Perceptions of Welfare Participants." *Affilia* 15, no. 2 (Summer 2000): 173–92.

The authors review the assumptions and models of public policy underlying the welfare system in the United States. To demonstrate "the disparities between the top-down goals of welfare policy and the bottom-up perceptions of their outcomes" (p. 174), focus groups were selected as the method of choice for obtaining these perspectives. The sample was drawn from women on welfare living in four rural Appalachian counties in Ohio. Four 90-minute audiotaped focus groups were conducted with 18 white, self-selected participants between the ages of 18 and the late 50s. The sessions produced wide-ranging views of the welfare programs. Four major themes were identified: doubts about the purposes, goals, and outcomes of welfare reform; concern over sanctions; the distinction between deserving and undeserving recipients; and the women's allegiance to their families. The research undertaken was part of a larger study using focus groups, surveys, and in-depth interviews to collect data in 29 counties in the state.

396. Urwin, Charlene A., and Dennis T. Haynes. "A Reflexive Model for Collaboration: Empowering Partnerships through Focus Groups." *Administration in Social Work* 22, no. 2 (1998): 23–39.

The term *collaboration* is defined as follows: "[T]wo or more parties work toward common goals by sharing responsibility, authority, and accountability for achieving results" (p. 23). Based on the models of B. Gray (1985) and J. O'Looney (1994), the authors developed the "Reflexive Model for Collaboration," which shifts a task-oriented problem to one that is "solution-oriented and visionary." In the context of a university-agency program designed to encourage more effective staff training in Texas, focus groups were conducted with trainers and supervisors to add "detail and substance" following needs assessment. Focus groups offer three processes relating to collaboration: relationship building, planning, and implementation. The authors demonstrate how each process contributes to the development of more "comprehensive and sophisticated" collaboration. A fourth dimension, visioning, was also identified. The focus group effort provided "a partnership with a common vision through a reflexive collaboration process" (p. 37).

397. Weitzman, Patricia Flynn, Robert Dunigan, Robert L. Hawkins, Eben A. Weitzman, and Sue E. Levkoff. "Everyday Conflict and Stress among Older African American Women: Findings from a Focus Group Study and Pilot Training Program." *Journal of Ethnic & Cultural Diversity in Social Work* 10, no. 2 (2001): 27–45.

The purposes of the research were to add to the body of literature that deals with sources of everyday stress and conflict among African-American women, and to explore the applicability and usefulness of a training intervention in constructive conflict strategies for this population. To inform this topic, three 90-minute audiotaped focus groups were conducted with 30 African-American women, ages 60 to 80, who were recruited from community organizations located in economically depressed inner-city neighborhoods of Boston. The primary and secondary authors moderated the sessions. The questions concerned the types of everyday stressors, how participants responded to them, and how they managed stress. Members of the last focus group, led by the third author, received an hour of instruction on healthy ways of addressing stressful situations. The discussions were transcribed and analyzed for emerging themes. Worries about functional disability and access to transportation were sources of everyday stress. Everyday conflicts occurred with adult children, grandchildren, neighbors, and peers. Stress and conflict were typically handled through avoidance and self-distraction. The value of the peer group format for improved mental health is discussed.

Theories

398. Munday, Jennie. "Identity in Focus: The Use of Focus Groups to Study the Construction of Collective Identity." *Sociology* 40, no. 1 (February 2006): 89–105.

The author reviews the theoretical perspectives of A. Touraine and A. Melucci [both sociologists] and then considers the concept of collective identity and how it is constructed within the context of social movements. Munday posits that the methods for examining social movements advocated by these sociologists "have not been fully developed or explored" (p. 93). The focus group approach is perceived to be "ideally suited" for investigating "the processes through which individuals work together to form a collective identity" (p. 95). The author reports on a pilot study carried out with members of the Women's Institute, the largest women's voluntary organization in Britain. A single focus group was conducted with five participants, with the author serving as moderator. Discussed are group composition, the appropriate degree of moderator control, and the importance of analyzing the process of interaction—not just the content of the discussion. The focus group method, described as "flexible and robust" for gathering data on collective identity, "overcame" the problems associated with the methodologies of Touraine and Melucci.

399. Myers, Greg. "Becoming a Group: Face and Sociability in Moderated Discussions." In *Discourse and Social Life*, edited by Srikant Sarangi and Malcolm Coulthard, 121–37. Harlow, England: Longman, 2000.

Myers considers the work of the German sociologist Georg Simmel, who developed the concept of "sociability," and the contribution of Erving Goffman in his essay titled "On Face-Work." The author relates these works to how a group emerges as an entity and to how the "development of talk through stages as a group is defined" (p. 124). The focus group data utilized came from a study titled "Global Citizenship and the Environment," which was conducted in northwest England. The first half hour of each group concerned local communities and everyday activities of the participants. At the same point in the topic guide, participants started to talk to each other. Myers considers in detail two passages from the focus group transcript, one as an example of the development of topics as a collaborative activity, and the second demonstrating the beginnings of conversational patterns. The author concludes by suggesting that talk in focus groups provides "a chance to explore how society emerges" (p. 135).

400. North, Peter. "Exploring the Politics of Social Movements through 'Sociological Intervention': A Case Study of Local Exchange Trading Schemes." *Sociological Review* 46, no. 3 (1998): 564–82.

Two theories of social movements are discussed. The first, called Sociological Intervention (SI), was devised by Alain Touraine in 1981. SI is a method for understanding and analyzing social movements. The second, by Alberto Melucci (1989), extends the work of Touraine, but differs from it in some important ways. Both sociologists provide "methodological recommendations centered around focus group work that complement traditional ethnographic approaches, longitudinal or life history studies, or interview-based research" (p. 565). North examines the two theories in the context of a case study of Local Exchange

Trading Schemes, a proposed bartering system. Three audiotaped focus groups were conducted with 15 participants. The appropriateness of SI is discussed as is the importance of triangulation. The author found that attempts to use SI as a stand-alone method were "less useful" than a multimethod approach — in this case participant observation and depth interviews.

Women's Studies

401. Brandwein, Ruth A., and Diana M. Filiano. "Toward Real Welfare Reform: The Voices of Battered Women." *Affilia* 15, no. 2 (Summer 2000): 224–43.

This article describes women's work experiences both before and after the implementation of the Family Violence Option of the Temporary Assistance to Needy Families (TANF) program, a part of the Personal Responsibility and Work Opportunity Reconciliation Act of 1996. The sample was drawn from five organizations in two states: a self-help advocacy group, two battered women's shelters, a health counseling program for battered women, and a welfare-to-work program. Two of the organizations were located in a large city in the Rocky Mountain West; three were located in suburbs of a Northeast metropolitan area. Five 60- to 90-minute audiotaped focus groups were conducted with 24 ethnically mixed women (ages 20 to late 40s), who were victims of domestic violence and who also were receiving public assistance. The authors moderated the discussions. A wide range of topics was addressed, including the women's attempts at employment, obstacles to employment, and how the welfare system helped or hindered them. The perspectives expressed in the focus groups led to both short- and long-term policy changes in TANF.

402. Braun, Virginia. "Heterosexism in Focus Group Research: Collusion and Challenge." *Feminism & Psychology* 10, no. 1 (2000): 133–40.

The term *heterosexism* found in the article title and throughout the text has been selected in preference to the word *homophobia*. Braun writes about the "everyday" heterosexism found in talk by people who are "tolerant" or "liberal." The nature of focus groups provides the participants the opportunity to interact with each other, during which it is possible that "offensive talk" may occur. The author draws her research in this area from the data produced in 16 small focus groups talking about the vagina. In eight of the groups at least one participant identified herself as lesbian, bisexual, or "unsure." Two types of heterosexism are described. The first, by commission, is where "explicit articulation or heterosexist assumptions" occur, with three categories presented: (1) "generic woman equals heterosexual woman"; (2) "sex equals heterosex"; and (3) "generic man equals heterosexual man." The second type is by omission. Braun discusses the lack of challenge to heterosexist talk, as well as the failure to follow up on lesbian "topics." Silence is noted as a form of "action." An example is presented in which heterosexism is challenged when talking about "whether and how the vagina is important in 'sex.'" The potential of focus groups to serve as agents of change with respect to talk and "attitudes" is discussed. The author views the need to eliminate heterosexism as "everyone's responsibility."

403. Buzi, Ruth S., Susan R. Tortolero, Peggy B. Smith, Michael W. Ross, and Robert E. Roberts. "Young Minority Females' Perceptions of Sexual Abuse: A Focus Group Approach." *North American Journal of Psychology* 4, no. 3 (2002): 441–56.

A qualitative data-collection method was selected to elicit the perceptions of adolescent females about issues related to a sexual abuse experience. The authors review prior literature indicating that a history of sexual abuse produces "a cluster of negative effects." Eleven 75- to 90-minute audiotaped focus groups were conducted with 60 African-American (80 percent) and Hispanic (20 percent) 16- to 22-year-old females, who were receiving family planning services at the Teen Health Clinic, located in the southeastern United States. Each was given a $20 gift certificate for participation. NUD*IST assisted with the identification of eight major themes and concepts. Among the results are the following: (1) participants expressed concern about sexual abuse in their community, considering it underreported; (2) sexual abuse was perceived to incorporate both contact and noncontact behaviors that were "nonconsensual and violate the rights of the victim"; and (3) sexual risk-taking behaviors were often a consequence of earlier sexual abuse. A variety of individual, family, community, and cultural factors contributing to sexual abuse were identified as a result of the focus group discussions. Multilevel intervention strategies are needed.

404. Claridge, C. "Rural Women, Decision Making and Leadership within Environmental and Landcare Groups." *Rural Society* 8, no. 3 (1998): 182–95.

Male hegemony is described as "pervasive" in Australian rural communities. As part of a larger study to develop and test a method to facilitate women's empowerment, the author sought to identify and understand women's perspectives with regard to the issues of decision making, leadership, and power structure in environmental management. (Women residing in urban areas were the subject of a prior study.) To accomplish this goal, a series of six focus group interviews were conducted with a sample of 51 women drawn from environmental, Landcare, and other community organizations in the South Burnett area. The questions discussed related to the participants' level of satisfaction concerning their involvement in the environmental groups, impediments to more prominent roles, and situations that encourage empowerment. Three categories of perceived barriers were identified: socialized, situational, and structural. Claridge discusses these categories in the context of a review of the literature and with excerpts from the interviews. The "most important" outcome of the study is the "overwhelming" evidence that rural Australian women want to increase their level of empowerment.

405. Dryburgh, Heather. "Work Hard, Play Hard: Women and Professionalization in Engineering—Adapting to the Culture." *Gender & Society* 13, no. 5 (October 1999): 664–82.

Three data-gathering approaches were used to examine the special challenges encountered by female students preparing for a career in engineering. Two dimensions were investigated: adjusting to the professional norms and culture of a male-dominated discipline and internalizing the professional identity. Undergraduates at all levels were recruited from an engineering department at a Canadian university. Observation took place in a variety of formal and informal sites on campus. Three focus groups and 15 individual in-depth interviews were conducted. Given the nature of the research, most participants were female. However, one male participated in the focus groups, and others were involved in the observation activities. The results indicate that these women experienced "tremendous" anxiety resulting from their gender identification rather than from their academic abilities. "Impression management" is one coping technique discussed.

406. Frith, Hannah, and Celia Kitzinger. "Talk about Sexual Miscommunication." *Women's Studies International Forum* 20, no. 4 (1997): 517–28.

Miscommunication (or "misunderstandings" or "misperceptions") about sex are very common between men and women—a "clash" of conversational styles. Miscommunication theory, widely acclaimed and criticized in academic circles, holds that the problem of sexual violence can be solved through improved communication skills. Frith and Kitzinger (Loughborough University) offer a different perspective by stating the following: "In perpetuating the notion of pretheoretical or presocialized 'experience,' we disguise or obscure the social framework within which our experience is constructed" (p. 522). The research reported was part of a larger study titled "Women Saying 'No' to Sex." Fourteen 30- to 90-minute focus groups, moderated by Frith, were conducted with 58 female school and university students to discuss their experiences with saying "no" to sex. Miscommunication theory was found to be the basis for how the young women explained men's behavior and as a rationale for building and sustaining heterosexual relationships. The authors highlight some of the reasons for the popularity of the theory: it avoids blaming men, it provides women with an "illusory" sense of control, and it "obscures" institutional power relations. Frith and Kitzinger's analysis of this study is found in "'Emotion Work' as a Participant Resource: A Feminist Analysis of Young Women's Talk-In-Interaction," *Sociology* 32, no. 2 (May 1998): 299–320.

407. Hughes-Bond, Linda. "Standing Alone, Working Together: Tensions Surrounding Young Canadian Women's Views of the Workplace." *Gender & Education* 10, no. 3 (September 1998): 281–97.

Young Canadian women often receive "disparate, often contradictory" messages about work and its role in their future lives. The authors observe that these young women expect to spend at least part of their adulthood in full-time employment; that work is frequently divided along gender lines; and that the concerns affecting this population exist worldwide. To identify the themes and issues surrounding young women's perceptions about work and the factors that shape these perceptions, two qualitative approaches—focus groups and individual interviews—were selected to collect the data. Three one-hour focus group discussions were conducted with a sample of 12 girls (ages 16 to 19) attending a secondary school in rural eastern Ontario. The results indicate that the girls were confused about the role of work in their future lives and that the combination of family and career remains problematic.

408. Kaplan, Elaine Bell. "Women's Perceptions of the Adolescent Experience." *Adolescence* 32, no. 127 (Fall 1997): 715–35.

The goal of the research was twofold: to examine through qualitative means women's thoughts about their preadolescent and adolescent years and to gain an understanding of the issues, consequences, and coping strategies that emerged during this transition period. Adolescents face a number of issues, such as those relating to body image, unwanted sexual advances, mental and emotional health, and societal pressures and expectations. Two two-hour audiotaped focus groups were conducted with 24 middle-class, ethnically mixed undergraduate students recruited from a local university. All were apparently without teenage pregnancy, drug use, or gang involvement. The majority of women (14) felt that their adolescence was mainly negative, with some becoming emotional upon recollection. This pivotal period was perceived as very stressful and sometimes had long-term consequences.

409. Kitzinger, Celia, and Hannah Frith. "Just Say No? The Use of Conversation Analysis in Developing a Feminist Perspective on Sexual Refusal." *Discourse & Society* 10, no. 3 (1999): 293–316.

To gain insight into why young women find it difficult to say "no" to unwanted sex, the authors employed techniques from conversation analysis (CA). CA relies on small details of naturally occurring conversation—pauses, hesitations, silences, and self-correction—for interactional relevance. Kitzinger and Frith provide data from their research to demonstrate (among other findings) that both men and women can convey and comprehend sexual refusals, including those refusals that do not specifically use the word "no." Further, the authors maintain that it should not be necessary for a woman to specifically have to use the word "no" for her to be understood as refusing sex, and that the "just say no" program ("a simplistic prescription" and "counterproductive") implies that other refusal techniques are "open to reasonable doubt." Analysis of audiotaped focus group transcripts of 58 female school and university students indicates that refusals are delayed and indirect, with a direct "no" perceived as rude or hostile by the women. The root of the problem is "not that men do not understand sexual refusals, but that they do not like them" (p. 310). The implications of CA for feminist psychology are discussed.

410. Lamana, Mary Anne. "Living the Postmodern Dream: Adolescent Women's Discourse on Relationships, Sexuality, and Reproduction." *Journal of Family Issues* 20, no. 2 (March 1999): 181–217.

Two data-collection methodologies—semistructured interviews and focus groups—were used to gain insight into this question: "Why do teen women risk pregnancy in a social context calling for deferred parenthood?" The setting for the research was a medium-sized Midwestern city and its suburbs. Convenience sampling aided recruitment from a variety of socially diverse environments: schools, churches, and social programs for teen mothers. Discourse on relationships, sexuality, and reproduction was obtained through interviews with 63 African American and white, "ever-pregnant" or never-pregnant adolescent women. Following the interviews, 23 one- to two-hour focus groups were conducted with 225 African-American and white men and women recruited from similar sources. In addition to a wide range of questions, hypothetical situations were incorporated into the focus group discussions. Both of the data-collection formats were conducted by the author (white) and four assistants (three white, one African American). The 32-page analysis (including quotations from the respondents) is organized around the four thematic categories of discourse identified: accidental, pair bond, developmental, and protective. Lamana writes that the analysis suggests that "(American) adolescent women of all classes live in a social world lacking structural support for the modern narrative" (p. 186).

411. Madriz, Esther. "Focus Groups in Feminist Research." In *Collecting and Interpreting Qualitative Materials*, edited by Norman K. Denzin and Yvonna S. Lincoln, 363–88. 2nd ed. Thousand Oaks, CA: Sage, 2003.

Madriz, a Latina feminist, discusses the use of focus groups "from a feminist/postmodernist framework," noting that in the past, social science researchers have ignored certain population groups, specifically women of color. A brief history of focus groups is provided, and the methodology is compared and contrasted to two other qualitative data-gathering approaches: participant observation and individual interviews. Focus groups are viewed as a "particularly well-suited" method for examining women in general as well as oppressed groups of women of color (African Americans, Latinas, and Asian Americans) "to unveil specific and little-researched aspects of women's daily existences, their feelings, attitudes, hopes, and dreams" (p. 365). The author discusses how feminist researchers prefer ethnographic over positivistic research approaches; how shattering the concept of "others" promotes social change; and the utility of focus groups for gathering collective testimony. Eighteen 1.5- to 2-hour focus groups, with between 5 and 12 participants each, were conducted with a sample of white, African American, and Latina women of lower socioeconomic background. Challenges were encountered with recruitment, matching the race/ethnicity of the moderator to the participants, reticent respondents, costs, and other areas.

412. Montell, Frances. "Focus Group Interviews: A New Feminist Method."
     NWSA Journal 11, no. 1 (Spring 1999): 44–71.

The presentation is divided into three main sections. In the first, Montell demonstrates how focus group interviews can strengthen and broaden the principles of feminist qualitative research. The prime advantages of group discussions are the following: the interaction of the participants generates valuable data for examining issues of gender and sexuality; consciousness raising, and empowerment are promoted for both the participants and the researcher; and a more egalitarian relationship between the researcher and the research subjects is fostered. The author addresses two practical issues in the second section: recruiting the participants (sample bias is a concern) and the unique dynamics of the group interview (relationships among participants, and between participants and moderator). The last section deals with discourse analysis of focus group data, a method that concentrates on people's talk as the subject of interest (rather than on the beliefs and experiences of individuals). Examples are based on the author's study of the influence of popular culture on the construction and maintenance of normative sexuality for women. Throughout the article, comparisons are made to individual interviews.

413. Pini, Barbara. "Focus Groups, Feminist Research and Farm Women: Opportunities for Empowerment in Rural Social Research." *Journal of Rural Studies* 18, no. 3 (July 2002): 339–51.

In a discussion of feminism and feminist research methods, Pini points out that the focus group technique is "rarely used" in rural social research, and is "much less" utilized than individual interviews by feminist researchers. Further, the author writes that "feminist research is not tied to a particular method nor to a particular discipline, but to the goal of women's emancipation" (p. 340). Focus groups were conducted as part of a larger study that examined women's contributions to the Australian sugar industry, the reasons for the lack of representation in leadership roles, and how women could become more involved in Canegrowers, an agri-political organization. A total of 80 farm women participated in 16 initial and follow-up two-hour focus groups (the follow-up sessions were conducted six months later). The author served as moderator. Based on extracts from the discussions, four examples are provided that demonstrate the effectiveness of focus groups. The author discusses their potential as an "empowering strategy" by giving voice to otherwise neglected populations in rural social research.

414. Pollack, Shoshana. "Focus-Group Methodology in Research with Incarcerated Women: Race, Power, and Collective Experience." *Affilia* 18, no. 4 (Winter 2003): 461–72.

Pollack reviews numerous studies that support the value of focus groups for feminist-related research. Using a sample of incarcerated women in Canada, the present study employed both focus groups and individual interviews (the latter referred to as "life-history methodology"). The goals of the study were to examine the effects of marginalization and oppression on these prisoners and to gain an understanding of the social context that leads to criminalization. (Data were also gathered through interviews with staff, analysis of documents, and participant observation.) The participants were recruited from a medium-sized Canadian federal women's prison. Of the three focus groups conducted, one, comprised of four African Americans, is reported here. Six women took part in five life-history interviews. The two data-collection approaches produced different kinds of data. The focus groups not only provided a conceptual framework for the project but also a "richer and more complex" understanding of individual accounts of racism, sexism, and classism and their relation to lawbreaking.

415. Tang, Catherine So-Kum, Day Wong, Fanny M. C. Cheung, and Antoinette Lee. "Exploring How Chinese Define Violence against Women: A Focus Group Study in Hong Kong." *Women's Studies International Forum* 23, no. 2 (2000): 197–209.

The authors review the patriarchal thought and practices that are fundamental to Chinese society, noting that violence against women not only continues to the present, but worst of all, "may largely be condoned." The first part of the article considers the differences between feminist and criminal approaches as to how the phrase "violence against women" is defined. Feminist theory holds that preexisting legal categories are insufficient to cover women's wide range of experiences of violence and abuse. To examine how a sample of Chinese people in Hong Kong define, comprehend, and conceptualize the meaning of the phrase, six two-hour focus groups, consisting of 4 to 10 members each, were convened with male and female college students, blue-collar workers, professionals, and homemakers. Two trained moderators led the discussions, which were conducted in Cantonese. The results indicate that nearly all the participants were unfamiliar with the terminology. The authors maintain that the "power" of the phrase lies in directing attention from violence in general to violence directed against women. The population examined is seen as "able to move beyond a narrow crime approach toward a feminist approach" (p. 207). To obtain a broader perspective, similar studies were undertaken in Taiwan and mainland China.

416. Tangenberg, Kathleen. "Marginalized Epistemologies: A Feminist Approach to Understanding the Experiences of Mothers with HIV." *Affilia* 15, no. 1 (Spring 2000): 31–48.

The author observes that, in the field of social work, different forms of knowledge are seen to possess varying degrees of value and professional relevance. Two "ways of learning" are discussed: empirically acquired ("privileged") and bodily and spiritual ("marginalized"). These different ways of knowing affect illness-related behaviors and responses to service providers of marginalized and stigmatized groups—in this case, mothers with HIV. This population typically experiences a wide range of social and psychological challenges. Focus group methodology was selected to examine how bodily and spiritual knowledge influences women's self-perception and experiences of illness. Six focus groups were conducted with 40 HIV-positive women of mixed ethnicity, all recruited from various sites in Philadelphia. Ten women had children with HIV. The narratives were analyzed, with specific attention to the forms of knowledge under investigation and their relationship to the social dynamics of power. Implications of the research for social work practice, education, and research are discussed.

417. Van Staveren, Irene. "Focus Groups: Contributing to a Gender-Aware Methodology." *Feminist Economics* 3, no. 2 (July 1997): 131–35.

Focus group methodology is reported to have had success in social science research—for analytical purposes as well as for policy-oriented studies. Van Staveren seeks to demonstrate how the approach can be utilized to study groups of women and/or gender issues, thereby adding to feminist research. The specific group work discussed was conducted in Nairobi, Kenya, in September 1996. The participants, undergraduate women studying economics, were from six different African countries. The author selected these respondents in order to "learn from the experiences of African women in combining their diverse and demanding roles in economic life" (p. 133). Van Staveren speaks of Western (and masculine) "value-ladenness of concepts" (p. 134) and notes that the focus group experience provided "a much richer spectrum of interpretations" (p. 133). Although not by design but rather as a development of the questioning, the author combined focus groups with personal life studies.

418. Wilkinson, Sue. "Focus Groups: A Feminist Method." *Psychology of Women Quarterly* 23, no. 2 (1999): 221–44.

Wilkinson, affiliated with Loughborough University (U.K.), provides a brief introduction to the key features of focus group methodology. It is observed that, despite over five decades of focus group research, feminist psychologists have begun to use the method only since the 1990s. The author identifies and discusses three primary ways that focus groups address "the feminist critique" of traditional methods in psychology: they are naturalistic in format, they provide a social context for generating meaning, and, compared to one-on-one interviews, they shift the balance of power from researcher to research participant. Thus, artificiality, decontextualization, and exploitation are avoided. In the final section, Wilkinson evaluates the potential of focus groups for feminist research, such as for work with underrepresented social groups, for action research, and for consciousness raising. Advantages and limitations are discussed. The author concludes by stating that, in a review of nearly 200 focus group studies published from 1946 to 1996, none concentrated on the conversation among participants, and that the "focus is on the content rather than the process of interaction" (p. 236).

419. Wilkinson, Sue. "Focus Groups in Feminist Research: Power, Interaction, and the Co-Construction of Meaning." *Women's Studies International Forum* 21, no. 1 (January–February 1998): 111–25.

Wilkinson's primary purpose for writing the article was to demonstrate the utility of focus group methodology for feminist psychology, and more generally, for feminist research. The British author reviews the historical development of the technique, comments on some contemporary applications, and laments the fact that, in a search of over 200 focus group studies published from 1946 to 1996, none concentrated on the conversation among participants. Further, very few included any quotations from more than one participant at a time. In order "to make the best possible case for the use of the method" (p. 113), direct quotations from the "(rare) published examples of *interactive* data" (p. 113) are cited. Also considered are how focus groups can address feminist ethical issues (such as the power structure between researcher and participant in the data-collection process); how high-quality data can be generated; and the value of studying an individual in social context, rather than in isolation. Despite limitations, such as being "ill-suited" for quantification and generalization, the technique has "the potential for future development into an approach *par excellence* for feminist research" (p. 123).

420. Wilkinson, Sue. "How Useful Are Focus Groups in Feminist Research?" In *Developing Focus Group Research: Politics, Theory and Practice*, edited by Rosaline S. Barbour and Jenny Kitzinger, 64–78. London: Sage, 1999.

The chapter is directed to the feminist researcher who wants to determine if focus group interviewing is potentially useful for a project. In Wilkinson's view, focus groups offer several features beneficial for feminist research principles and goals: they can examine the individual in social context and the ensuing interaction; research participants have more power and control; the method is useful for accessing minority groups and for action research; and focus groups contribute to consciousness-raising. The author concludes by highlighting some of the primary difficulties with how focus groups are currently used, namely, through inappropriate applications; by interaction among participants (the distinguishing characteristic) that is rarely analyzed and reported; and with epistemological frameworks that are not clearly identified.

IV.

Sciences

4.1 AGRICULTURE

421. Frederiksen, Boie S., and Anna H. Johannessen. "Using Focus Groups for Evaluation of the CAP Accompanying Measures." *International Journal of Environmental Technology and Management* 1, nos. 1–2 (2001): 127–39.

Part of the CAP (Common Agricultural Policy) Accompanying Measures, an element of a European Directive, refers to the improvements that can be made in connection with agricultural practices and the environment. Two focus groups were conducted in two Danish counties, involved six to eight farmers in each, and included individuals who were participating and those not participating in the environmentally beneficial agricultural program. The findings were that more emphasis on methods and content of information was needed, along with payment and the priorities concerning the environmental effects, as well as communicating the importance of the environmental significance. The authors compare the results of the focus group findings with those of a large-scale questionnaire. The results were "fairly close." The advantages of the focus groups were the "richness of the information," a greater degree of understanding of the details and reasons underlying the decisions, the depth possible, and therefore the more useful information collected. The authors maintain that had the questionnaire study had access to the focus group results, the information would have been more useful.

422. Howden, Peter, Frank Vanclay, Deirdre Lemerle, and John Kent. "Working with the Grain: Farming Styles amongst Australian Broadacre Croppers." *Rural Society* 8, no. 2 (1998): 109–25.

The research was undertaken to test the applicability of J. D. van der Ploeg's farming styles theory, a method for conceiving and understanding diversity in agriculture. To identify the possible farming styles that may be present in broadacre cropping, a series of 18 two- to three-hour audiotaped focus groups were conducted in the Riverina region of southwest New South Wales. The groups were comprised of the following categories: nine sessions involving farmers, six with farm men, two with farm women, and a mixed session consisting of government and private agronomists and a rural counselor. Participants were first asked to use index cards to describe themselves and other farmers in the area, and the perceived differences among themselves and others. A total of 20-plus styles were identified and discussed. An "expert" panel of seven members, including the authors of this article, created a taxonomy and refined the data collected. The authors provide detailed descriptions of the farming styles identified (such as innovative, lazy, hard driver, and secret). The farmers interviewed were not conscious of their own style or the styles of other farmers.

4.2 BIOLOGY

423. Bates, Benjamin R. "Public Culture and Public Understanding of Genetics: A Focus Group Study." *Public Understanding of Science* 14 (2005): 47–65.

The Bates study was part of a larger project designed to investigate the public's understandings of the relationships among genetic science, public policy, and ethnicity. To discuss the role of public culture in shaping the "lay" public's comprehension of genetics, focus groups were used "to examine how members of the public use the media to express their understanding of genetics research" (p. 50). A total of 25 two-hour audio- and videotaped focus groups were conducted with 216 male and female participants (ages 18 to 64) recruited from three cities in Georgia: Atlanta (urban), Gainesville (rural), and Athens (suburban). There were 12 focus groups with 118 African Americans; 7 groups with 71 whites; 2 groups with African Americans and whites; 2 groups with 11 multiracial persons; and 2 groups with 15 Hispanics or Latinos. The participants were chosen to represent a range of perspectives in their community and were paid $50 each. Moderators were matched to the self-identified race of the group members. Contrary to previous research, it was found that people not only draw from two common formats—the news media and science fiction—but also from a variety of other sources: documentaries, non-science-fiction films, and popular television. Information about genetics was processed "complexly and critically" by the study participants.

424. Beckwith, Jo Ann, Timothy Hadlock, and Heather Suffron. "Public Perceptions of Plant Biotechnology—A Focus Group Study." *New Genetics and Society* 22, no. 2 (August 2003): 93–109.

The authors maintain that "little has been done" to engage and educate the ordinary American citizen on the issue of food biotechnology. They write that "popular public debate on the acceptability of genetically modified (GM) or genetically engineered (GE) crops and food products has all too often taken the form of interest group propaganda steeped in vitriolic rhetoric" (p. 94). A focus group study conducted in 2000 by the U.S. Food and Drug Administration found that participants had a low level of knowledge and awareness of this field. To gain a greater understanding of the factors affecting the public's view of GM and GE, a qualitative data-collection approach was undertaken. In total, six 1.5- to 3-hour videotaped focus groups were conducted with 45 participants: environment graduate students, undergraduate students, plant biology researchers (all at Michigan State University), farmers, and members of environmental groups. A $30 honorarium was paid. The participants presented a "complex mental picture," identifying many environmental, socioeconomic, and value-driven issues. It was agreed that public debate was needed, but "support for food biotechnology may be fragile."

425. Kaplowitz, Michael D. "Statistical Analysis of Sensitive Topics in Group and Individual Interviews." *Quality & Quantity* 34, no. 4 (November 2000): 419–31.

Kaplowitz used two data-collection methodologies—focus groups and individual interviews (also known as in-depth or unstructured interviews)—to determine the extent to which participants in each format would raise socially sensitive topics for discussion. A total of 97 year-round residents of two coastal communities in Mexico took part in a study of the value of a shared natural resource—a mangrove ecosystem. The residents selected participated in either one of 12 focus groups or in 19 individual interviews in order to discuss difficulties in, and between, communities and community members. A professional moderator conducted both the focus group discussions and the interviews. The sessions and interviews resulted in over 500 pages, which were then coded with an iterative, grounded theory approach. The data were transformed into summary variables, permitting statistical analysis. The study findings indicate that the participants assigned to individual interviews were 18 times more likely to raise socially sensitive discussion topics than the participants in the focus group environment. The two qualitative methods yielded "complementary, not substitute information."

426. Kaplowitz, Michael D., and John P. Hoehn. "Do Focus Groups and Individual Interviews Reveal the Same Information for Natural Resource Valuation?" *Ecological Economics* 36, no. 2 (February 2001): 237–47.

A mixed-method data-collection approach—focus groups and individual in-depth interviews—was used for the initial stage of a valuation study of a mangrove ecosystem in Mexico's Yucatan Peninsula. Kaplowitz and Hoehn hypothesized that focus groups would yield the same or a similar range of ecosystem service data as do individual interviews, noting that previous empirical research is "not conclusive" as to the relative performance of the two approaches. A total of 97 year-round residents of two nearby communities participated in one of two protocols, each led by a professional Mexican moderator: 78 were interviewed in one of 12 60-minute focus groups and 19 took part in 30-minute individual interviews. The authors describe in detail the procedures employed to analyze the data. The findings indicate that focus groups and individual interviews yielded significantly different information in terms of quantity and type, leading the researchers to conclude that the two formats are not substitutes for one another.

4.3 ENGINEERING

427. Bruseberg, Anne, and Deana McDonagh-Philp. "Focus Groups to Support the Industrial/Product Designer: A Review Based on Current Literature and Designers' Feedback." *Applied Ergonomics* 33, no. 1 (2002): 27–38.

The authors observe the lack of use of focus group methodology in conventional design training and the "significant" gap in training materials for design research. To demonstrate how focus groups and related techniques have been applied to various design-related disciplines, Bruseberg and McDonagh-Philp list 17 relevant studies published from 1990 to 2000. The list includes the name of the authors, the field of application (human factors, 12; market research, 3; and design research, 2), and whether focus groups were used as part of several studies, incorporated with other data-collection techniques or modified in some way to achieve the goals of the project. The authors discuss the results from two case studies they conducted to elicit designers' feedback regarding the use of focus group methods. The goal was to establish information requirements for adapting the technique, based on the designer's needs and suggestions. The article concludes with a list of user-research techniques useful to product design and how focus groups are suitable for this task.

428. Bruseberg, Anne, and Deana McDonagh-Philp. "New Product Development by Eliciting User Experience and Aspirations." *International Journal of Human-Computer Studies* 55, no. 4 (2001): 435–52.

Although the authors acknowledge that a "paradigm shift" is required, they believe that potential users should be consulted during the design phase of new product development. Bruseberg and McDonagh-Philp report on a research project that was based on the collaborative efforts of an ergonomist, a design researcher, and a consultant. To elicit user needs and perspectives about a new kitchen product (kettles), 74 individuals were recruited for 14 focus groups conducted in the East Midlands, England. A variety of techniques from other disciplines (such as the social sciences, human factors, and market research) were evaluated, adapted, and incorporated into the focus group framework. These techniques included Mood Boards, the nominal group technique, visual stimuli, project personality profiling, and drawings by the participants. Focus groups are viewed as an "informal" and "flexible" technique for facilitating communication and informing the design process.

429. Engelbrektsson, Pontus. "Effects of Product Experience and Product Representation in Focus Group Interviews." *Journal of Engineering Design* 13, no. 3 (September 2002): 215–21.

In the author's opinion, the methods traditionally used for market research (surveys, complaints, and so forth) have proven "inefficient" for generating data required by engineers. The goal of the present research was to elicit customer requirements information about the design for a new tram by examining the effects of product experience versus product representation (PR) on focus group participants. PR refers to any kind of object, picture, or computer model that is presented to help participants visualize the form, texture, and/or function of the product being evaluated. Four 90-minute audiotaped focus groups were conducted with a total of 23 participants, divided by users and nonusers of public transportation. Two different PRs were presented: an actual tram or slides of the tram. Participants who were experienced with public transportation provided more information and were less dependent on PRs.

430. Hide, Sophie, Sarah Hastings, Diane Gyl, Roger Haslam, and Alistar Gibb. "Using Focus Group Data to Inform Development of an Accident Study Method for the Construction Industry." In *Contemporary Ergonomics 2001*, edited by Margaret A. Hanson, 153–58. New York: Taylor & Francis, 2001.

The authors of this chapter are associated with the Health & Safety Ergonomics (HSE) Unit at Loughborough University (U.K.). To determine the source of high injury rates for the construction industry, HSE undertook a preliminary study using focus groups to collect the data. A series of seven 90-minute focus groups were conducted with a group of industrial practitioners (five to seven participants per group) to obtain their perceptions of accident causality. The discussion areas concerned failure occurrence in four areas: project concept, design and procurement; work organization and management; task factors; and individual issues. The focus group discussions provided a "rich source of data" for future investigations.

431. Langford, Joe, and Deana McDonagh. "What Can Focus Groups Offer Us?" In *Contemporary Ergonomics 2002*, edited by Paul T. McCabe, 502–6. London: Taylor & Francis, 2002.

Traditionally, practitioners in the fields of ergonomics (human factors) and industrial/product design have employed a variety of methods (trials, surveys, and observation) to gain insight into users' needs and desires as well as how they use products and services. More recently, focus group methodology has been added to the "toolkit" as a way to gather qualitative information in this area. Advantages of the method include the synergistic effect of group interaction, efficiency, and flexibility. The primary disadvantages are the difficulty of keeping participants "on target," and time-consuming data analysis. The authors suggest some appropriate applications of the method for designers and ergonomists, such as identifying problems, evaluating existing or proposed designs, generating new design concepts, and influencing decision makers.

432. Langford, Joe, and Deana McDonagh, eds. *Focus Groups: Supporting Effective Product Design*. London: Taylor & Francis, 2003. 230p.

The book is directed to those involved in the fields of human factors/ergonomics and design, the goal of which is to develop products and systems that effectively meet the needs of their users. Twelve chapters, authored by 16 contributors, are organized into three main parts. Part I, consisting of a single chapter, considers the logistics of conducting a focus group project from the initial planning phase to the specifics of analyzing the data. The nine chapters of part II provide case studies and examples of how focus group interviewing has been used in a variety of human factors/ergonomics and design projects. Areas discussed include market research, new product development, user requirements analysis, health and safety research, focus groups with older participants, scenario-based discussions, visual communication, and participatory design. Part III, also consisting of one chapter, considers 38 techniques for enhancing the effectiveness of the focus group experience. These include tools for immersion and warm-up, problem analysis, idea generation and development, and concept evaluation.

433. Lin, Chin-Tsai, and Che-Wei Chang. "Focus Groups: Impact of Quality and Process Capability Factors on the Silicon Wafer Slicing Process." *International Journal of Manufacturing Technology and Management* 6, nos. 1–2 (May 10, 2004): 171–84.

Silicon wafer slicing is described as a "highly complex" manufacturing process, one that involves "multiple quality characteristics that occur synchronously" (p. 171). (Silicon wafers are used in the semiconductor industry, among other uses). The authors believe that quantitative methods, such as process capability indices and statistical process control charts, which have been frequently used for monitoring quality, are "severely limited." Other evaluative procedures, especially one devised by Tagushi, are reviewed. Lin and Chen report on the application of a qualitative approach, focus groups, to explore how engineers use their knowledge to reduce slicing damage. Four audiotaped focus groups were conducted with 15 participants who represented managers, engineers, quality control personnel, and consultants. A range of slicing problems were discussed, specific problems were identified, and solutions were proposed. The focus group discussions were successful for improving the productivity and effectiveness of decisions.

434. McDonagh-Philp, Deana, and Anne Bruseberg. "Using Focus Groups to Support New Product Development." *Institution of Engineering Designers Journal* 26, no. 5 (September–October 2000): 4–9.

The authors write from the perspective that designers should "widen their empathy" with customers and consider user needs at the "earliest possible stage" when developing new products—while concepts and prototypes are being generated. Focus groups are recommended to elicit users' input concerning their experiences, aspirations, and requirements relative to new design. The key characteristics of the method are reviewed: the rationale for its use; appropriate applications in the field; how to plan a research project; the development of the moderator and interview guides; proper participant recruiting procedures (normally through purposive sampling techniques); and analysis to relate the data to the project. Focus groups offer a "valuable," "flexible," and "direct" way for users to contribute throughout a product development project.

435. McDonagh-Philp, Deana, and Howard Denton. "Using Focus Groups to Support the Designer in the Evaluation of Existing Products: A Case Study." *Design Journal* 2, no. 2 (1999): 20–31.

The objectives of the study were to obtain useful design-related data from the product users themselves by means of focus groups; to heighten designers' awareness of users' needs; and to explore the value of having the designer serve as moderator. The authors (Loughborough University, U.K.) review the key characteristics of focus group interviewing, noting that this qualitative methodology is an activity that has "not fully been embraced" by product designers. Eight 45-minute audio- and videotaped sessions were conducted with a purposively selected sample of male and female participants, representing various socioeconomic levels, to discuss the features (cost, appearance, lifespan, and ease of use) of small kitchen appliances. Triangulation was used to validate the results, which are discussed in terms of the cost-benefit ratio ("complex"); the challenges faced by the designer-moderator; insufficient discussion time; and gender effects (the design-moderator was female and the sessions were gender specific). There were "clear benefits" from the use of focus groups in this context.

436. Prince, Mary M., Michael J. Colligan, Carol Merry Stephenson, and B. J. Bischoff. "The Contribution of Focus Groups in the Evaluation of Hearing Conservation Program (HCP) Effectiveness." *Journal of Safety Research* 35, no. 1 (2004): 91–106.

Relying exclusively on traditional methods (such as policy review, audiometric testing audits, and noise surveillance) to evaluate the effectiveness of hearing conservation programs in the workplace environment "fails" to reveal the impact of such programs on industrial workers. In this study, focus groups were used to "clarify and augment" data gathered through conventional audit measures and to determine the extent to which hearing loss prevention policies had been adopted by the organization. Three unionized manufacturing plants located in the Midwest were selected, based on the perceived level of hearing loss prevention practiced. A total of 93 employees, supervisors, and managers were recruited and paid $50 for participation. Trained moderators conducted four focus groups per plant. The interview guide covered a wide range of topics, including the use of hearing prevention devices, training, audiometric testing, and organizational commitment. The results from focus groups, interviews, audits, and other documentation are compared. Focus groups are deemed to complement and validate other qualitative methods.

4.4 ENVIRONMENTAL STUDIES

437. Jaeger, Carlo C., Ralf Schüle, and Bernd Kasemir. "Focus Groups in Integrated Assessment: A Micro-cosmos for Reflexive Modernization." *Innovation* 12, no. 2 (June 1999): 195–219.

The article deals with the use of focus groups for the Integrated Assessment (IA) of environmental risks. IA is an approach designed to deal with problems requiring many disciplines. It is most closely associated with efforts to analyze geo-, bio-, and sociosphere complexities. As modernization occurs, there is a capacity to look critically at older social traditions, and there is also the possibility to look at modernity itself—with public debate leading to reflexive modernity. To study this phenomenon, five audio- and videotaped focus groups were implemented, the first of which discussed the overall theme of climate change. The groups were directed by a moderator and assisted by a "model moderator" who provided computer presentations. The focus group members considered the model and the computed outcomes. Policy goals and measures were discussed in follow-up sessions. The sessions took place in Frankfurt, Germany. The focus groups enabled the researchers to introduce new arguments and to study "the cultural dynamics of new elements of everyday knowledge" (p. 212).

4.5 PHYSICS

438. Gerber, Theodore P., and Deborah Yarsike Ball. "The State of Russian Science: Focus Groups with Nuclear Physicists." *Post-Soviet Affairs* 18, no. 3 (July–September 2002): 183–212.

Gerber and Ball discuss the "crisis" that befell Russian science following the collapse of the Soviet Union as evidenced by a dramatic decrease in state funding, the diminished social standing of scientists, and a decline in the number of inventions, patent applications, and publications. The situation in the mid-1990s is described as "grim." At the time of the writing of this article, however, the authors write that "Russian science is less in a state of crisis than in a state of transition" (p. 184), arguing that the crisis had abated. This argument is supported by a review of the factors that contribute to increased productivity and effectiveness, and by a focus group study. In October 2001, four focus groups were conducted with 19 Russian nuclear physicists, with all but one having received support from Western grants. The goals were to ascertain the scientists' views about the new developments, how they have adapted to change, their future careers and social responsibilities, and the impact of Western funding. A sociologist from the Centre for Independent Social Research served as moderator. Positive and negative sentiments were expressed. The implications of the focus group results for international security and for Russia's "economic and political trajectories" are discussed.

Appendix: Source Journals

The numbers following each entry refer to item numbers in the text.

AAC: Argumentative and Alternative Communication, 336
Academic Exchange Quarterly, 219
Action in Teacher Education, 204
Administration and Policy in Mental Health, 289
Administration in Social Work, 396
Adolescence, 408
Advances in Consumer Research, 131
Affilia, 335, 391, 395, 401, 414, 416
Aging & Mental Health, 303
American Behavioral Scientist, 342, 364
American Demographics, 171
American Journal of Evaluation, 332
American Journal of Family Therapy, 347, 352
Analyses of Social Issues and Public Policy, 272
Applied Ergonomics, 300, 427

Best Practice Measurement Strategies, 143
British Educational Research Journal, 190, 217
British Journal of Educational Technology, 196
British Journal of Health Psychology, 95, 296
British Journal of Social Psychology, 58
British Journal of Social Work, 377
British Journal of Sociology of Education, 191, 222
Business Communication Quarterly, 36
Business Strategy and the Environment, 152

Author Index

The numbers following each entry refer to item numbers in the text.

Subject Index

The numbers following each entry refer to item numbers in the text.

MORI [Market and Opinion Research International], 261
Morris, Charlotte Wortz, 229
MP3, 67
mushroom industry, 345
musical identities, 92

Name Game [technique], 127
National Library Power, 259
National Science Foundation, 168
National Survey of Student Engagement, 203
Native American, 289, 330, 344, 392
naturalistic, 26, 247, 418
natural resource valuation, 426
Naval Training Center, 80
needs assessment, 144, 281, 301, 353, 390, 396
Nepal, 101
Netherlands, 163, 272, 370
Network Library System, 237
neuroimaging, 171
newscasters, female 167
news media, 423
newsroom style, 160
New Zealand, 281
Nigeria, 274
noise surveillance, 436
nominal grouping sessions, 121
nominal group technique, 17, 31, 128, 428
Non-English-Speaking-Background Women's Sexual Health Project, 359
normative discourses, 47
North Carolina Academy of Trial Lawyers, 229
Norway, 47, 313
nuclear waste, 275
nuclear weapons, 271
NUD*IST [software], 21, 107, 216, 287, 335, 372–73, 385, 403
nutraceuticals, 141

observation, 98, 194, 222, 253, 276, 323, 327, 400, 405, 411, 414, 431
unobtrusive, 253
Office of Consumer Affairs [Canada], 135

old-age security [Thailand], 170
O'Looney, J., 396
On Face-Work, 399
online: anonymity, 70; catalogs, 237; chat room, 360; chauffeur, 76; connections, 342; discussion board, 68, 79; focus groups, 55, 65–67, 69–70, 72, 74–75, 77, 89, 97, 239, 245, 360; help screens, 240. *See also* Internet; Web
opinion, 58, 128, 276–77
opinion polls, 262–63, 268, 270, 275
OptionFinder, 28
organizations, 12, 32, 143, 167, 398
outreach projects, 238
Oxford Concordance Program, 28

Pacific Islander, 289, 330
Parasuraman, A., 234
parenting, 22, 410
participatory action, 26, 37, 101, 297
peer, 42, 195, 208, 321, 358
peer-to-peer filesharing, 67
pension plans, 109
perceptual mapping, 50
Personal Responsibility and Work Opportunity Reconciliation Act, 401
personification, 84
pharmacists, 177
Philip Morris campaign, 230
Philippines, 304, 306
physiological changes, 376
planning policy, 270
playacting, 87
plus-minus method, 163
poetic displays, 85
police, 34
portals, 321–22
Portugal, 47
positivist, 18, 146, 411
postmodernist framework, 411
poverty, 323, 394
practicum, 224
prayer, 94
pregnancy, 367, 410
pretest, 13, 157, 224, 307
pricing strategy, 52
prison, 293–94, 414. *See also* incarcerated

About the Author

Graham R. Walden is professor at The Ohio State University. He has been with university libraries for 25 years and has subject responsibilities for Communication and Journalism, Germanic Languages and Literatures, and General Reference. His previous publications include *Public Opinion Polls and Survey Research* (1990); *Polling and Survey Research Methods 1935–1979* (1996); and *Survey Research Methodology, 1990–1999* (2002). Articles on polling sources, interviewing, and focus groups appear in *Reference Services Review* and *Communication Booknotes Quarterly*. Walden is a reviewer for *Choice, American Reference Books Annual (ARBA)*, and *Library Journal*.

In 2006, Walden was the recipient of the Marta Lange/CQ Press Award granted by the Law and Political Science Section (LPSS), Association of College and Research Libraries, American Library Association. The award, established in 1996 by LPSS and CQ Press, "honors an academic or law librarian who has made distinguished contributions to bibliography and information science in law or political science."